FORT WILLIAM, 1837
From a sketch by A. J. Miller

FORT LARAMIE
and the Pageant of the
West, 1834–1890

by
LeRoy R. Hafen
and
Francis Marion Young

University of Nebraska Press
Lincoln and London

First Bison Book printing: September 1984
Most recent printing indicated by the first digit below:
     4 5 6 7 8 9 10

Library of Congress Cataloging in Publication Data
Hafen, Le Roy Reuben, 1893–
  Fort Laramie and the pageant of the West, 1834–1890.
  Reprint. Originally published: Glendale, Calif. : A.H.
Clark, 1938.
  Includes index.
  1. Fort Laramie (Wyo. : Fort)—History. 2. Indians
of North America—West (U.S.)—Wars—1815–1875. 3. West
(U.S.)—History. I. Young, Francis Marion. II. Title.
F769.F6H34 1984   978   84-5196
ISBN 0-8032-2331-5
ISBN 0-8032-7223-5 (pbk.)

Reprinted by arrangement with the Fort Laramie Historical Association.

∞

Contents

Illustrations

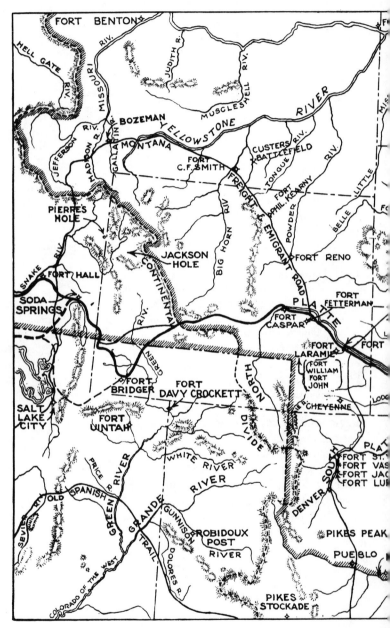

MAP OF THE Fo

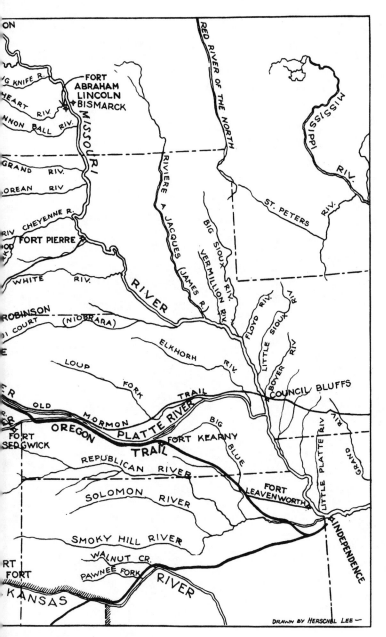

DRAWN BY HERSCHEL LEE

RAMIE REGION

Preface

Persons too numerous for individual enumeration have assisted with material or suggestions for this work. The following institutions with their staffs have been especially helpful: the Henry E. Huntington library, Bancroft library, L. D. S. church historian's office of Salt Lake City, state historical society of Colorado, Denver public library, Wyoming state historian's office, Kansas state historical society, Nebraska state historical society, Missouri state historical society, Missouri historical society, Kansas City public library, St. Louis public library, William Jewell college library of Liberty, Missouri, Salt Lake City public library, the Walters art gallery and the Municipal museum of Baltimore, Fort Myer, Virginia, Congressional library, Adjutant-general's and Advocate-general's offices in the war department, and the Bureau of Indian Affairs in the interior department at Washington.

Inasmuch as contemporary journals, letters and reports not only give a first hand record of events but reflect as well the flavor and the spirit of the times, the authors have felt it desirable to make numerous quotations from such sources. The fact that many of these original accounts are in rare volumes and inaccessible records is added reason for their reproduction.

Introduction

The story of Fort Laramie is the story of the conquest of Western America. Founded in the days of the fur-trapper, it faded only with the American frontier, and during that epic interval, was identified with the principal factors of western expansion.

Fort Laramie saw the trappers pack to rendezvous, the first missionaries venture to Oregon, the first home-seekers cross the Rockies.

It was the first trade center of an inland empire. Beaver skins and buffalo robes from a wide field were gathered in to its protecting walls. It was a place of rendezvous and of outfit for the mountain men, that restless breed of trappers and traders who were the trail blazers of unknown land.

Located on the mighty Oregon trail, over which trekked the commonwealth founders of Western America, it watched the great caravan pass and gave succor. Guardian and outpost of the overland trail, protecting emigrant train, mail service and telegraph line, it was the extended hand of a fostering government.

Throughout its days, it was identified with the Indian. Here was the scene of extensive barter with wild tribes, the setting of great peace councils, the base of military operations in expelling the red man from his ancient home.

In depicting the story of this great American outpost we shall not confine ourselves to the scene within its walls, but shall portray also the historical background which gave the fort significance. With lens focused on Fort Laramie, we shall open the shutter to encompass a panoramic view of the conquest and development of the Far West, America's last frontier.

Fur-trade Post

The First Fort on the Laramie

Near the eastern border of present Wyoming the Laramie and North Platte rivers unite their waters. Before the days of the reservoir and the irrigation ditch these were impressive streams. The tall grass of the bottomlands beside the Laramie and the short curly buffalo grass of the surrounding plains sustained large herds of native game – buffalo, deer and antelope. So to this land, before the days of white invasion, came regularly large bands of nomad tribes to hunt and feast, to "make meat" for winter needs.

It was an interesting country, this border land between the plains and the mountains. To the east stretched a level expanse to the faint horizon; to the west rose the Black Hills, dark with scrub cedar and pine, and beyond, the shining Laramie Peak. As the meeting place of mountain and plain, it became also the meeting ground of red man and white. Here, a little over one hundred years ago, was founded the first post to accommodate their trade. But the establishment of a fort on the banks of the Laramie in 1834 was not the first white entry into the region; it was rather the culminating event marking the end of the first phase of the history of this land. That preceding development – the coming of the first white men, their gradual acquaintance with the country and its denizens, the mounting interest in the region and its resources – need only for our present purposes, to be treated in the briefest outline.

White contact with the interior of Western America had begun in the sixteenth century, when Francisco Coronado pushed north from Mexico seeking the Seven Cities of Cibola and their rumored gold. Disappointed at Zuni and the Pueblo towns of the upper Rio Grande, he made one further thrust, venturing far out on the plains of Texas and Kansas in the hope of reaching the wealth of fabled Quivira. Then disillusioned and disheartened, he straggled back to Mexico and to obscurity.[1]

But white magic had touched the plains and they were never the same again. The Querechos (herdsmen), or buffalo Indians, had seen the hornless elk, the thunder stick and shining knives. These they must have for war and the hunt. They followed the white man, offering dried meat and tanned skins. Barter, here begun, grew with the years and spread in an ever-widening circle from the New Mexico base.

The Indian's manner of life was noticeably altered by his acquisition of the horse, firearms and metal. Mounted, and with improved weapons, he became a more formidable warrior, carrying his raids farther afield. Horse stealing became a fine art and a brave's wealth was reckoned in horseflesh. The red man acquired also a taste for various white man goods, including cloth and blankets for dress, beads and gewgaws for adornment.

Other white men reached the plains. They came from the East, traveling in canoes instead of on horseback. They accepted the Indian as brother and brought articles for trade. In 1743 Verendrye reached the western mountains, probably the Big Horn range, and may

---

[1] G. P. Winship, "The Coronado expedition, 1540-1542," in *Fourteenth annual report, Bureau of Ethnology*, Part I.

have reached the North Platte above the site of Fort Laramie.[2]

Spanish and French contacts with the natives continued, but were never intimate in the Fort Laramie region. Not until the early years of the nineteenth century and the coming of another people, did such relations develop. By this time a number of tribes were at home in the North Platte country – Crows, Shoshones and Utes, and, as more recent arrivals, Arapahos and Cheyennes. These last, pushed westward from the upper Missouri to the plains by the powerful Sioux, were soon followed by the aggressors. Before the middle of the century the Fort Laramie region was to be recognized as predominantly Sioux country.

Following the Louisiana Purchase in 1803, Americans boated up the Missouri river to share in the fur-trade that heretofore had been carried on by Frenchmen and Spaniards. The three nationals combined their interests in the Missouri Fur company and St. Louis continued as the great outfitting point and market. Through various reorganizations, this company was to be for some years the principal operator on the Great Muddy.[3]

Then John Jacob Astor of New York organized the American Fur company and entered the field. In 1811 he sent a party overland under Wilson Price Hunt, headed for the mouth of the Columbia. After turning from the Lewis and Clark path in present South Dakota, Hunt and his men took a generally westward course, across Wyoming, Idaho and Oregon to the Pacific coast.[4]

---

2 Francis Parkman, *A half-century of conflict*, II, 20-34.

3 For an excellent treatment of the general subject see H. M. Chittenden, *The American fur trade of the far west* (3 vols.).

4 Washington Irving, *Astoria, or anecdotes of an enterprise beyond the Rocky mountains.*

The following summer a small group of Astor's men,
led by Robert Stuart, set out from Astoria to carry dispatches back to the United States. They struck the upper
North Platte by a new trail and continuing down the
stream, reached the vicinity of the future Fort Laramie
on december 22, 1812. Here, writes Stuart, a "well
wooded stream apparently of considerable magnitude
came in from the south west." [5] This appears to be our
first recorded description of the Laramie river and of
the country at its mouth. Stuart's party may have been
also the first white men to visit this section, although it
is likely that Ezekiel Williams and his fellow trappers
of the Missouri Fur company passed this way when
going from their fort on the Big Horn to the upper
Arkansas river in 1810.[6] And it is possible that back of
them, wandering Spanish or French traders may have
touched this ground. But if so, we have found no record
of the visits.

Now enters a shadowy character on the scene, one
made famous only by his death. Of his life and his ante-
cedents we know nothing. Even his name is in doubt.
This man, a trapper, called Laramé (given various
forms of spelling), is reported to have been killed by
Indians in 1821, on the stream that thereafter took his
name.[7] From the river the name was to go to the mountain range, the peak, the plains, the fort, a town, a city,
and a county in Wyoming.

The spring of 1822 saw the beginning of what was to

[5] Philip Ashton Rollins (ed.), *The discovery of the Oregon trail. Robert Stuart's narratives,* etc., 196.

[6] *Ibid.,* p. cxxxiii. See also *Missouri historical society collections,* IV, 194, 202-8.

[7] "Diary of Rev. Jason Lee," in *The quarterly of the Oregon historical society,* XVII, 129; H. M. Chittenden, *The American fur trade of the far west,* 469; Hebard and Brininstool, *The Bozeman trail,* I, 102, II, 233; C. G. Cout-ant, *History of Wyoming,* 298.

become the Rocky Mountain Fur company – the company first to exploit the resources of the Fort Laramie region. William H. Ashley and Andrew Henry of St. Louis launched this enterprise.[8] After operating in the upper Missouri country, Ashley sent a party west from Fort Kiowa in the fall of 1823. This group, led by Jedediah S. Smith and Thomas Fitzpatrick, spent most of the winter in the Wind river region, north of the Laramie country, and then in the spring crossed South Pass and entered the Green river valley of southwestern Wyoming. After taking a fine catch of beaver in this virgin fur-field, they recrossed the continental divide, and Fitzpatrick made his way back to the Missouri by way of the Sweetwater and the Platte – a route soon to become famous as the Oregon trail.[9] Being apprised by Fitzpatrick of the practicable South Pass route and of the rich beaver country in the valley of the Green, Ashley led a party back, in the winter of 1824-25, to this trapper's paradise. Here he divided his men into small bands and with the thawing of the mountain streams, sent the brigades forth in various directions to make their spring catch of beaver. All were ordered to bring their harvest to a central meeting place (near the mouth of Henry's Fork) about july first. Here supplies would be replenished, noses counted, and wages paid. Accordingly, there assembled in 1825, the first of those famous summer gatherings – the trappers' rendezvous.[10]

For sixteen years thereafter similar midsummer meetings took place. The trading companies found

---

[8] H. C. Dale, *The Ashley-Smith explorations and the discovery of a central route to the Pacific, 1822-1829.*

[9] L. R. Hafen and W. J. Ghent, *Broken hand; the life of Thomas Fitzpatrick, chief of the mountain men,* 33-47; C. L. Camp (ed.), *James Clyman, American frontiersman, 1792-1881,* 22-37.

[10] Dale, *op. cit.,* 117-139.

business good at the rendezvous. From the East they brought supplies and equipment for their hired trappers and large assortments of goods attractive for the Indian trade. For the trapper the rendezvous was the great occasion of the year. Here was opportunity for trading, for social life, for reckless hilarity. In this brief holiday he found respite from what was otherwise a rather lonely life, and in a few days of prodigal living frequently spent the earnings of a year. Indians in great numbers came to the fair, bringing their skins and furs to trade for beads and gewgaws, for knives and firewater. Indeed, the rendezvous was a fiesta, a market day, a carousal, all in one. It was the highlight of trapper life, outstanding institution of the early Far West.

General Ashley continued in the mountain fur-trade until 1826, when he sold his business to three of his employees – Jedediah S. Smith, William L. Sublette and David E. Jackson.[11] These partners carried on through four years, captaining fur brigades, exploring the Rocky mountains and the Pacific coast for beaver, and bringing annually a large train of supplies and goods to the appointed rendezvous. The earlier supply caravans were pack trains, but in 1830 wagons were used – the first on the Oregon trail.[12]

In this year Smith, Jackson and Sublette sold their business to another group of seasoned trappers – Thomas Fitzpatrick, James Bridger, Milton G. Sublette, Henry Fraeb, and Jean Baptiste Gervais – who were to adopt the firm name of the Rocky Mountain Fur company.[13]

---

[11] *Ibid.*, 168, 183-184.

[12] Report of Smith, Jackson and Sublette to the secretary of war, in *Sen. ex. docs.*, cong. 21, sess. 2, no. 39.

[13] Chittenden, *American fur trade of the far west*, 292.

Thus far this company and its predecessors had had the central Rocky mountain country largely to themselves, save for some little competition from Ogden's brigade of the Hudson's Bay company pushing southeast from the Columbia, and a few trappers from the Taos country. But now a more formidable rival was entering. Astor's powerful American Fur company, which had heretofore confined itself largely to the upper Missouri river country and to the regions north and east, decided to exploit the area of the central Rockies.[14] With ample financial backing and an efficient organization for marketing furs, it had distinct advantages over the Rocky Mountain Fur company.

In 1831, another partnership, Gant and Blackwell, entered the fur-trade, bringing seventy men to trap the upper waters of the Arkansas, the branches of the Platte and the country between.[15] Nathaniel J. Wyeth and his New Englanders entered the field in 1832,[16] and Captain Benjamin L. E. Bonneville, late of the army, with 110 well-equipped men, reached Green river the same year.[17] Sinclair with a party from Arkansas [18] and other minor groups swelled the numbers at the great rendezvous of 1832.

The field was becoming over-crowded, the competition ruthless. With fewer beavers and more trappers, the possible catch was inadequate for all. Throughout a number of years the contest was to continue, however,

---

[14] *Ibid.,* 295, 328.

[15] Zenas Leonard, *Narrative of the adventures of Zenas Leonard.* Leonard was an employee of Gant and Blackwell.

[16] F. G. Young (ed.), *Correspondence and journals of Captain Nathaniel J. Wyeth, 1831-6.*

[17] Washington Irving, *The adventures of Captain Bonneville.*

[18] W. H. Ellison (ed.), *The Life and Adventures of George Nidever.* Nidever was a member of Sinclair's party.

with certain companies dropping out and others entering the lists.

It was in december, 1832, that William L. Sublette and Robert Campbell formed a partnership to venture a fur-trade project of their own.[19] They, it was, who were to found the first post on the Laramie. Both men were capable and experienced in the fur-trade, having, during the preceding decade, trapped, conducted supply trains and fought Indians in the Rocky mountain West.[20] Supported by their former leader, General William Ashley – now a member of congress – and with friendly relations with the Rocky Mountain Fur company, they were in a position to challenge the primacy of Astor's powerful organization.

In the summer of 1833, while Campbell led a land caravan up the Platte heading for the Green river rendezvous with goods for the Rocky Mountain Fur company, Sublette ascended the Missouri by steamboat with extensive equipment. He left parties at various points along the river with instructions to build posts to compete with those of the American Fur company. One post, Fort William, was located on the upper Missouri near the rival's Fort Union.

But in this upper country they found themselves bucking an established and resourceful – not to say un-

---

[19] Chittenden, *American fur trade of the far west*, 350.

[20] William L. Sublette was the most gifted and famous of five brothers, all of whom figured in early fur-trade annals. He was born in Kentucky in 1799 and came to Missouri when he was nineteen. Soon thereafter he entered the fur-trade, in which he rose to leadership and accumulated a modest fortune. He died in 1845.

Robert Campbell was born in Ireland, came to America, and made his first trip to the Rocky mountains in 1824. For the next ten years he was active in the fur-trade, and for another decade was identified with it through business connections. He became one of the richest and most influential citizens of St. Louis. He died there on october 16, 1879.

scrupulous – organization. One of its factors, McKenzie, instructed his agents to pay any price to secure the furs from the Indians and thus forestall all efforts of the intruders to procure trade. His measures were most effective. Sublette and Campbell finally proposed to sell out, but McKenzie rebuffed their advance, reporting that he saw no reason to "buy out" competitors whom he could "drive out." Head officials, however, in New York and St. Louis were thoroughly alarmed at the rival company's activity and came to terms with it. They purchased Sublette and Campbell's fort and merchandise on the upper Missouri to retain control in that quarter; and agreed to retire, for the ensuing year, from the central Rocky mountain region.[21] Thus Sublette and Campbell were free to pursue a lucrative trade in the Rocky mountain region during 1834.

They did not have the field entirely to themselves, however. N. J. Wyeth, ambitious Bostonian, was bringing out another caravan of trade goods. In fact he had a conditional contract with the Rocky Mountain Fur company leaders to supply them goods at the summer rendezvous on the Green river.[22] The two preceding years Sublette had furnished trade goods to that company and meant not to have this lucrative business cut in upon by an outsider. He must outmaneuver this green New Englander.

To assure their position, the new partners planned to establish a great central trading post that would control the fur traffic of a vast interior region.

These farseeing men saw a change coming over the fur-trade of the Rocky mountain West. So long as

[21] Chittenden, *op. cit.*, 353. Letter of april 8, 1834, to McKenzie.

[22] For a discussion of this contract see Hafen and Ghent, *Broken hand, the life of Thomas Fitzpatrick*, 109, 112-114.

beaver skins were the principal objects and white trappers the chief agents of the fur-trade, the annual rendezvous was adequate. It afforded the necessary facilities for distributing supplies and receiving the skins. But as the beaver were depleted and as their skins decreased in price – through the introduction of invented substitutes, such as silk hats for beaver hats – the rendezvous declined. When the bulky buffalo robes took the place of the neat packs of beaver skins, the trader replaced the trapper, and the fixed trading-post displaced the shifting rendezvous. A strong-walled fort was necessary to house trade goods and to store the buffalo hides brought in by the Indians for barter. While in the catching of beaver, white men did the trapping, in the procuring and tanning of buffalo skins the white men could not, or else would not compete with the Indian. Hence, in the new conditions, the white trader and his post were the effective agents.

But this important change in the western trade did not come suddenly. For a time the rendezvous and some of the earliest forts were to operate side by side.

Where to locate their new fort, was a matter of importance to Sublette and Campbell. Already the junction of the Laramie and the Platte was known as a favorable location for trade with the Indians. When Wyeth had secured his trader's license at St. Louis, among the places named for conduct of the trade was "a point of timber on the south side of the grand river Platte, called Laremars' point, about ten miles below the Black Hills" [23] [not to be confused with the Black Hills of present South Dakota]. Pratte, Chouteau and

---

[23] "Abstract of licenses issued to trade with the Indians, etc.," in *House docs.* cong. 33, sess. 2, no. 97. This reference was found through the kindness of Miss Sarah Guitar, reference librarian, Missouri state historical society, Columbia, Missouri.

company, too, had obtained a license to trade at the aforesaid place. Sublette and Campbell's license, issued april 15, 1834, provided the right to trade "for one and one-half years, with twenty-five men employed" and named many places on the Missouri and Colorado rivers and their branches for trading, including "Laremais' point." [24]

As planned, the partners with their loaded pack train bound for rendezvous, overtook and passed Wyeth's train. Late in may, 1834, Sublette and Campbell reached the Laramie river. Here Campbell appears to have remained with part of the men and a portion of the goods, while Sublette hurried on to the Green river rendezvous ahead of his opponents. Presently Wyeth reached the Laramie region and recorded:

"JUNE 1 [1834]. Made 15 miles to Laramies fork . . . At the crossing we found 13 of Sublettes men camped for the purpose of building a fort   he having gone ahead with his best animals and the residue of his goods   he left about 14 loads." [25]

Accompanying Wyeth were the first overland missionaries bound for the Oregon country. Jason Lee, leader of the little band of five, recorded in his diary:

"SUNDAY, JUNE 1, 1834. Started about the usual [time] and arrived at Laramas [Laramie's] Fork and forded it without difficulty before dinner. It receives its name from the circumstance that a man by that name was killed by the Indians on that branch. This stream is generally very difficult to cross, it being very rapid. Some of Sublett's men who are building a trading-fort

---

[24] *Ibid.* The amount of Sublette and Campbell's bond was listed at $1,500 and the capital employed at $2,957.12. The license of "Astor, Bonneville and company" of april 16, 1834, authorized them "to trade at Laremais' Point" also. The licenses issued the preceding year did not mention Laremais' Point.

[25] Wyeth's journal, *op. cit.*, 223.

a little distance came to us   they are planting corn.
Three of our party free trapers left us here with the intention to catch beaver in the Black Hills and thus they
expose themselves their lives yea they run greater risks
for a few beaver skins than we do to save souls and yet
some who call themselves Christians   'tell it not in
Gath'   would have persuaded us to abandon our enter-
prize because of the danger which attended it." [26] In a
letter to the *Christian Advocate and Journal* the missionary reports Sublette as saying that this was "a most
favorable location for missionary operations, it being
a central place where hundreds of Indians of various
tribes will in future assemble every year." [27]

The building of the fort progressed rapidly. Lucien
Fontenelle, who brought back furs from the mountains
in the summer of 1834, writes to Pierre Chouteau upon
returning to the Missouri:

"William Sublette has built such a fort as Fort Clark
(Mandans) on Laramie's Fork of the river Platte and
can make it a central place for the Sioux and Cheyenne
trade. He has now men running after these Indians to
bring them to the river Platte. Buffalo is in abundance
on that river during all seasons of the year, and the situation may turn out to be an advantageous one for the
trade." [28]

Sublette appears to have returned immediately to the
states after obtaining the furs from the rendezvous,[29]

[26] *Quarterly of the Oregon historical society*, XVII, 129. John K. Townsend, who accompanied the N. J. Wyeth party and wrote an account of the journey, does not mention the building of the fort. See Thwaites, *Early western travels*, XXI, 181. Nor does Osborne Russell, also with Wyeth, mention the post. See his *Journal of a trapper*, 8.

[27] Letter written from the rendezvous, october 3, 1834. This reference was kindly supplied by Nellie Pipes of the Oregon historical society.

[28] Letter dated at Bellevue, september 17, quoted in Chittenden, *American fur trade of the far west*, 305.

[29] *Missouri Republican*, august 26, 1834. "Mr. W. L. Sublette and Captain

while the junior partner must have remained on the Laramie to attend to construction of the post and promotion of the Indian trade. But we are not even certain of this. Louis Vasquez, an employee of Sublette and Campbell in 1833-34, writes to his brother Benito from the rendezvous at Ham's Fork (Green river valley), july 9, 1834: "I am not coming down [to Missouri] this year. You will find in the letter which I am writing and sending through Mr. Wm. L. Sublette a draft for 50 *piastre*. . . Mr. Sublette or Campbell are coming up this fall. I beg you to write to me and give me the detail news from all. . . If you could procure for me a few novels Mr. Campbell would be pleased to bring them to me." [30] Campbell, or one of his men, must have made the trip to the states and returned to the mountains that fall, for Vasquez again writes his brother, on december 30, 1834 from Fort Convenience [believed to be a fort at the mouth of Vasquez creek, or Clear creek, about four miles north of present Denver] acknowledging receipt of a letter answering his of july 9, and adds: "Write me care of the company. Address your letter to Ft. William (Black Hills) and if I do not come down I will write you my intentions." [31]

This is one of the earliest appearances, in the scant records of the time, of the name Fort William for the post on the Laramie. It was named in honor of William

Cerre with Bonneville's furs have perhaps arrived at Independence by this time – the former with 60 or 70 packs, and the latter with about 20 packs of beaver." The information was from a man who had just returned from the mountains.

[30] Vasquez letters in possession of the Missouri historical society. These letters are written in French. They are made available through the kindness of Stella M. Drumm, librarian of the Missouri historical society. For a biographical sketch of Louis Vasquez see L. R. Hafen, "Mountain men – Louis Vasquez," in *Colorado magazine*, X, 14-21. Louis Vasquez was later a partner of William's brother, Andrew W. Sublette.

[31] Vasquez letters.

Sublette, senior partner of the founders.[32] In this they
were following a common practice of the time.[33] In fact
there were two other Fort Williams already in existence. One, located on the north bank of the Arkansas
near present La Junta, Colorado, was built by Bent and
St. Vrain and was named in honor of William Bent
[Bent's Fort]. The other was Sublette and Campbell's
abandoned post near Fort Union on the upper Missouri.
The fact that the partners had been forced by the
American Fur company to give up their Fort William
on the Missouri may have been a reason for the transfer
of the name to their new post on the Laramie.

The actual construction of the fort is usually credited
to Mr. Campbell.[34] Mr. Coutant, early historian of
Wyoming, who interviewed many old trappers, gives
details as to its establishment:

"The force was completely organized, a detachment
was sent to the woods for the timber, and a band of hunters supplied buffalo, elk, deer and mountain sheep. By
the time winter approached there was an abundant
larder and plenty of fuel had been gathered to keep
up cheerful fires during the long winter months. Mr.
Campbell had with him a stock of merchandise which
he traded for furs with independent trappers who came
along, and also with the Indians. There was at the fort

[32] See Chittenden, *American fur trade of the far west,* 967; Coutant, *History of Wyoming,* 300; Irving, *Bonneville,* 39; and practically all writers
who tell of the founding of the fort. William M. Anderson, one of Sublette's
men, records in his diary on june 1, 1834: "This day we laid the foundation
log of a fort on Laramee's fork." Anderson's grandson, Charles Gauld, III,
in "A trip to the Yellowstone and the Oregon country in 1834," in the *Washington historical quarterly,* XXVI, 28, says: "He [Anderson] and Captain
Sublette each wanted to name it for the other. They compromised, both being
named William, and so Fort William was christened."

[33] Others are Fort Manuel, Fort George, Fort Lancaster (Fort Lupton).

[34] Wislizenus, *A journey to the Rocky mountains in the year 1839,* 69;
Coutant, *op. cit.,* 299; description of the artist A. J. Miller, cited below.

that winter a motley collection of American trappers, hunters, French Canadians, half-breeds, Mexicans and Indians. Robert Campbell presided over the multifarious assembly with that true dignity which was a part of his nature. He was at this time still a young man, scarcely in his prime. He is spoken of as being tall, with a fair complexion and rather light colored hair. His figure was erect and his bearing that of a man of much reserved power. He settled disputes and bickerings with a word, and so that neither side could feel aggrieved." [35]

The new post was rectangular in form. Hewn cottonwood logs about fifteen feet high formed the palisade. At diagonal corners were protruding log bastions, or blockhouses, provided with loopholes for defense. A third blockhouse rose over the front gate and, supported by high posts, projected beyond the wall line. Against the inside of the stockade was a row of rooms, whose flat roofs reached to within three feet of the top of the palisade. One side of the fort was fenced off as a horse corral, leaving the rest of the interior as a courtyard. The rooms were devoted to various uses. One was the store room, another the smithy, and others were quarters for the men. Altogether, it was a substantial post adapted for trade in the Indian country.[36]

While Fort William was being established on the

---

[35] Coutant, *op. cit.*, 300. Mr. Coutant does not specify the source of this information. It probably came from old timers whom he interviewed. Though Campbell may have spent part of the winter at the fort, he could not have been there the entire season. He was in St. Louis in early april, 1835; see below.

[36] Contemporary descriptions of this first fort are few and brief. See the indirect description by Mrs. Marcus Whitman (1836) in Myron Eells, *Marcus Whitman, pathfinder and patriot*, 70-71; another lady missionary's description in Myra F. Eells' journal (1838) in *Transactions, Oregon pioneer association, 17th annual reunion*, june 8, 1889; A. J. Miller's description (1837); and Dr. Wislizenus' report of 1839, in Wislizenus, *op. cit.*, 67-68. These accounts are to be given in their chronological order in the following chapter.

Laramie (1834), important changes in company align-
ments were taking place in the western fur field. On
june 1, 1834, Astor withdrew from the western fur-
trade, selling the northern department of his American
Fur company to Ramsay Crooks and associates, and the
western department (which had operated in the central
Rockies) to Pratte, Chouteau and company of St. Louis.
The principals in this last named company had been
associated with the American Fur company for some
years. After the purchase of Astor's interest in 1834
they operated under the name Pratte, Chouteau & Company (changed to Pierre Chouteau Jr. & Company in
1838), but in popular usage the firm was still referred
to in the West as the American Fur company, and we
shall so use the name.[37]

Shortly thereafter the Rocky Mountain Fur company was dissolved (june 20, 1834), Fraeb and Gervais
being paid off in goods, and the remaining three forming a partnership under the style, Fitzpatrick, [Milton]
Sublette and Bridger.[38] These three thereupon made an
agreement with Lucien Fontenelle to turn over their
furs to him. Inasmuch as Fontenelle was an agent of, or
at least in close affiliation with, Pratte, Chouteau and
company, this agreement has significance. It meant that
the remnant of the expiring Rocky Mountain Fur company was being absorbed by the more powerful organization, popularly known as the American Fur company.[39]

In the spring following the building of the fort, Sub-

---

[37] Chittenden, *American fur trade of the far west,* 364.

[38] *Ibid.,* 304. The dissolution agreement is reproduced opposite p. 864.

[39] *Ibid.,* 365, and Fontenelle's letter of September 17, 1834, published, *ibid.,*
304-305. In this letter, written to Pierre Chouteau, he says: "I have entered
into a partnership with the others [Fitzpatrick, Sublette and Bridger] and
the whole of the beaver caught by them is to be turned over to us by agreement made with them in concluding the arrangement."

lette and Campbell brought out a fresh supply of goods from St. Louis. They spent fifteen days at the fort trading and making ready for the return shipment of the furs. It was at this time, presumably, that they sold Fort William on the Laramie to Fitzpatrick and his associates.[40] Exact data in regard to the transfer have not come to light.

The water being high in the Platte, Sublette and Campbell decided to attempt to float their furs downstream to St. Louis. They "constructed a batteaux, loaded it with a large number of packs of buffalo robes, and by the employment of small boats made of skins" were able to "descend the river a distance of six hundred miles in safety." [41] In its lower stretches, however, the river became so wide and shallow that the navigators had to forsake their boats for land transportation. They finally reached St. Louis on july 15. Thus the fort on the Laramie witnessed the construction and the launching of the first boats to successfully navigate a long stretch of the Platte river – the stream whose name in various languages meant always the same flat river – Chato [Spanish], Nebraska [Pawnee], and Platte [French]. In its account of their arrival the *Missouri Republican* called attention to the fact that "deducting days lost, it took only three months for the accomplishment of this perilous adventure [out to the fort and back]," and added: "By and by we shall think nothing of making excursions to the mountains."

While on the eastbound journey, at the Elkhorn branch of the Platte, Sublette and Campbell, with their twelve men, had met Fontenelle [june 27]. Having

40 *Ibid.,* 365, 967.

41 *Missouri Republican,* july 18, 1835, quoted in *Publications of the Nebraska state historical society,* XX, 64. Another account of the expedition is found in *Niles Register,* august 8, 1835, p. 406.

previously obtained a trading license from William Clark for Fontenelle, Fitzpatrick and company, april 21, 1835,[42] he was now leading a trader's caravan up the north bank of the Platte, headed for Fort William and the rendezvous. Accompanying him were Reverend Samuel Parker and Dr. Marcus Whitman, missionaries, on their way to the Oregon country.[43] Fontenelle had between fifty and sixty men, six wagons and nearly 200 horses and mules.[44] On july 26, 1835, he came to a point opposite the mouth of the Laramie.

"At evening," writes Reverend Parker, "we passed over the Platte, and went a mile and a half up to the fort of the Black Hills,[45] [Fort William] and encamped near the fort in our usual form. . .

"At this place the caravan halted, and according to immemorial usage, the men were allowed a 'day of indulgence,' as it is called, in which they drink ardent spirits as much as they please, and conduct as they choose. Not unfrequently the day terminates with a catastrophe of some kind, and today one of the company shot another with the full intention to have killed him. The ball entered the back, and came out at the side. The wounded man exclaimed, 'I am a dead man,' but after a pause, said, 'No, I am not hurt.' The other immediately seized a rifle to finish the work, but was prevented by the bystanders, who wrested it from him and discharged it into the air." [46]

A band of some two thousand Oglala Sioux had come

[42] Manuscript found in the office of Indian Affairs, Washington, D.C.

[43] Samuel Parker, *Journal of an exploring tour beyond the Rocky mountains*, 49, and "Journal and report by Dr. Marcus Whitman," etc., in *Oregon historical quarterly*, XXVIII, 239-57.

[44] Dr. Whitman's journal, *op. cit.*, 245.

[45] Dr. Whitman also calls it "the company's fort at Black Hills," and the "Fort Black Hills" (Journal, *op. cit.*, 247, 250). He also speaks of James Bridger as "one of the partners of the company" (p. 247).

[46] Parker, *op. cit.*, 68-70. Parker does not speak of the fort by name.

in to the fort to trade. They brought dressed skins, moccasins and belts which they wanted to exchange for knives, awls, combs and vermilion. The missionaries thought these were the finest looking Indians they ever had seen. But the Reverend Parker was not well impressed with the dance which the Indians presented at the fort. He writes: "In the buffalo dance, a large number of young men, dressed with the skins of the neck and head of buffalos with their horns on, moved round in a dancing march. They shook their heads, imitated the low bellowing of the buffalo, wheeled, and jumped. At the same time men and women sung a song, accompanied with the beating of a sort of drum. I cannot say I was much amused to see how well they could imitate brute beasts, while ignorant of God and salvation. The impressive enquiry was constantly on my mind, what will become of their immortal spirits? Rational men imitating beasts, and old gray-headed men marshaling the dance! and enlightened white men encouraging it by giving them intoxicating spirits, as a reward for their good performance." [47]

The wagons brought to Fort William by Fontenelle were left at the post, while the goods intended for the rendezvous were transferred to pack mules for the remaining portion of the trip. Leaders were changed here. Fontenelle remained at the fort but sent a letter on to rendezvous by Thomas Fitzpatrick, who conducted the pack train westward.[48] Fontenelle's letter to his friend and partner Andrew Drips reads:

"Fort William, august 1, 1835
"DEAR FRIEND . . . I have concluded that it was better for our mutual interest for me to remain at this place until the return from the mountains should get in and then go down with them according

---

[47] *Ibid.*, 70-71.
[48] *Ibid.*, 72.

to our agreement with Messrs Fitzpatrick, Sublette & Bridger – I regret however that I could not make it convenient to go up and see you not only on account of business but on account of friendship – it would be too tedious for me at the present to undertake to give you a full view of our business, suffice it to say that it stands fair. Mr. Fitzpatrick may be able to give you some information on the subject.

"I wish that you would have the goodness to settle all accounts (separately) which regards our old and new concern and send me if you should not come down yourself a copy of the same, inclosed is a copy of an acc Messrs Fitzpatrick Sublette & Bridger which you will please include in the arrangement. . . He [John Gray] takes up some beans, corn meal & pumpkins which are sent up by my woman for yours [both had Indian wives]. . . Send down if you can all those hard hands – or if you could you ought to pay them in goods, even by diminishing or lowering the old prices. . . You will also receive a bridle from Capt. Walker which I send up to you. Bridger has a fine coat, cap, pantaloons etc. baled up for him among the goods, present him if you please my respects. There are two gentlemen going up with the party who are Gentlemen [Rev. Parker and Dr. Whitman] and I wish you would treat them as such. The Doctor particularly. He has been of great service to us.

"If you should want to come down this fall you will have to get some person to stay in your place to conduct a party it will be paid by you and myself – If Bridger should also want to come down He has to furnish a man in his place (that is an able man). . . Howell is to trap by the skin, you will have to furnish him with traps, horses, etc.

Goodby my dear friend   L. FONTENELLE" [49]

The train from Fort William reached the Green river rendezvous august 12. Reverend Parker writes of the assemblage: "The American Fur company have between two and three hundred men constantly in and about the mountains, engaged in trading, hunting and trapping. These all assemble at rendezvous upon the arrival of the caravan, bring in their furs, and take new

[49] This, one of the few extant letters written by Fontenelle, is among the Drips papers in possession of the Missouri historical society and was made available through the kindness of Miss Stella M. Drumm, librarian of the society.

supplies for the coming year, of clothing, ammunition, and goods for trade with the Indians. But few of these men ever return to their country and friends. Most of them are constantly in debt to the company, and are unwilling to return without a fortune; and year after year passes away, while they are hoping in vain for better success.

"Here were assembled many Indians belonging to four different nations; the Utaws, Shoshones, Nez Perces, and Flatheads, who were waiting for the caravan, to exchange furs, horses, and dressed skins, for various articles of merchandise." [50]

Two events at this rendezvous of 1835 are rather far famed. First of these was a surgical operation performed by Dr. Whitman. He cut from the back of Jim Bridger a three-inch iron arrowpoint, which the old scout had been carrying since a skirmish with the Blackfeet three years before. Then there was a famous duel, with Kit Carson as hero. It came near the close of "another day of indulgence" when "all restraint was laid aside. These days are the climax of the hunter's happiness." Shunar, "the great bully of the mountains, mounted his horse with a loaded rifle, and challenged any Frenchman, American, Spaniard, or Dutchman, to fight him in single combat. Kit Carson, an American, told him if he wished to die, he would accept the challenge. Shunar defied him. C. mounted his horse, and with a loaded pistol, rushed into close contact, and both almost at the same instant fired. C's ball entered S's hand, came out at the wrist, and passed through the arm above the elbow. Shunar's ball passed over the head of Carson; and while he went for another pistol, Shunar begged that his life might be spared. Such scenes, some-

---

[50] Parker, *op. cit.,* 79-80.

times from passion, and sometimes for amusement, make the pastime of their wild and wandering life." [51]

With the rendezvous over, Bridger and other brigade captains led their men in various directions toward the mountains for another season of trapping. Fitzpatrick, accompanied by Dr. Whitman, who was returning to the states for more missionaries, packed up the product of the trading and conducted the string of mules loaded with furs back to Fort William.

[51] *Ibid.*, 80, 84.

Fur-traders and Missionaries, 1836-1840

The next spring (1836) saw a large caravan headed for Fort William on the Laramie. Trade goods had been freighted by steamboat to Council Bluffs, where they were packed in wagons and on the backs of mules. Seventy men and about four hundred animals comprised the caravan, all under the leadership of Thomas Fitzpatrick, captain of the train. Seven six-mule wagons were loaded with goods and supplies for the fort, while a large band of mules carried great packs bulging with attractive items destined for the summer rendezvous.[52] Accompanying the captain was his partner Milton Sublette, still suffering with a leg that had already been amputated a time or two without relief. Milton rode in a cart drawn by two mules hitched tandem.

An unusual missionary party was to join the traders on the Loup Fork of the Platte. It comprised Dr. Marcus Whitman and his young bride, Rev. and Mrs. H. H. Spalding, and W. H. Gray. The two Indian boys, whom

[52] Mrs. Marcus Whitman, quoted in Eells, *Marcus Whitman*, 60-61. W. H. Gray in *History of Oregon* (1870), 115, says the caravan consisted of "nineteen carts, with two mules to each, one in the shafts and one ahead, one light Dearborn wagon, two mules and two wagons belonging to an English nobleman." Mrs. Victor, in *The river of the West* (1870), 203, gives a similar report. The Mrs. Whitman report being contemporary has been accepted. The other two were written later and their agreement may be accounted for by one having copied from the other. The trains of 1836 and 1838 are doubtless confused by Gray and Mrs. Victor. Dr. Whitman, writing from Vancouver, sept. 18, 1836, says: "Fitzpatrick headed the caravan this year. We travelled hard, but more comfortably than last year, as we always took breakfast before starting in the morning. Capt. Fontanell had become so intemperate that the company had disposed [deposed] of him."—A. B. and D. P. Hulbert, *Marcus Whitman, crusader*, 230.

Whitman had taken to the states the previous year, were members of the party, as was sixteen-year-old Miles Goodyear, destined to be the first white settler in Utah.[53]

Accompanying the caravan went the redoubtable Sir William Drummond Stewart who, having spent the winter in New Orleans, was again answering the call of the mountains. The English nobleman and his companion, Mr. Celam, had three servants, two dogs, and four extra horses with which to run buffalo. With these blooded horses, says missionary Gray, the Englishmen would give chase to antelope and when outdistanced "Sir William and his companion would come charging back to the train, swearing the antelope could outrun a streak of lightning, and offering to bet a thousand pounds that if he had one of his English 'orses he could catch 'em." [54]

Along the north bank of the Platte, in the trail of the previous year, the caravan moved westward. "If you want to see the camp in motion," writes Mrs. Whitman, "look away ahead, and see the pilot, and the captain, Fitzpatrick, just before him; next the pack animals, all mules, loaded with great packs. Soon after you will see the wagons, and in the rear our company. We all cover quite a space. The pack mules always string along, one after the other just like Indians." [55]

Near Scott's Bluffs some hunters from Fort William were met, descending the Platte in boats. They were taking advantage of the june rise to make a trip back to Missouri.

Upon arriving opposite the mouth of the Laramie the train was greeted by men from the fort. And not only

---

[53] W. H. Gray, *A History of Oregon* (1870), 114. Goodyear located on the site of Ogden, Utah, before the Mormons settled there.

[54] *Ibid.,* 115.

[55] Eells, *op. cit.,* 61.

men, but Indian wives and half-breed children formed a lively part of the welcoming hosts.

To cross the high river, two dugouts, made by hollowing large tree trunks, were lashed together by means of poles and ropes and converted into a ferry boat. In this the vehicles and goods were crossed to the west bank of the Platte, just above the mouth of the Laramie, and from thence were taken up to Fort William.[56]

The arrival of the company caravan was the event of the year to the fur-men and employees who had spent the winter at the trading-post. Letters and news from the East were eagerly read, while fresh supplies and new trade goods gave a sort of Christmas morning atmosphere to the fort. Fitzpatrick and Sublette were equally anxious to learn the state of business at their post. Had many buffalo robes and furs been brought in; had cordial relations with the Indians been maintained? Yes, everything seemed to be well at Fort William.

The hospitality of the post was extended to the visitors, with special consideration for the ladies – the first white women to honor the fort with a visit. Mrs. Whitman and Mrs. Spalding had had Sir William, Captain Fitzpatrick and other notables of the train "to tea" on the banks of the Platte some weeks before. Though the table then was the ground covered with an India rubber cloth and dishes were "of tin, basins for tea cups, iron spoons and plates for each," [57] the occasion was none the less remembered. Now the courtesy could be repaid – and in a room provided with tables and chairs. Mrs. Whitman especially remembered the chairs; they were so comfortable, with their buffalo skin bottoms.[58]

---

56 Gray, *op. cit.*, 116. See also, C. M. Drury, *Henry Harmon Spalding,* 139.
57 Eells, *op. cit.*, 62.
58 *Ibid.*, 71. Rev. Spalding, in a letter of september 20, 1836, speaks of Fort

Mrs. Spalding records in her journal: "JUNE 15. Fort William. We are camped near the fort, and shall remain here several days, as the co. are to leave their wagons at this post and make arrangements to transport their goods the remainder of the journey on mules. It is very pleasant to fix my eyes once more upon a few buildings, several weeks have passed since we have seen a building.

"JUNE 17, 1836. Fort William. Today is the sabbath and the first we have spent in quietness and rest, since the 8th of may. . . Mr. S[palding] in compliance with the request of the chief men of the expedition, met with the people under the shade of a few trees near our camp for religious services. A large assembly met, and were very attentive while Mr. S. made a few remarks upon the parable of the prodigal son." [59]

The wagons, according to plans, were to be left at the fort. But Whitman insisted on taking one of the mission wagons farther, for the convenience of the women. So the fur company leaders decided to join him in the project, and send one of their carts along, both to be under the charge of the missionary. The trade goods for rendezvous were to continue by mule back.

On the first day's travel from the fort, Whitman had considerable difficulty in getting his vehicles through a cottonwood bottom along the river. He "came into the camp puffing and blowing, in good spirits, all right side up, with only one turn over with the wagon and two with the cart. The fur company being interested in exploring a wagon route to Green river, next day gave the

---

William but does not describe it. This is quoted in J. C. Bell, *Opening a highway to the Pacific,* 83-84.

[59] Typescript in Oregon historical society library. Copy kindly supplied by Nellie B. Pipes of the Oregon historical society.

Doctor two additional men to assist in exploring and locating the road, and getting the wagon and cart over difficult places." [60]

Below the Red Buttes the party stopped to prepare for crossing the Platte. While some of the men made a willow frame for a boat, others pursued and killed buffalo to procure hides for a covering. The green hides were sewed together and stretched over the willow frame. Seams were plugged with a mixture of tallow and ashes. The whole was dried over a slow fire and the bullboat was ready. With it the goods were successfully transported across the stream. [61]

As they journeyed up the Sweetwater toward South Pass, the health of Mrs. Spalding failed noticeably. It was feared that she could never reach her destination. Once she fainted and upon being revived spoke to her husband: "I cannot live much longer. Go on and save yourself, and carry the Book of God to those Indians. I shall never see them; my work is done, but bless God, he has brought me thus far. Tell my mother I am not sorry that I came." [62] But she did go on; she lived to see Oregon.

An express having been dispatched to Green River to announce the coming of the train, a motley band of trappers and Indians came forward to meet it. Upon coming in sight of the caravan the leader of the greeting delegation tied a white cloth to the end of his gun and led the charge. On came the mountaineers, yelling and whooping, their horses jumping the sage brush as they dashed past the train. Over the heads of the excited missionaries they sent a volley of bullets; then whirling

[60] Gray, *op. cit.,* 117.

[61] *Ibid.,* 117.

[62] Eells, *op. cit.,* 34.

back they circled the caravan and quieted down to hand-shake greetings.[63]

Arrived at the rendezvous, the pack animals were unloaded and the goods placed in a large log storeroom which had previously been built for such occasions. The clerks brought out their books and the trading began. Free trappers and Indians crowded around to barter their furs for powder and knives, sugar and coffee, bright colored cloth and spangles, and the numerous articles that appealed to primitive tastes.

The tents of the women missionaries became reception chambers. Braves admired the genial and gracious Mrs. Whitman, while the squaws were drawn to the enfeebled Mrs. Spalding. Trappers were reminded of mothers and sisters and of homes left behind.

On the sixth day of the rendezvous, the Indians entertained with a gorgeous procession and a brilliant display of military maneuvers. The braves were painted and dressed (or undressed) for war, and with their weapons and battle paraphernalia needed only the presence of scalps to make the war scenes complete.[64] The demonstration was enjoyed by the spectators almost as much as by the participants.

To the rendezvous of this year came an agent of the American Fur company who purchased the business interests of Fitzpatrick and the other mountain partners. Writes Dr. Whitman in september, 1836: "Major Pilcher joined us at Fort William and came on to rendezvous, as agent of Pratt, Choteau & co., in whose behalf he bought out the 'mountain partners,' so that the whole [fur] business now belongs to them." [64a]

[63] F. F. Victor, *The river of the West*, 202. Also Gray, *op. cit.*, 118. The similarity of wording in these two accounts indicates that one was copied from the other.

[64] Gray, *op. cit.*, 122.

[64a] Hulbert, *Marcus Whitman, Crusader*, 230.

The rendezvous over, the missionaries continued toward Oregon under the guidance of some Hudson's Bay company traders, while Fitzpatrick and Milton Sublette packed the furs obtained in barter, and those brought in by their trapper employees, and started the mule train back to Fort William.

Within the walls of the fort the rendezvous furs were added to the buffalo robes, buckskin, and furs gathered at the trading post during the winter, and the total product was loaded on mules for the journey back to the states. Fitzpatrick captained the caravan on its return.

Little is known of events at Fort William during the succeeding winter. We know that Milton Sublette remained at the post and that after continued suffering caused by his leg, he died there in december, 1836.[65]

With the trader and trapper supply train that left St. Louis the next spring (1837), came again the English sportsman, Sir William Drummond Stewart. And, fortunately for history, Sir William brought with him, to make sketches in the far West, the artist A. J. Miller. This capable portrayer of western scenes made several paintings of the fort, the two principal ones of which are reproduced here for the first time. Miller's drawings are the only ones extant of the original fort, and their importance can scarcely be overestimated.[66] Mr. Miller also wrote a brief description of the fort and of his reception there. The post, he says, "is of a quadrangular form, with block houses at diagonal corners to sweep the fronts in case of attack.

---

[65] Chittenden, *American fur trade of the far west,* 254.

[66] The existence of these important paintings and the acompanying notes by Miller was made known to us by Mr. C. P. Russell of the National park service. Copies of the paintings and permission to reproduce were kindly given by Mr. Morgan Marshall, administrator of the Walters Art Gallery and by Mr. Macgill James, director of the municipal museum of the city of Baltimore.

"Over the front entrance is a large block house in which is placed a cannon. The interior of the fort is about 150 feet square, surrounded by small cabins whose roofs reach within 3 feet of the top of the palisades against which they abut. The Indians encamp in great numbers here 3 or 4 times a year, bringing peltries to be exchanged for dry goods, tobacco, beads and alcohol.

"The Indians have a mortal horror of the 'big gun' which rests in the block house, as they have had experience of its prowess and witnessed the havoc produced by its loud 'talk.' They conceive it to be only asleep and have a wholesome dread of its being waked up.

"On entering the principal room of the fort we noticed 5 or 6 first class engravings, one of which was Richard and Saladin battling in the Holy land and from these immediately surmised that the commander of the fort was a refined gentleman. When he came in we found our surmise correct. He tendered at once the hospitalities of the place and attendants and gave orders for crocks of milk to be brought to us, a luxury we had been deprived of for a length of time and to which we did ample justice; and while we rested here seemed never tired of extending to us every comfort and aid that he could command.

"The view [Interior, reproduced herewith] is from the great entrance looking west and embraces more than half the court or area. When this space is filled with Indians and traders as it is at stated periods the scene is lively and interesting. They gather here from all quarters; from the Gila at the south, the Red river at the north, and the Columbia river west, each has its quota and representatives, Sioux, Bannocks, Crows, Snakes, Pend-Oreilles, Nez Perces, Cheyennes and Delawares, all except the Black Feet who are 'betes noirs' and con-

INTERIOR OF FORT WILLIAM, 1837
From a sketch by A. J. Miller

sidered 'de trop.' As a contrast there are Canadian trappers, free and otherwise, half-breeds, Kentuckians, Missourians and Down-Easters. A saturnalia is held the first day and some excesses committed. But after this trading goes briskly forward." [67]

Late in june Captain Fitzpatrick moved on from Fort William toward the rendezvous with forty-five men and twenty mule carts loaded with trade goods.[68] Upon reaching the mouth of Horse creek on Green river, he found Captain Drips and his trappers assembled and anxiously awaiting the arrival of the train. Captain Thing from the Hudson's Bay company's Fort Hall on Snake river was also there.[69]

W. H. Gray, one of the missionaries who had gone to Oregon the previous year, was returning with some Flathead companions and was at the rendezvous. He records in his journal:

"JULY 18. tuesday The company from St. Louis have arrived. A young man by the name of Mr. Ewing has called upon me. Capt. Stewart and others are with the company; also a Mr. Miller, etc. They have been since the 27th of june, coming from Fort William, on Laramie's Fork. Mr. Ewing and L. Phillipson called and took dinner with me. Mr. Miller, who is a portrait painter, called at tea or supper." [70]

The rendezvous was again a gay and colorful assemblage. Writes Osborne Russell, one of the participants: "Joy now beamed in every countenance. Some received

---

[67] Notes accompanying Miller's paintings. Supplied by Mr. C. P. Russell.

[68] Osborne Russell, *Journal of a trapper*, 63.

[69] "Journal of Wm. H. Gray," in a volume privately printed for Mrs. Jacob Kamm by the American historical society, 666.

[70] *Ibid.*, 668. Osborne Russell appears to be in error in placing the arrival of the fur company train at rendezvous on July 5. See his *Journal of a trapper*, 63.

letters from their friends and relations; some received the public papers and news of the day; others consoled themselves with the idea of getting a blanket, a cotton shirt or a few pints of coffee and sugar to sweeten it just by way of a treat, gratis, that is to say, by paying 2,000 per cent on the first cost by way of accommodation. For instance, sugar $2 per pint, coffee the same, blankets $20 each, tobacco $2 per pound, alcohol $4 per pint, and common cotton shirts $5 each, etc. And in return paid $4 or $5 per pound for beaver. In a few days the bustle began to subside. The furs were done up in packs ready for transportation to the States and parties were formed for the hunting the ensuing year. One party, consisting of 110 men, was destined for the Blackfoot country, under the direction of L. B. Fontanelle as commander and James Bridger as pilot." [71]

Gray left the rendezvous on july 25 and reached Fort William on august 2. On this date he records: "Proceeding at a quick pace we arrived at this fort on Laramie's Fork at half past seven A.M., coming about ten miles. We find it in the charge of Mr. Woods.

"Finding some of my horses' feet worn, I have got four of them shod. We find a number of Sioux at this fort. The chief gave us an invitation to a feast this evening, which he has provided with roots, beaten up and boiled in water and marrow grease, presented us in a dish, made of a nut, and horn spoons. The chief made many apologies for not being able to procure a dog for us, which they consider as a great treat to a white man, and a valuable animal among themselves." [72]

Though warned at the fort that Sioux had recently killed a half-breed near Chimney Rock and that to con-

[71] Russell, op. cit., 63-64.
[72] Gray's journal, op. cit., 671.

tinue with his small party would be dangerous, Gray
decided to proceed. Near Ash Hollow he was attacked
by Sioux. He escaped but his Flathead companions
were killed.[73]

Fort William had already become a gathering place
for trappers, and especially for such as were robbed and
pillaged by hostile Indians. Osborne Russell, with a
little party of mountain men detached from Fontenelle's
main band, headed for this fort after being robbed by
the Crows in early november, 1837. With their horses
gone, the trappers had cached their beaver skins, burned
their saddles and set out toward a new base of supplies.
After almost three weeks of tedious travel on foot, much
of the time through rain or snow, they finally welcomed
the sight of the high log enclosure of Fort William.
Their treatment there, however, fell short of what they
had expected.

"When I entered this fort," writes Russell, "I was met
by two of my old messmates, who invited me to their
apartments. I now felt myself at home, as Mr. Fontanell
was one of the chief proprietors of the establishment,
and who had been partly, and I may say wholly, the
cause of our misfortunes [having failed to leave a message for them at the appointed place]. At night I lay
down, but the pains in my legs and feet drove sleep
from me. The next day I walked around the fort as
well as I could in order to get my joints limber, and on
the third day after our arrival I felt quite recovered and
at breakfast I asked my messmates where the man was
who had charge of the fort. They replied he was in his
house, pointing across the square. I inquired if he was
sick, for I had not seen him. They said he was unwell,

<hr />

[73] Gray's journal, op. cit., 672-75. Gray has been accused of sacrificing the
Flatheads for his own safety. See Victor, op. cit., 233-34.

but not so as to confine him to his room. I observed I must go and see him, as I discovered he was not coming to see me, so saying, Allen and myself started across the square and met him on the way from the storehouse to his dwelling room. We bid him 'good morning,' which he coldly returned and was on the point of turning carelessly away, when we told him we would like to get some robes for bedding, likewise a shirt or two and some other necessary articles. 'Well,' said he, 'as for blankets, shirts or coats, I have none, and Mr. Fontanell has left no word when there will be any come up.' 'If that is the case,' I replied, 'you can let us have some buffalo robes and epishemores.' 'Yes,' said he, 'I believe I can let you have an epishemore or two. Here, John, go up into yonder bastion and show these men those epishemores that were put up there some time ago.' 'I don't think there are any there,' replied John, 'but some old ones, and them the rats have cut all to pieces.' 'Oh, I guess you can find some there that will do,' he replied, turning around and swinging a key on his thumb as the insignia of his dignified position and with a stiff stride walked to his apartments, while we followed the major-domo of this elevated quadruped to the bastion, where I took the best epishemore I could find, which was composed of nine pieces of buffalo skin sewed together. But necessity compelled me to take it, knowing at the same time there were more that 500 new robes in the warehouse which did not cost a pint of whisky each. But they were for the people in the U.S. and not for trappers." [74]

Russell does not give the name of the man in charge of the fort, but it probably was Mr. Wood, whom Gray had met there in august.

Shortly after Russell's arrival, Thomas Biggs with a

[74] Russell, *op. cit.,* 79-80.

small trapping party came in to the fort, there to await further orders from Fontenelle. Within a month (december 20) Fontenelle himself with fifteen men arrived, "bringing the furs he had collected during the hunt, for the purpose of depositing them at the fort." [75] He had met with the Crows that robbed Russell's party and had forced them to give up their spoils.

Fontenelle remained at Fort William the rest of the winter. The post was coming to be the capital of the fur empire of the central Rocky Mountain West. It was headquarters. From this post supplies were obtained and to its shelter was brought the product of trapping and the Indian trade.

In late january, 1838, Fontenelle sent a small brigade of men, including Russell, up to the winter rendezvous on Powder river, where Jim Bridger was encamped with the main body of trappers. This valley was a furman's paradise, even in winter. Writes Russell: "Here we found the camp living on the fat of the land. The bottoms along Powder river were crowded with buffalos, so much so that it was difficult keeping them from among the horses, which were fed upon sweet cottonwood bark, as the buffalos had consumed everything in the shape of grass along the river." [76]

In this camp was Kit Carson, already becoming somewhat famous as a trapper. Of the winter on Powder river Kit is reported to have said: "We had to keep the buffalo from our camp by building large fires in the bottoms. They came in such large droves that our horses were in danger of being killed when we turned them out to eat of the branches of trees which we had cut down. When [we] broke up camp and started two men for

---

[75] *Ibid.*, 83.
[76] *Ibid.*, 84.

Fort Laramie where the American Fur company had established a trading post. They never reached this. I presume they were killed by the Sioux Indians." [77]

With the early spring, the trappers set out to make their catch. "A trapper's equipment in such cases," says Russell, "is generally one animal upon which is placed one or two epishemores, a riding saddle and bridle, a sack containing six beaver traps, a blanket with an extra pair of moccasins, his powder horn and bullet pouch, with a belt to which is attached a butcher knife, a wooden box containing bait for beaver, a tobacco sack with a pipe and implements for making fire, with sometimes a hatchet fastened to the pommel of his saddle. His personal dress is a flannel or cotton shirt (if he is fortunate enough to obtain one, if not antelope skin answers the purpose of over and undershirt), a pair of leather breeches with blanket or smoked buffalo skin leggings, a coat made of blanket or buffalo robe, a hat or cap of wool, buffalo or otter skin, his hose are pieces of blanket wrapped around his feet, which are covered with a pair of moccasins made of dressed deer, elk or buffalo skins, with his long hair falling loosely over his shoulders, completes his uniform. He then mounts and places his rifle before him on his saddle." [78]

The summer supply train of 1838 was led by Captain Andrew Drips, in charge of sixty men. Accompanying them and bound for the Oregon country was another party of missionaries – Reverend and Mrs. W. H. Gray, Reverend and Mrs. E. Walker, Mr. and Mrs. C. Eells, and Mr. and Mrs. A. B. Smith. Writes Mrs. Eells of

---

[77] B. C. Grant (ed.), *Kit Carson's own life story,* 39. The story was dictated in later years, which probably accounts for the use of the name Fort Laramie instead of Fort William. The editor mistakes the date as the spring of 1837 instead of 1838.

[78] Russell, *Journal of a trapper,* 85.

the caravan: "The company have about two hundred horses and mules; we have twenty-two horses and mules; they have seventeen carts and wagons, we have one. We have twelve horned cattle. The wagons are all covered with black or dark oil cloth." [79] Traveling with the company was a Swissman destined for fame – August Johann Sutter.[80]

Up the valley of the Platte the caravan moved without important incident. It reached the vicinity of Fort William at the end of may. An interesting record is preserved in the diary of Mrs. Eells:

"WEDNESDAY, MAY 30. Last night a number of Indian women came to see us. They were neatly dressed and ornamented with beads. Suppose they are wives of white men at the fort and in the mountains. Moved camp at six, rode two hours, crossed Laramie's Fork and came to Fort William five miles. Sell Mr. Walker's horse to Capt. Fontenelle for forty dollars. Three Indian women, wives of Capt. Drips, Fontanelle, and Wood, with their children call on us. The children are quite white and can read a little. Rainy.

"THURSDAY, MAY 31. The ladies engaged in washing, mending, etc., our husbands making repairs and arrangements for the remainder of the journey. Give the wagon to Capts. Drips and Fontanelle. They with Mr. Wood take tea with us.

"FRIDAY, JUNE 1. Attend to writing. Indian women and children continually calling on us. The company gave us a horse. Mr. Gray takes one he left here a year ago.

"SATURDAY, JUNE 2. Leave here this morning, ride into Fort William. It is a large hewed log building with

79 Myra F. Eells, Journal, in *Transactions, Oregon pioneer association.* Seventeenth annual reunion (1889).

80 Gray, *op. cit.*, 177.

an opening in the center; partitions for various objects. It compares very well with the walls of the Connecticut state prison. A fort in this country, is a place built to accommodate the company as they go and come from the mountains to trade with the Indians. Start at seven, ride five and one-half hours twenty-eight miles. Encamp in the open prairie at a clear spring at the foot of the Black Hills. Left four of our cattle because their feet were so sore they could not travel." [81]

From the fort the train continued with the carts on up the Platte and the Sweetwater. A little beyond Independence Rock it turned north to the junction of the Popo Agie and Wind river, where the rendezvous of 1838 was to be held. Here, near present Riverton, Wyoming, the train waited for two weeks before the trapping band came in. Of their arrival Mrs. Eells writes:

"THURSDAY, JULY 5. Capt. Bridger's company comes in about ten o'clock with drums and firing – an apology for a scalp dance. After they had given Capt. Drips' company a shout, fifteen or twenty mountain men and Indians came to our tent with drumming, firing and dancing. If I might make a comparison, I should say that they looked like the emissaries of the devil worshipping their own master. They had the scalp of a Blackfoot Indian, which they carried for a color, all rejoicing in the fate of the Blackfoots in consequence of the smallpox." [82]

On the 8th some Hudson's Bay company trappers came in to rendezvous and with them were Jason Lee and P. L. Edwards, returning to the states to recruit missionaries for Oregon.[83] With the break up of the rendezvous on the 20th, the carts set out on the return

---

[81] Eells, Journal, *op. cit.*
[82] *Ibid.*
[83] Russell, *op. cit.*, 93; C. J. Brosnan, *Jason Lee,* 93, 97.

to Fort William. Drips and Bridger remained in the mountains at the head of trapping brigades. The conductor of the furs back to the states is not identified.[84]

The fur-trade caravan was much smaller than usual in 1839. The beaver trade was decidedly on the decline, the rendezvous about to be abandoned. The fur company, Chouteau, Pratt & Co.,[85] had but four two-wheeled carts, each drawn by two mules and carrying 800 to 900 pounds each. In charge of these goods was a veteran mountain man, "Black" Harris, assisted by eight company employees. Missionaries and independent travelers increased the number in the party to twenty-seven. Among these latter was a German physician from St. Louis, Dr. Wislizenus, on a tour of recreation and adventure to the mountains. His account of the expedition, published in German the following year, gives interesting sidelights on the trip and valuable data respecting the fort on the Laramie.

After journeying up the south side of the Platte to its forks, the company encountered large bands of Indians, Sioux and Cheyennes, traveling up the river on the opposite side. Although they appeared friendly, Capt. Harris feared for his goods. So after dark, by way of precaution, he "caused the few barrels of spirits which he had with him to be buried and enjoined on all" the greatest vigilance.[86] Next day the Indians set up nearly one thousand tepees on the bank opposite the white caravan. Many bucks and even squaws crossed the river on horseback or by means of a bullboat of their own manufacture, to visit the white camp. "We obtained by barter with them several articles," says Wis-

---

[84] Russell, *op. cit.,* 94.

[85] F. A. Wislizenus, *A journey to the Rocky mountains in the year 1839* (a translation of the original German and published in 1912), 28-29.

[86] *Ibid.,* 55.

lizenus, "such as tanned skins, moccasins, buffalo hides
and the like. For a piece of chewing tobacco as big as
a hand one could get a fine buffalo hide. Some Indians
would sell everything they had on. But all showed immense curiosity.

"They were continuously about us in our tents; all objects that were new to them they stared at and handled,
not failing to appropriate some when unobserved. The
two wives of the missionaries were special objects of
their curiosity. . .

"All night through matters were lively in the Indian
camp. Dreadfully piercing notes came to us over the
water; and then a chorus of some thousand dogs howled
such night music as I have never yet heard. The next
morning we saw with pleasure how the Indians struck
their tents, packed their horses and dogs, and gradually
set themselves in motion toward the North Fork. . .
Glad to be rid of our guests, we set in earnest about
finishing the canoe at which we had hitherto worked
but slowly. These canoes are made in the following manner: Small trunks of some wood that bends easily are
split; out of these a boat-shaped frame work is made
with some cross pieces inside; this is firmly bound with
thongs of buffalo leather and willow bark, and all gaps
are stopped with withes; and buffalo hides, sewed together, with the hair inside, are stretched as taut as can
be over the whole. Then it is dried in the air, and the
outside daubed over with a mixture of buffalo tallow
and ashes. Our canoe was covered with three buffalo
hides, and was about fifteen feet long by a width in the
middle of five to six feet. It was finished towards evening, but we still spent the night here, to dig up the
buried barrels of spirits." [87]

[87] *Ibid.*, 58-59.

After traveling some distance farther up the South Fork, the stream was successfully crossed by means of the bullboat and the company moved over the divide to the North Platte. Before reaching the fort they met the first whites encountered on the journey. "They were French Canadians," says the German doctor, "clad half Indian fashion in leather, and scurrying along on their ponies, bedight with bells and gay ribbons, as if intent to storm some battery. . . Meanwhile we came in view of the fort.

"At a distance it resembles a great blockhouse; and lies in a narrow valley, enclosed by grassy hills, near by the left bank of the Laramie, which empties into the North Platte about a mile below. Toward the west a fine background is formed by the Black Hills, a dark chain of mountains covered with evergreen trees. We crossed the Laramie toward noon, and encamped outside the fort. The fort itself first attracted my attention. It lies on a slight elevation, and is built in a rectangle of about eighty by a hundred feet. The outside is made of cottonwood logs, about fifteen feet high, hewed off, and wedged closely together. On three sides there are little towers on the wall that seem designed for watch and defense. In the middle a strong gate, built of blocks, constitutes the entrance. Within, little buildings with flat roofs are plastered all around against the wall, like swallows' nests. One is the store house; another the smithy; the others are dwellings not unlike monks' cells. A special portion of the court yard is occupied by the so-called horse-pen, in which the horses are confined at night. The middle space is free, with a tall tree in it, on which the flag is raised on occasions of state. The whole garrison of the fort consists of only five men; four Frenchmen and a German. Some of them were married

to Indian women, whose cleanliness and neat attire
formed an agreeable contrast to the daughters of the
wilderness whom we have hitherto seen. . . As far as
I know, there is no fort on the North Platte save Fort
Laramie [Fort William]; but several American trading companies have built forts along the South Platte,
the Arkansas, the Green river, and the Missouri. Beyond the Rocky mountains are only English forts. Fort
Laramie was built in 1835 [1834] by Robert Campbell,
and was then called Fort William. Later it passed into
other control, and was rechristened Fort Laramie after
one Laramie, who was killed here by the Indians. . .[88]
The fort is at present in possession of Piggit, Papin and
Jaudron. [89] In many respects it has a very favorable
location. There is sufficient wood in the vicinity and
good pasture. A few days' journey further there is abundance of buffalo and other game, and the Platte from
this point is navigable for small boats; at least Campbell has already gone down from here to the Missouri
in buffalo boats. Then, too, it is a very suitable center
for trade with important Indian tribes, especially the
Sioux and Crows. The last named Indians had recently
levied a small contribution from the fort, in that they
had driven off sixteen horses grazing in the vicinity in
full daylight and in view of two guards. Luckily the
fort had a superfluity of horses, so that the loss was not
serious. In addition to horses, the fort owns property
that is of very great value in this region; that is, several
cows. No attention is paid to agriculture, although the

[88] *Ibid.*, 67-69. The name "Laramie" appears gradually to have been applied to the fort on the Laramie river. Neither the name Fort William nor
the later one, Fort John, were generally accepted.

[89] *Ibid.*, 69. Just when this company came into possession of the fort is not
clear. It is significant that the company in possession of the fort is distinct
from the one carrying goods to the rendezvous – granting that Wislizenus is
correct in his statements.

ground seems suitable for it. Hunting is the sole reliance for food. All we found in stock at that time was dried buffalo meat, of which we took a supply with us. As we stayed there the rest of the day, several races took place between our horses and those of the fort; and of course there was betting and swapping of horses. I swapped my horse, which was somewhat run down by the journey and thin, for a swift, well fed Indian horse trained to hunt buffalo." [90]

The fur-trade caravan destined for the rendezvous remained only a half day at the fort, continuing up the Platte on the morning of the 15th. Past Independence Rock, the Rocky Mountain Album,[91] and through South Pass they journeyed toward Green river. Shortly before reaching the place of rendezvous they were met by "two agents of the fur company, Trips [Drips] and Walker. These agents were accompanied by their Indian wives and a lot of dogs. The two squaws, quite passable as to their features, appeared in highest state. Their red blankets, with the silk kerchiefs on their heads, and their gaudy embroideries, gave them quite an oriental appearance. Like themselves, their horses were bedight with embroideries, beads, corals, ribbons and little bells. The bells were hung about in such number that when riding in their neighborhood, one might think one's self in the midst of Turkish music. The squaws, however, behaved most properly. They took care of the horses, pitched a tent, and were alert for every word of their wedded lords. From the agents we learned that this year's meeting place had been fixed on the right bank of the Green river at the angle formed by its junction with Horse creek." [92]

[90] *Ibid.,* 69-70.
[91] *Ibid.,* 78.
[92] *Ibid.,* 84.

The next day [july 5] they reached the rendezvous. "What first struck our eye," says Wislizenus, "was several long rows of Indian tents [lodges], extending along the Green river for at least a mile. Indians and whites were mingled here in varied groups. Of the Indians there had come chiefly Snakes, Flatheads and Nez Perces, peaceful tribes, living beyond the Rocky mountains. Of whites the agents of the different trading companies and a quantity of trappers had found their way here, visiting this fair of the wilderness to buy and to sell, to renew old contracts and to make new ones, to make arrangements for future meetings, to meet old friends, to tell of adventures they had been through, and to spend for once a jolly day. These trappers, the 'knights without fear and without reproach,' are such a peculiar set of people that it is necessary to say a little about them. The name in itself indicates their occupation. They either receive their outfit, consisting of horses, beaver traps, a gun, powder and lead, from trading companies, and trap for small wages, or else they act on their own account, and are then called freemen. The latter is more often the case. In small parties they roam through all the mountain passes. No rock is too steep for them; no stream too swift. . . In manners and customs, the trappers have borrowed much from the Indians. Many of them, too, have taken Indian women as wives. Their dress is generally of leather. The hair of the head is usually allowed to grow long. In place of money, they use beaver skins, for which they can satisfy all their needs at the forts by way of trade. A pound of beaver skins is usually paid for with four dollars worth of goods; but the goods themselves are sold at enormous prices, so-called mountain prices. A pint of meal, for instance, costs from half a dollar to a dollar; a pint of coffee-beans, cocoa-beans or sugar, two dollars each; a pint of diluted alcohol (the only spiritous liquor to be had), four dollars; a piece of chewing tobacco of the commonest sort, which is usually smoked, Indian fashion, mixed with herbs, one to two dollars. Guns and ammunition, bear traps, blankets, kerchiefs, and gaudy finery for the squaws, are also sold at enormous profit. At the yearly rendezvous the trappers seek to indemnify themselves for the sufferings and privations of a year spent in the wilderness. With their hairy bank notes, the beaver skins, they can obtain all the luxuries of the mountains, and live for a few days like lords. Coffee and chocolate is cooked; the pipe is kept aglow day and night; the spirits circulate; and whatever is not spent in such ways the squaws coax out of them, or else it is squandered at cards. Formerly single trappers on such occasions have often wasted a thousand dollars. But the days of their glory seem to be past, for constant hunting has very much reduced the number of beavers. This diminution in the beaver catch made itself noticeable at this year's [1839] rendezvous in the quieter behavior of the trappers. There was little drinking of spirits, and almost no gambling. . .

"The Indians who had come to the meeting were no less interesting than the trappers. There must have been some thousands of them. Their tents are made of buffalo hides, tanned on both sides and sewed together, stretched in cone shape over a dozen poles, that are leaned against each other, their tops crossing . . . groups of whites and Indians were engaged in barter. The Indians had for the trade chiefly tanned skins, moccasins, thongs of buffalo leather or braided buffalo hair, and fresh or dried buffalo meat. They have no beaver skins. The articles that attracted them most in exchange were powder and lead, knives, tobacco, cinnabar, gaily colored kerchiefs, pocket mirrors and all sorts of ornaments. . .

"The rendezvous usually lasts a week. Then the different parties move off to their destinations and the plain that today resounded with barbarous music, that was thronged with people of both races, with horses and dogs, returns to its old quiet, interrupted only now and then by the muffled roar of the buffalo and the howl of the wolf." [93]

Andrew Drips led the fur-trade caravan of 1840. It set out from Westport on the last day of april with carts and pack animals laden with goods for Fort William and the rendezvous.[94] With the traders went the protestant missionaries, Harvey Clark, A. T. Smith, and P. B. Littlejohn with their wives, and Father De Smet, famous catholic missionary. There was also an avowed emigrant settler, Joel P. Walker, with his wife and five children.[95]

The route was again up the south side of the Platte. "On the 4th of june," writes Father De Smet, "we crossed the Fourche-a-la-Ramee [Laramie fork] one of the principal tributaries of the Platte, in a buffalo canoe, or bullboat. Here we found some forty lodges of the Cheyennes, who received us with all the signs of good will and esteem; they were polite, cleanly and decent in their manners. . .

---

[93] *Ibid.*, 86-90.

[94] Chittenden and Richardson, *Life, letters and travels of Father Pierre-Jean De Smet, S.J.*, 201. Hereafter this work will be referred to as *De Smet*. See also Joel P. Walker's Narrative, MS., in Bancroft library, university of California.

[95] H. H. Bancroft, *History of Oregon*, I, 239-40. See also Walker, Narrative, *op. cit.* Walker says that he had two wagons and the missionaries had two. In one place he says the American Fur company had 30 carts and forty men; in another place he says they had fifty men, fifty two-wheeled carts and about sixty pack mules.

"The head chiefs of this village invited me to a feast, and put me through all the ceremonies of the calumet, . . .

"Fort la Ramee [Laramie] is at the foot of the Black Hills. There is nothing observable, either in the color of the soil of these mountains or in that of the rocks, that can have given them this name; they owe it to the sombre verdure of the little cedars and pines that shade their sides." [96]

Unfortunately, neither De Smet or Walker give any description of the fort or of conditions there. The party must not have stayed long at the post for they were at the Red Butte, near the mouth of the Sweetwater, on june 14. At Independence Rock, "the great register of the desert," [97] De Smet added his name to the many already scratched or painted upon this famous landmark.

The caravan reached the Green river rendezvous on june 30, two months after its departure from Westport on the Missouri. Shoshones in great numbers were there to greet the traders and missionaries and give an exhibition in their honor. Says Father De Smet: "Three hundred of their warriors came up in good order and at full gallop into the midst of our camp. They were hideously painted, armed with their clubs, and covered all over with feathers, pearls, wolves' tails, teeth and claws of animals, outlandish adornments, with which each one had decked himself out according to his fancy. Those who had wounds received in war, and those who had killed the enemies of their tribe, displayed their scars ostentatiously and waved the scalps they had taken on the ends of poles, after the manner of standards.

[96] *De Smet*, 210-13.
[97] *Ibid.*, 214.

"After riding a few times around the camp, uttering at intervals shouts of joy, they dismounted and all came to shake hands with the whites in sign of friendship." [98]

This was the last great fur-trade rendezvous [1840], the finale of those spectacular mountain assemblages that for sixteen years had been the outstanding annual event, the unique institution of the Rocky mountain West. To grizzled trappers who had seen the rise and the fall of the beaver skin business, this final gathering brought bewilderment and regret.

Men who had become attached to this fascinating, dangerous life were loath to leave it. But there was no choice left them. A livelihood no longer could be made by trapping beaver; and no fur company would agree to bring trade goods to the Green river valley to barter for beaver pelts. The rendezvous was dead. Trappers must look for employment elsewhere. Some would go to Santa Fe, some to California or Oregon, others would return to Missouri.

"Come," said Doc. Newell to Joe Meek, "we are done with this life in the mountains – done with wading in beaver-dams, and freezing or starving alternately – done with Indian trading and Indian fighting. The fur-trade is dead in the Rocky mountains, and it is no place for us now, if ever it was. We are young yet, and have life before us. We cannot waste it here; we cannot or will not return to the states. Let us go down to the Wallamet [Oregon] and take farms." [99]

---

[98] *Ibid.*, 217.
[99] F. F. Victor, *The river of the West*, 264.

Rival Posts - Fort Platte and Fort John, 1840-1845

The abandonment of the annual rendezvous only increased the importance of the trading-post. For although beaver skins were both scarce and cheap, trade in buffalo robes could still flourish. Indians would procure and tan these skins and bring them in to the traders' forts to barter for white man goods. Rival companies built rival forts and employed all the devices known to unscrupulous traffickers to confine to themselves the choice products of the trade.

For six years preceding 1840, Fort William, or Laramie, had been alone in the country of the North Platte. In fact, when it was founded, its closest neighbors were Fort Bent [to the south, on the Arkansas], Fort Hall [to the west, on the Snake river], and the forts on the Missouri. In the interval, four fur-trade posts had arisen on the South Platte river, less than two hundred miles to the south of Fort William. These were forts Lupton, Jackson, Vasquez and St. Vrain.[100] Their establishment resulted from the keen competition there, which may be outlined as follows:

After Sublette and Campbell sold Fort William on the Laramie, they continued to supply goods to itinerant traders in the South Platte region, rich buffalo country of the Arapahos and Cheyennes. Then into this section

---

100 These forts were founded respectively by Lancaster P. Lupton, Henry Fraeb and P. A. Sarpy, Louis Vasquez and Andrew W. Sublette, and Bent and St. Vrain.

came an ambitious young lieutenant, Lancaster P. Lupton, to enter the fur-trade. He had come west in 1835 with Colonel Dodge and his Dragoons, saw the possibilities of trade, and forthwith resigned from the army. In 1836 he built the first adobe fort on the South Platte – Fort Lupton – near the present town of Fort Lupton, Colorado.[101] To compete with this intruder, Pratte, Chouteau and company (American Fur company) advanced trade goods and money the following year to Peter A. Sarpy and Henry Fraeb for establishing an opposition fort. This resulted in the building of Fort Jackson within six miles of Mr. Lupton's post.[102] To retain their Indian trade in this region, Louis Vasquez and Andrew Sublette, backed by the founders of Fort William, erected their post, Fort Vasquez, also in 1837.[103] And Bent and St. Vrain, finding the trade of their fort on the Arkansas cut in upon, hurried to build a fort on the South Platte. This post, known in turn as Fort Lookout, Fort George and Fort St. Vrain, completed a chain of four rival adobe trading-posts on the South Platte within a distance of fifteen miles.[104]

The Indian trade in that quarter by no means justified the maintenance of so many posts there. In october, 1838, Fort Jackson was sold to Bent and St. Vrain and abandoned. Fort Vasquez was sold to Lock and Randolph in 1840 or 1841 and was abandoned in 1842. Fort Lupton and Fort St. Vrain continued active until the middle forties.

---

[101] See L. R. Hafen, "Old Fort Lupton and its founder," in *Colorado magazine*, VI, 220-26.

[102] See L. R. Hafen, "Fort Jackson and the early fur trade on the South Platte," in *Colorado magazine*, V, 9-17.

[103] L. R. Hafen, "Mountain men – Louis Vasquez," in *Colorado magazine*, X, 16-19.

[104] L. R. Hafen, "The early fur trade posts on the South Platte," in the *Mississippi valley historical review*, XII, 334-341.

While Fort William on the Laramie was, prior to 1840, the only post in the North Platte section, the buffalo country of the Sioux, independent traders for some years had operated there. In february, 1838, P. A. Sarpy, wrote from the Laramie to his partner Fraeb, complaining about the competition of Mr. St. Vrain, of Papin and Picotte, and of B. Orrick and company on the North Platte.[105] And a rival trading post in this area was not to be much longer delayed.

This opposition fort must have been built in the fall of 1840 or spring of 1841.[106] It was named Fort Platte and appears to have been built by L. P. Lupton, owner of the fort on the South Platte. Travelers through the region in the summer of 1841 are the first to mention it. John Bidwell, principal contemporary historian of the emigration of 1841, writes under date of june 22: "Eight miles this morning took us to Fort Laramie, which is on Laramie's fork of Platte about 800 miles from the frontiers of Missouri. It is owned by the American Fur company. There is another fort within a mile and a half of this place, belonging to an individual by the name of Lupton." [107]

Fort Platte was a commodious adobe structure, located on the right bank of the North Platte, about three-fourths of a mile above the mouth of the Laramie. Its erection doubtless stimulated the rebuilding of Fort William in a more substantial form. The fact that the logs of the old stockade fort were decaying and the post was in need of repair was an added argument for replacing the old structure with one built of adobes. The

---

[105] Letter in the Chouteau-Maffitt collection, Missouri historical society, calender no. 720.

[106] De Smet in the summer of 1840 mentions only one fort on the Laramie, see above.

[107] J. Bidwell, *A journey to California* (in Bancroft library, university of California).

owners of the post now adopted the New Mexican type of adobe building already employed by the builders of Fort Bent on the Arkansas and the four forts on the South Platte. This new adobe fort that replaced Fort William was christened Fort John, presumably in honor of John B. Sarpy, an officer of the company that built and owned it. But this name did not "take." Instead, the name Laramie, given to the river and the region, and frequently applied to the preceding wooden fort, soon attached itself to the new adobe structure.

When Joseph Williams, eccentric missionary, came by in the summer of 1841, the new fort was under construction. He writes that after crossing the Laramie river, he "went up to a new fort that they were building, called Fort Johns. . . There are two forts here, about one mile apart. . ." [108] Dr. H. S. Schell, who was later stationed at Fort Laramie, made a report in which is incorporated a brief history of the fort. He says that when the picket fort [Fort William] "began to rot badly" the American Fur company "rebuilt it of adobes at an expense of $10,000. The people who lived inside of the fort at this time named it Fort John, but the name could not be popularized." [109] Alexander Culbertson, American Fur company official, said that Fort John [or Laramie] was built at a cost of $10,000 and was the best built stronghold in the company's possession.[110]

Furs from the fort were sent to St. Louis in the spring of 1841 both by wagon and by boat. The first California-

---

[108] J. Williams, *Narrative of a tour from the state of Indiana to the Oregon territory, 1841-2,* 38.

[109] Assistant Surgeon Schell's report, circular no. 4 (1870), Barracks and hospitals. Dr. Schell gives 1836 as the year of this rebuilding with adobes, but in this he is clearly mistaken, as is proved by the contemporary descriptions given in the preceding chapter. Unfortunately, Bancroft, Coutant and others have followed Schell and given the year 1836 as the date for the building of the adobe fort.

[110] Thwaites, *Early western travels,* XXX, 60.

bound emigrant party met the fur-laden wagons east of Fort Kearny on may 31, 1841. John Bidwell writes: "We met six wagons with 18 men, with fur and robes on their way from Ft. Laramie to St. Louis. . . The waggons were drawn by oxen and mules – the former looked as though they received a thousand lashes every day of their existence! The rusty mountaineers looked as though they never had seen razor, water, soap or brush." [111] On june 5 the emigrants saw several boats descending the Platte with furs and robes for the American Fur company.[112]

Considerable data regarding Fort Platte and Fort John and especially of their rivalry in 1841-42 are recorded for us by Rufus B. Sage in his *Rocky Mountain Life*. Mr. Sage enlisted with the party that set out from Independence, Missouri, early in september, 1841, to bring goods and supplies to Fort Platte for the winter trade. He does not give the name of the leader of the party, but from the description and the biographical data given, one is able to determine that it was Lieutenant Lancaster P. Lupton.[113] Mr. Sage's declination to name. his commandant was no doubt induced by considerations relating to the liquor trade. The party was bringing out 24 barrels of alcohol to barter to the Indians. Not only was this contrary to law, but Sage charges that the government officials winked at enforcement. He also presents in considerable detail the disastrous effects upon the Indians of the use of alcohol.

The Lupton party made its way up the Platte valley along the road on the south side of the river. Above Ash Hollow, on the North Platte, they met Chief Bull Tail and his band of Brulé Sioux. The Indians anxiously

---

111 John Bidwell, *A journey to California* (copy in Bancroft library).

112 *Ibid.*

113 R. B. Sage, *Rocky mountain life,* 39.

inquired as to the amount of liquor brought in the wagons. "It was right," they said, "the Long-knife should bring the fire-water to GIVE to the red man, but wrong to SELL it." "Our company," writes Sage, "was designated by the Indians as the Long-knife, or American company – a term by which all Americans are known among them. The American Fur company, employing almost exclusively Frenchmen, or individuals speaking the French language, receives the appellation of Wah-ceicha, or Bad-medicine company – a phrase universally applied to the French among the mountain tribes." [114]

On november 2, 1841, the party reached Fort Platte, their destination. Writes Mr. Sage: "This post occupies the left [right] bank of the North Fork of Platte river, three-fourths of a mile above the mouth of Larramie, in lat. 42° 12′ 10″ north, long, 105° 20′ 13″ west from Greenwich, and stands upon the direct waggon road to Oregon, *via* South Pass.

"It is situated in the immediate vicinity of the Oglallia and Brulé divisions of the Sioux nation, and but little remote from the Cheyennes and Arapaho tribes. Its structure is a fair specimen of most of the establishments employed in the Indian trade. Its walls are 'adobies,' [sun-baked brick], four feet thick, by twenty high – enclosing an area of two hundred and fifty feet in length, by two hundred broad. At the northwest and southwest corners are bastions which command its approaches in all directions.

"Within the walls are some twelve buildings in all, consisting as follows: office, store, warehouse, meathouse, smith's shop, carpenter's shop, kitchen, and five dwellings, so arranged as to form a yard and *corel*,

114 *Ibid.*, 83-84.

sufficiently large for the accommodation and security of more than two hundred head of animals. The number of men usually employed about the establishment is some thirty, whose chief duty it is to promote the interests of the trade, and otherwise act as circumstances require.

"The fort is located in a level plain, fertile and interesting, bounded upon all sides by hills, many of which present to view the nodding forms of pines and cedars, that bescatter their surface, – while the river bottoms, at various points, are thickly studded with proud growths of cottonwood, ash, willow, and box-elder, thus affording its needful supplies of timber and fuel.

"One mile south of it, upon the Larramie, is Fort John, a station of the American Fur company. Between these two posts a strong opposition is maintained in regard to the business of the country, little to the credit of either. . .

"The night of our arrival at Fort Platte was the signal for a grand jollification to all hands, (with two or three exceptions,) who soon got most gloriously drunk, and such an illustration of the beauties of harmony as was then perpetrated, would have rivalled bedlam itself, or even the famous council chamber beyond the Styx.

"Yelling, screeching, firing, shouting, fighting, swearing, drinking, and such like interesting performances, were kept up without intermission – and woe to the poor fellow who looked for repose that night – he might as well have thought of sleeping with a thousand cannon bellowing at his ears.

"The scene was prolonged till near sundown the next day, and several made their egress from this beastly carousal, minus shirts and coats – with swollen eyes, bloody noses, and empty pockets – the latter circumstance will be easily understood upon the mere mention of the fact that liquor, in this country, is sold for four dollars per pint." [115]

Two villages of Indians, encamped near the forts, were soon imbibing freely and were whooping and dancing in wild imitation of the white celebrants. At this stage, so it was charged, the American Fur company began dealing out strongly drugged liquor free, with the object of winning the Indian trade to itself. The results of this were being manifest when a somewhat sobering event occurred. Susu-ceicha, one of the Brulé chiefs, while riding at full speed from Fort John to Fort Platte and being too drunk to maintain his balance, fell from his horse and broke his neck. Wails loud and long now filled the air and mingled with bitter denunciations of the traders whose firewater had caused the chief's death.

Preparations for the burial rites were commenced. A scaffold was erected for reception of the body, which "was first washed, then arrayed in the habiliments last worn by Susu-ceicha during life, and sewed in several envelopes of lodge-skin, with the bow, arrows, and pipe once claiming him as their owner. This done, all things were ready for the proposed burial.

"The corpse was then borne to its final resting place, followed by a throng of relatives and friends. While moving onward with the dead, the train of mourners filled the air with their lamentations and rehearsals of the virtues and meritorious deeds of their late chief.

"Arrived at the scaffold, the corpse was carefully reposed upon it, facing the east, while beneath its head

[115] *Ibid.*, 96, 98.

was placed a small sack of meat, tobacco and vermillion, with a comb, looking-glass, and knife, and at its feet, a small banner that had been carried in the procession. A covering of scarlet cloth was then spread over it, and the body firmly lashed to its place by long strips of rawhide. This done, the horse of the chieftain was produced as a sacrifice for the benefit of his master in his long journey to the celestial hunting ground." [116]

The sudden death and burial of their chief put a stop to the Indians' dissipation. Presently the Sioux took down their lodges and moved away.

By the end of the second day, everything about the forts was decidedly calm. Preparations were now made for the winter trade. Small quantities of goods were to be sent from Fort Platte to the different Indian villages, and larger consignments were to be taken to Lupton's fort on the South Platte and to the White river [present South Dakota].

The owners of Fort John [Laramie] pursued a similar course, sending traders with goods to the various Indian bands. F. X. Matthieu, one of the American Fur company traders at Fort John in 1841-42, reports: "They furnished me with goods, man and horses and all that was necessary. They generally gave us some alcohol in ten gallon casks, one on each side of a pack animal; blankets, tobacco, vermillion and beads; very little powder and lead. . . They had a great many other traders like myself as far as the Blackfoot nation. Probably they sent out ten or twenty traders from each fort, and there were about six forts along the Missouri. On the Platte they had but one fort but from that the traders would go in pack trains and stay with the camps

---

[116] *Ibid.,* 101-2.

of the Indians." He speaks of some little opposition: "On the Platte there was Sybil Sambran [St. Vrain(?)] and other one horse companies." [117]

The most potent article of trade was fire water. "The liquor used in this business," writes Sage, "is generally third or fourth proof whiskey, which, after being diluted by a mixture of three parts water, is sold to the Indians at the exorbitant rate of three cups per robe – the cups usually holding about three gills each.

"But, notwithstanding the above unconscionable price, a large share of the profits result from the ingenious roguery of those conducting the trade.

"Sometimes the measuring-cup is not more than half full – then, again the act of measuring is little other than mere feint, (the purchaser receiving not one fourth the quantity paid for.)

"When he becomes so intoxicated as to be unable to distinguish the difference between water and liquor (a thing not rare), the former is passed off upon him as the genuine article.

"Another mode of cheating is, by holding the cup in such a manner that the two front fingers occupy a place upon the inside, and thus save to the trader nearly a gill at each filling.

"Some have two cups, (one of the usual size, and the other less), which are so exchanged as to induce the purchaser to believe he is obtaining a third more than he actually receives; and others yet more cunning, fill the measure half full of tallow and deal out the liquor from off it – the witless dupe, not thinking to examine the bottom, supposes he receives the requisite quantity." [118]

117 F. X. Matthieu, MS. in Bancroft library, university of California.
118 Sage, op. cit., 121-122.

Mr. Sage, who was engaged in this trade, recites numerous quarrels and fights and murders that occurred through the winter, directly caused by the imbibing of liquor.

"In the present state of things," writes a visitor at the fort in 1842, "when the country is supplied with alcohol, when a keg of it will purchase from an Indian every thing he possesses – his furs, his lodge, his horses, and even his wife and children – and when any vagabond who has money enough to purchase a mule can go into a village and trade against them successfully, without withdrawing entirely from the trade it is impossible for them [the large companies] to discontinue its use. . . . The difference between the regular trader and the *coureur des bois,* (as the French call the itinerant or peddling traders), with respect to the sale of spirits, is here, as it always has been, fixed and permanent, and growing out of the nature of their trade. The regular trader looks ahead, and has an interest in the preservation of the Indians, and in the regular pursuit of their business, and the preservation of their arms, horses, and every thing necessary to their future and permanent success in hunting: the *coureur des bois* has no permanent interest, and gets what he can, and for what he can, from every Indian he meets, even at the risk of disabling him from doing any thing more at hunting." [119]

In the early spring of 1842, Fort Platte changed hands. Presumably, it was sold to Sybille, Adams and company, for this company was in possession of the post when Fremont visited it in July.[120] Details as to the terms of the transfer have not come to light.

Preparations were made for sending the products of

[119] J. C. Fremont, *An exploring expedition,* etc., 40.
[120] *Ibid.,* 35.

the winter's trade down the Platte with the spring rise. Three boats were to be launched from Fort John and two from Fort Platte. A brief description of one of those from the latter post is given by Rufus Sage, who had charge of the craft: "She measured fifty feet keel by thirteen beam, and, without her lading, drew but an inch and a half of water. Her intended burthen was between two and three tons." [121] She was made of pine and ash timber from the neighboring hills, sawed by hand with a pit-saw. This boat was loaded with sixty packs of robes and with provisions for four weeks. The crew consisted of five men.

The boats from Fort Platte set forth on may 7. During the first two days they floated easily with the current, lying by at night. Then in the vicinity of Scott's Bluffs, the water became so shallow that it was decided to camp and wait for a rise of water. After a two week's wait, the river rose somewhat, the voyageurs "again loosed cable, and, after toiling all day, and tugging with might and main, by hand-spikes and levers – twisting, screwing, and lifting, now in water up to our necks, and now on dry sand-bars – we succeeded in dragging, or rather carrying, our craft for a distance of about five miles, and again lay by for four succeeding days to await a still further rise." [122]

By similar exertions they finally succeeded in reaching a point about 200 miles below the fort by june 10. But the spring rise had failed and with it the hopes of completing the voyage. The crews of the two boats piled their furs on the bank, covered them with two thicknesses of lodgeskins, dispatched two men on foot back

[121] Sage, *op. cit.*, 180.
[122] *Ibid.*, 187.

to the fort, left two men to guard the furs, and the remainder embarked in one of the emptied boats to try to make their way on to the Missouri.

After floating some thirty miles down stream, the boat crew overtook the three American Fur company barges, their men still struggling with the cargoes. But they, too, gave up presently, and piled their freight on the bank to await carriage the remaining distance on land. The crews of the five boats now joined forces to float farther in the unloaded boats; but the difficulties of travel on the shallow sandbar-studded river became so great that they finally deserted the stream in the Thousand Islands region to make their way on foot to Council Bluffs.[123]

This experience was not unique in the fur-trade of the Platte river region. While boatloads of furs sometimes made the journey all the way to the Missouri, they frequently were stranded en route. And oftentimes navigation was not attempted at all, the furs being transported to the states by pack train or by wagons.

The men who had been sent back to the forts on the Laramie, having apprised the company officials of the failure to navigate the Platte, teams and wagons were assembled for transportation of the robes the remaining distance to the states. This was accomplished in due time, for L. W. Hastings, one of the Oregon emigrants of 1842, writes of meeting the caravan near the Missouri frontier: "In a few days we met a company of fur-traders from Fort Laramie on their way to the states, with their returns of furs and buffalo robes, which they had accumulated during the previous year.

---

[123] *Ibid.,* 187-197. Matthieu (*op. cit.,* 8) was sent from Fort John with provisions to the men with the stranded boats.

These furs and robes were transported in wagons, drawn by oxen." [124] The traders had with them eight or ten buffalo calves which they were taking to the states with some domestic cows.

The robes from Fort Platte also reached Missouri successfully. William Sublette, in writing from St. Louis to W. D. Stewart in september, 1842, says: "Adams, Sabelle and Richard with a small outfit from Pratte got in and has returned with another small one." [125]

When Lieutenant John C. Fremont, on his first exploring expedition to the Rocky mountains, visited the forts on the Laramie in july, 1842, he wrote: "Issuing from the river hills, we came first in view of Fort Platte, a post belonging to Messrs. Sybille, Adams, & co., situated immediately in the point of land at the junction of Laramie with the Platte. Like the post we had visited on the South fork [Fort St. Vrain], it was built of earth, and still unfinished, being enclosed with walls (or rather houses) on three of the sides, and open on the fourth to the river. A few hundred yards brought us in view of the post of the American Fur company, called Fort John, or Laramie. This was a large post, having more the air of military construction than the fort at the mouth of the river. It is on the left bank, on a rising ground some twenty-five feet above the water; and its lofty walls, whitewashed and picketed, with the large bastions at the angles, gave it quite an imposing appearance in the uncertain light of evening. A cluster of lodges, which the language told us belonged to Sioux Indians, was pitched under the walls, and, with the fine

[124] L. W. Hastings, *The emigrants' guide to Oregon and California,* 7.

[125] Letter in the Sublette collection, Missouri historical society. This note reveals Pratte, former partner of Chouteau, as the backer of Adams, Sybille and company.

FORT LARAMIE, 1842

From a sketch accompanying Fremont's report

background of the Black Hills and the prominent peak of Laramie mountain, strongly drawn in the clear light of the western sky, where the sun had already set, the whole formed at the moment a strikingly beautiful picture. From the company at St. Louis I had letters for Mr. Boudeau, the gentleman in charge of the post, by whom I was received with great hospitality and an efficient kindness, which was invaluable to me during my stay in the country. . .

"I walked up to visit our friends at the fort, which is a quadrangular structure, built of clay, after the fashion of the Mexicans, who are generally employed in building them. The walls are about fifteen feet high, surmounted with a wooden palisade, and form a portion of ranges of houses, which entirely surround a yard of about one hundred and thirty feet square. Every apartment has its door and window – all, of course, opening on the inside. There are two entrances, opposite each other, and midway the wall, one of which is a large and public entrance; the other smaller and more private – a sort of postern gate. Over the great entrance is a square tower with loopholes, and, like the rest of the work, built of earth. At two of the angles, and diagonally opposite each other, are large square bastions, so arranged as to sweep the four faces of the walls.

"This post belongs to the American Fur company, and, at the time of our visit, was in charge of Mr. Boudeau. Two of the company's clerks, Messrs. Galpin and Kellogg, were with him, and he had in the fort about sixteen men. As usual, these had found wives among the Indian squaws; and, with the usual accompaniment of children, the place had quite a populous appearance. It is hardly necessary to say, that the object of the establishment is trade with the neighboring tribes, who, in the course of the year, generally make two or three visits to the fort. In addition to this, traders, with a small outfit, are constantly kept amongst them. The articles of trade consist, on the one side, almost entirely of buffalo robes; and, on the other, of blankets, calicoes, guns, powder, and lead, with such cheap ornaments as glass beads, looking-glasses, rings, vermilion for painting, tobacco, and principally, and in spite of the prohibition, of spirits, brought into the country in the form of alcohol, and diluted with water before sold. . .

"The fort had a very cool and clean appearance. The great entrance, in which I found the gentlemen assembled, and which was floored, and about fifteen feet long, made a pleasant, shaded seat, through which the breeze swept constantly; for this country is famous for high winds.

". . . I dined today at Fort Platte, which has been mentioned as situated at the junction of Laramie river with the Nebraska [Platte]. Here I heard a confirmation of the statements given above [of Indian hostility ahead]. . . Mr. Bissonette, one of the traders belonging to Fort Platte, urged the propriety of taking with me an interpreter and two or three old men of the village; in which case, he thought there would be little or no hazard in encountering any of the war parties." [126]

Trade at the Laramie forts must have continued during the winter of 1842-3 much as in the preceding winter. The Indians had come to consider this as the great trading center and came in large bands. During the winter of 1842-3, one of the emissaries sent out to the Indian villages, Raphael Carrofel, suffered a long and terrible ordeal in the snow, from which he escaped by a combination of luck and endurance. He finally

[126] J. C. Fremont, *op. cit.,* 35-42.

dragged himself back to Fort Platte, after "as keen
and prolonged suffering as was ever known among the
mountains." [127]

At least a part of the winter's trade was again embarked in bullboats in the spring of 1843. The Sir
William D. Stewart company of hunters and health
seekers met the "trappers returning down the river in
batteaux, little boats, which were pushed with poles or
paddled, as the river was shallow most of the way." [128]
William L. Sublette, one of the founders of Fort Laramie, but now a leader of the Stewart party, records:
"Met John Rishan [Richau, Richard] this evening
(june 6, 1843) one of the party of the company of
Sabille and Adams who has a fort on the river Platte
near the mouth of Larami's fork. He had some cows
& 6 buffalo calves & one young elk also 5 or 6 one
(horse) waggons loaded with robes." [129]

Fort Platte, owned by Sybille, Adams and company,
was being managed by Mr. Bisonette when Fitzpatrick's division of the Fremont expedition later visited
the post [august, 1843]. Theodore Talbot, journalist
of this party, reports that the post, though smaller, was
more active than its competitor, Fort Laramie, and that
many Indians were continually about it.[130] It soon
changed apparent owners, for in september, 1843, it
was in possession of Pratte and Cabenna, with Bisonette
still in charge of the fort.[131]

---

[127] Matthew C. Field in the *St. Louis Reveille,* september 4, 1844.

[128] Kennerly papers (Missouri historical society).

[129] H. C. Dale, "A fragmentary journal of William L. Sublette," in *Mississippi valley historical review,* VI, 110.

[130] *The journals of Theodore Talbot, 1843 and 1849-52.* (Charles H. Carey,
editor), 34.

[131] Letter of John Hill to Mr. Drips from Fort John, september 17, 1843;
also, letter of Drips to Mitchell, dated Fort Pierre, september 7, 1843; in
Drips papers, Missouri historical society.

Free use of liquor had been working havoc in the Indian trade on the North Platte. Now a determined effort was made to curtail or eliminate it. The American Fur company, smarting under the competition of opposition liquor traders advocated enforcement of the prohibition laws of the United States government. Not that they had been free from the use of liquor in the Indian trade, but they realized that it was a powerful weapon in the hands of the small trader.

Back in 1832, when congress was considering a prohibition law, the American Fur company had been most active in opposing its enactment, contending that inasmuch as the Hudson's Bay company used liquor the American company must be permitted its use or lose to the British company all the Indian trade in the upper country. But the law was passed, nevertheless.[132] However, by cunning devices of traders and by negligence of government officers, the traffic had continued much as before.

By the early '40s the ill effects on the Indians were becoming so marked, and the competition of opposition traders was so keen that the American Fur company vigorously championed strict enforcement of the law. The company succeeded in having one of its own men, Andrew Drips, appointed Indian agent for the upper Missouri and especially commissioned to stop the liquor trade.

His instructions, dated october 6, 1842, were given by the superintendent of Indian affairs at St. Louis, D. D. Mitchell – also a former employee of the American Fur company. Drips was directed to proceed to Fort Pierre [present South Dakota] on the Missouri, thence

---

[132] Act of july 9, 1832. See Chittenden, *American fur trade of the far west,* I, 22-31, for discussion of the traffic.

to Laramie's Fork. There, wrote Mitchell, "you will, in all probability, find quantities of liquor brought in from Santa Fe; with these violators of all law, who have neither the privileges of a license nor citizenship, I would deal in a very summary and severe manner, and if physical force be necessary, I doubt not but that it will be cheerfully furnished by the American traders." [133]

Agent Drips was authorized to appoint subagents. He chose Joseph V. Hamilton, another American Fur company employee, to be stationed in the Laramie region in 1843.[134] Pratte, Cabanne and company, Sybille, Adams and company, and traders from Taos provided the chief opposition in that section. The new prohibition enforcement officers appeared to serve the American Fur company first and the government afterwards. They were empowered to confiscate and destroy liquor in the Indian country and to revoke licenses of offending parties. At the same time Drips authorized the American Fur company to establish trading posts or conduct trade wherever the opposition companies were located.[135]

Drips sent Hamilton to Fort Platte to confiscate the liquor known to be there and to expel the guilty traders. But the Fort Platte men learned of his coming; they raised the cached liquor within the fort and took it elsewhere. So Hamilton found only the empty caches. He procured affidavits that the traders had sold liquor, but failed to get the article itself.[136] Mr. Richards, asso-

---

[133] Reproduced in *South Dakota historical collections*, IX, 174.

[134] *Ibid.*, 192.

[135] Drips's letter of november 4, 1843, *ibid.*, 177.

[136] Chittenden, *American fur trade of the far west*, 369. See also affidavit of John Hill, dated at Fort John, september 17, 1843, and the letter of september 7, from O. Sarpy, and endorsed by J. Loughborough, and the letter of A. R. Bouis from Fort Pierre, october 4, 1843, in Missouri historical society papers.

ciated with Sybille and Adams, of whom we shall hear more hereafter, brought in liquor from New Mexico and appears to have been the principal offender. Apparently he was operating without a license, so Pratte and Cabanne arranged to have him included under theirs.[137]

In the early fall of 1843 Mr. Cabanne arrived at Fort Platte with wagons loaded with goods. He "brought no liquor," writes Hamilton to Drips, "but brought a very fine assortment of goods and has about 20 traders to scatter over the country and about 40 voyageurs and 70 head of horses and mules, oxen, wagons and they intend scattering in every direction." [138]

This meant real competition for the American Fur company, owners of Fort Laramie. In addition, their Missouri river field was being vigorously invaded by the Union Fur company (Ebbetts and Cutting, backed by Fox, Livingston and company of New York), and Sybille and company, both of whom brought boatloads of goods up the Missouri river in the fall of 1843.[139] In addition there was the competition of Lupton and others on the South Platte and the various traders from New Mexico.

The trade in the Laramie region through the winter of 1843-4 was rather brisk. Upon returning to St. Louis with part of his company, early in the spring of 1844, Mr. Cabanne reported the trade as successful on the North Platte, but unsuccessful on the South Platte and the Arkansas.[140]

---

137 *Ibid.* On november 5, 1843, Pratte and Cabanne "engaged John Pichard [Richard?], Peter Richard," etc., and requested Drips to permit them to be included under the Pratte and Cabanne licenses, *South Dakota historical collections,* IX, 175.

138 *Ibid.,* 196. Hamilton's letter to Drips, dated at Fort John.

139 *Ibid.,* 177, 196, 198.

140 *Niles Register,* may 4, 1844, p. 160.

Mr. Bissonette set out from the Missouri frontier in the spring of 1844 with a train of pack mules loaded for Fort Platte. He passed the emigrant companies in the latter part of may.[141]

Six mackinaw boats loaded with peltries from the North Platte arrived in St. Louis on june 21. "A party of Pawnee Indians attacked them on their way down, but they repulsed them without loss of life." [142] These boats probably brought the furs of Pratt and Cabanne from Fort Platte, for on the 27th the Fort Laramie traders came in to St. Louis. They were led by Major Hamilton and Frederick Lafou and had set out from Fort John on may 14 "in seven boats, laden with about seven hundred packs of buffalo robes and furs. On the day they started two of the boats were swamped and their cargoes were taken on board the other five." [143]

The unusually high water of the spring of 1844 was a boon to the traders, who were able to bring down their robes and furs by boat without serious difficulty. But to the emigrants who set out on the Oregon trail that spring, it was a source of great distress. The persistent storms of that year raised the Missouri and Mississippi to the highest mark since 1785.[144]

No doubt the returns of this year produced the encouraging outlook expressed in the *St. Louis Reveille* as follows: "In reference to the great and profitable trading in furs, which has been so extensively instrumental in building up the West, and particularly St. Louis, it has been estimated that notwithstanding the steady increase in consumption, the required animals abound still in numbers every way sufficient to maintain

[141] *James Clyman, American frontiersman, 1792-1881* (ed. by Charles L. Camp), 60.
[142] *St. Louis Reveille,* june 22, 1844.
[143] *Ibid.,* june 27, 1844.
[144] *Ibid.,* june 22, 1844.

the trade, and keep in full activity all the hunters and trappers sent out in pursuit. It is supposed that the buffalo increase in a ratio of at least three to every one destroyed." [145]

The American Fur company, owner of Fort Laramie, was prospering, as is evidenced by the recent building of two large fireproof structures in St. Louis. The city's pride in the new buildings is voiced in a description of them in the *St. Louis Reveille* of june 26, 1844: ". . . Spacious vaults and cellars, constructed of native rock, range beneath the front warehouse, and offices of convenience extend under the sidewalks of the street. . . Upon the first floor, ranging level with the street, are the directors rooms, and clerks' offices. . . Above this is an extensive room, running the whole length of the building, where huge bales of blankets, furs, boxes of hardware, and other necessaries of the trade are stored. The floors above are divided into various wholesale and retail stores, some exclusively for traders, others for Indians. The large trader is led to one store, the poor trapper to another, and the Indian to another. There is great subtlety and skill required in managing well the complicated peculiarities of the trade.

"The rear warehouse presents the appearance of an immense factory. A great number of men are constantly in active employ, sorting and arranging skins, packing, pressing, and putting them away in bales."

Our data on the trade during the following winter are meagre, but the spring express to the American Fur company from the forts reported good trade in buffalo robes on the Laramie but little at Fort Pierre – due to prairie fires that had driven the buffalo away.[146]

---

[145] *Ibid.,* july 31, 1844.

[146] *Missouri Republican,* april 28, 1844. In publications of the Nebraska state historical society, XX, 130.

Captain Cooke gives us some figures on the amount of the trade as reported to him in the early summer of 1845. "The trade at this post [Fort Laramie]," he writes, "is principally for buffalo robes; nine thousand were lately sent off by the American Fur company and how many by the other company I do not know. They get about two thousand pounds of beaver skins a year." [147]

In the spring of 1845, again skins were started down the North Platte in bullboats, but the spring rise subsided as the voyageurs reached the vicinity of Chimney Rock. Writes Captain Cooke, west-bound with the First Dragoons: "We met here [on North Platte, a little above Ash Hollow] a number of boats laden with buffalo robes; and although drawing but eight inches of water, they had been some two months descending the hundred miles from Fort Laramie; the hardy boatmen, who are also the trappers, hunters, etc., of the Fur company, spending perhaps half the time in the water. Only for a short season in favorable years, is the river navigable at all." This attempt was now abandoned; and wagons and carts had been sent for to transport the packs back to the Fort.[148]

Instead of transporting these robes by wagon down the Oregon trail, it was decided to freight them across country to Fort Pierre on the Missouri, whence they could be sent to St. Louis by boat. Thus was inaugurated the general use by the American Fur company of the Fort Laramie-to-Fort Pierre road for transportation of its buffalo robes. Traders had broken a trail in their frequent journeys between these posts, but now a

---

[147] Cooke, *Scenes and adventures in the army*, 336.

[148] *Ibid.*, 312. See also Joel Palmer, *Journal of travels over the Rocky mountains to the mouth of the Columbia river, made during the years 1845 and 1846* (ed. by R. G. Thwaites), 55.

regular wagon road was established. It was approximately 300 miles long and followed the general course of the White and then the Teton rivers.[149]

In the *St. Louis Reveille* of june 3, 1845, we read: "Twelve men, of Pratte and Cabanne's company from Fort Larrameé, came down on the steamer Tobacco Plant, yesterday evening." Whether they came with or without furs is not stated. It may have been that they were giving up the trade in the Laramie region, as indicated below.

On august 27, 1845, Mr. Kellogg brought in to Fort Pierre twelve wagons and two carts loaded with 387 packs of robes from Fort Laramie. And these were in addition to 520 packs still near Chimney Rock on the North Platte awaiting transportation.[150] This unexpected demand for boats found the company unprepared. Writes Mr. Bouis at Fort Pierre to Joseph Picotte at Fort Laramie on august 30: "We have had to make three boats and repair several that came from above [and here is introduced Fort Laramie in a new role], our rosin is out and if you do not send us some tar, we will not be able to make boats next spring." [151]

Midsummer of 1845 saw the end of the rivalry between Fort Laramie [or Fort John] and Fort Platte and the triumph of the former. Details as to who brought this about are lacking. Writes Mr. Bouis from Fort Pierre on august 31: "Mr. Cabanne has abandoned Fort Platte. Bissouet is stationed a few miles below that fort with a few articles of trade that remained on hand last spring. [This is doubtless the beginning of Fort

---

149 A detailed description of the route is found in the *South Dakota historical collections*, XI, 259.

150 Letter from A. R. Bouis, dated at Fort Pierre, august 31, 1845. Found in *South Dakota historical collections*, IX, 206.

151 *Ibid.*, 205.

Bernard, on the North Platte eight miles below Fort Laramie, of which we shall hear more later. It was probably named for Bernard Pratte, partner of Mr. Cabanne.] It is supposed that if Cabanne comes up next fall it will be with but a small outfit. The prospect of trade in that section of the country is very flattering, plenty of buff and there will be more Indians there this season than ever. Part of the Minniconajous and 200 lodges of Cheyennes will winter in the neighborhood of the fort. Joe [Picotte, who had been sent to take charge of Fort Laramie in june, 1845][152] thinks he will trade 12 to 1500 packs." [153]

In the early fall of this year Bridger and Vasquez brought to Fort Laramie articles new to the trade of that post. Since the recent establishment of their Fort Bridger, in the extreme southwest corner of present Wyoming, they had been operating as a sort of subdivision of the American Fur company and had conducted most of their trade through Fort Laramie. The new articles were California sea shells procured by Bridger on his recent trip to the Pacific coast. He delivered to Mr. Picotte at Fort Laramie, "840 beaver skins and castoram, 675 dressed deer skins, 28 mules, 24 horses, 1400 California sea shells H.C., the whole amounting to about $5000 exclusive of the California shells." [154]

While other forts on the north and south forks of the Platte rose and fell during the decade following the founding of Fort Laramie, this post lived on. Through the shifting fortunes of the traffic in beaver skins and buffalo robes, it managed a generally profitable business. Then with the coming of the emigrant tide it

[152] *Ibid.*, 203.
[153] *Ibid.*, 206.
[154] *Ibid.*, 210. Letter of A. R. Bouis, september 17, 1845.

adapted itself to new conditions and a new type of trade. Located at a strategic point on the highroad of the west-ward advance, it was in a position to render assistance to the caravans and to play an important part in the travel over the Oregon trail. To this phase of the Fort Laramie picture we turn next in our story.

The Coming of the First Emigrants, 1841-1845

The Trapper had opened the trails to the Rocky mountains. The Missionary had followed his paths to carry the white man's religion to the Indian. The home-seeker was next in line. Missionaries had written back letters about the western land; trappers told enticing stories of far-away places. The border settlers of the Missouri country, restless and migratory, listened eagerly to descriptions of the fertile acres of Oregon and the verdant paradise that was California.

As early as 1829, the American Society for Encouraging the Settlement of Oregon Territory, had been organized at Boston by Hall J. Kelley, enthusiastic school teacher. The movement was a little premature. A second Oregon emigrating Society began in 1838 the publication in Massachusetts of *The Oregonian and Indians' Advocate,* to promote interest and enlist recruits. By 1840 conditions were ripe for emigration. Explorers, missionaries, sportsmen and scientists had visited the far West. Speeches, pamphlets and newspaper stories publicized the region. Soon emigration societies were formed in Pennsylvania, Ohio, Michigan, Illinois, Indiana and Missouri.[155]

A variety of motives actuated recruits. Hard times precipitated by the panic of 1837; a desire to escape the torments of the ague; opportunity visioned by poor

---

[155] H. C. Dale, "The organization of the Oregon emigrating companies," in the *Quarterly of the Oregon historical society,* XVI, 207-9.

whites to achieve social equality in the new land; the very momentum of the westward movement – all were to make contributions to swell the ranks of westbound emigrants.

In early may, 1841, the initial band, composed of homeseekers and missionaries, to a total of about 80, set forth from the Missouri frontier. Under the guidance of the veteran mountain man, Thomas Fitzpatrick, they made their way westward over the route soon to be known as the Oregon trail. The emigrants traveled in covered wagons drawn by horses or oxen; the missionaries used Red River carts (two wheeled) drawn by mules hitched tandem.

The party's first Indian scare came shortly after reaching the Platte. A young man named Dawson, while out hunting, ran into a band of Indians. He made his escape and came dashing into camp without mule, gun or pistol, and lacking most of his clothes. The emigrants and missionaries became excited and started their teams on the run. Fitzpatrick spurred ahead and as fast as the wagons and carts reached the river, formed them into a circle. Presently the Indians came in sight, but there were only about fifty of them, instead of the thousands the frightened hunter had reported. Nor were they hostile, but came peacefully into camp near the whites.

Upon reaching the buffalo country the train was supplied with fresh meat. Of the buffalo herds Bidwell, principal historian of the journey, writes: "I have seen the plains black with them for several days' journey as far as the eye could reach. They seemed to be coming northward continually from the distant plains to the Platte to get water, and would plunge in and swim across by thousands – so numerous that they changed not only the color of the water, but its taste, until it was unfit to drink – but we had to use it. One night when we were encamped on the south fork of the Platte they came in such droves that we had to sit up and fire guns and make what fires we could to keep them from running over us and trampling us into the dust. We were obliged to go out some distance from the camp to turn them; Captain Fitzpatrick told us that if we did not do this the buffaloes in front could not turn aside for the pressure of those behind. We could hear them thundering all night long; the ground fairly trembled with vast approaching bands, and if they had not been diverted, wagons, animals and emigrants would have been trodden under their feet." [156]

The party continued without important incident along the south side of the Platte to the crossing of the South Fork. In fording this stream the water was so high that men had to accompany each wagon to prevent the boxes from being carried down the current. After crossing to the North Fork and passing the landmarks of Chimney Rock and Scott's Bluffs they came finally to the Laramie river.

How welcome was the site of the trading post to these weary emigrants who had traveled for weeks without seeing a white habitation. A day and a half of rest was now enjoyed. Here the belongings of James Shotwell, who some days before had been killed by the accidental discharge of his own gun, were auctioned off. Two of the emigrant party, George Simpson [157] and Mast, left the train to remain at the forts, but their places were taken by two trappers and an Indian who joined the westbound caravan. [158]

---

[156] John Bidwell, *Echoes of the past in California.* 14-15.

[157] This appears to be the Mr. Simpson who became one of the founders in 1842 of Fort Pueblo on the Arkansas, and later was a prominent pioneer of Trinidad, Colorado.

[158] Bidwell, *op. cit.,* 18.

One of the travelers, an eccentric preacher named Joseph Williams, was not well impressed with the denizens of the forts. "Here is a mixture of people," he writes, "some white, some half breeds, some French. Here is plenty of talk about their damnation, but none about their salvation; and I thought about the words of David, 'Woe is me that I sojourn in Mesech, that I dwelt in the tents of Kedar' . . . I tried to preach twice to these people, but with little effect. Some of them said they had not heard preaching for twelve years." [159]

Beyond the forts the emigrants continued their journey, up the Platte and the Sweetwater, across the Green river valley and on to the Soda Springs of present Idaho. Here the party divided, about half going to California and the remainder continuing on along the route to Oregon.

The year 1842 saw the second emigrant party trekking west over the Oregon trail. It left Elm Grove, twenty miles southwest of Independence, Missouri, about the middle of may, and numbered at starting some 112 persons, including men, women and children. There were 18 wagons, with horses and mules, and large herds of cattle. Dr. Elijah White, former missionary to Oregon and now newly appointed Indian agent for that country, in organizing the company, had been careful to insist that all members come well provided and equipped for the long journey. Each man was to have one gun, three pounds of powder, twelve pounds of lead, 1,000 caps (or suitable flints), fifty pounds of flour and thirty pounds of bacon, with a proper proportion of provisions for women and children.[160]

---

[159] Joseph Williams, *Narrative of a tour from the state of Indiana to the Oregon territory, in the years 1841-2*, 38-39.

[160] A. J. Allen, *Ten years in Oregon. Travels and adventures of Doctor E. White and lady west of the Rocky mountains*, 144.

At setting out, writes L. W. Hastings, one of the party, "all was high glee, jocular hilarity, and happy anticipation, as we thus darted forward into the wild expanse of the untrodden regions of the 'western world.'" All was harmonious for a few days but soon "the 'American character' was fully exhibited. All appeared to be determined to govern, but not to be governed." [161] Dissensions split the company into factions, and as separate units they reached the Laramie. Here, writes Hastings, "we were received in a very kind and friendly manner by the gentlemen of those forts, who extended every attention to us, while we remained in their vicinity." [162]

Weary from the long journey and with footsore cattle, the emigrants were glad to spend a week at the forts on the Laramie, repairing their outfits, purchasing supplies, and giving their animals needed rest. Some of their wagons and many of their cattle, they traded here for horses and supplies. Mr. Bordeau purchased thirty head of fine cattle for Fort Laramie, while the trader at Fort Platte obtained eighty head. The emigrants traded in their wagons and cattle at the prices paid for them in the states and received in exchange coffee and sugar at $1 per pound and flour at 50 cents per pint.[163]

Having learned of Indian danger ahead, the factions reunited and procured the services of Thomas Fitzpatrick to guide them through the Indian country. On two occasions as they journeyed on toward South Pass, serious Indian troubles arose, but through the management of their experienced guide, the company escaped without serious injury.

It was not until 1843 that the first great migration

161 L. W. Hastings, *The emigrants' guide to Oregon and California* (1932 edition), 6.

162 *Ibid.,* 9.

163 Fremont, *Report,* 40-41.

passed the Laramie forts. Thereafter during the next quarter century, a great annual caravan of covered wagons bore westward the pioneer founders of commonwealths.

About the outfitting town of Independence the wagons began to assemble early in may.

The election of officers, as witnessed by Matt Field, newspaperman, was conducted in an interesting fashion: "The candidates stood up in a row behind the constitutents, and at a given signal they wheeled about and marched off, while the general mass broke after them 'lick-a-ty-split,' each man forming in behind his favorite, so that every candidate flourished a sort of a tail of his own, and the man with the longest tail was elected! These proceedings were continued until a captain and a council of ten were elected." [164]

The emigrants engaged as their guide, Captain John Gant, former army man, more recently a trapper and trader in the far West, agreeing to pay him $1 per head for each emigrant guided to Fort Hall.

The courageous Dr. Marcus Whitman was to accompany the emigrants this year. In addition to administering to the sick, he was to become the real leader of the band.

A census taken on the Big Blue, according to *Niles Register* of july 29, 1843, showed 121 wagons, 698 oxen, 296 horses, 973 loose cattle and 1,000 persons. It is significant to note the character of the band as revealed in this report, for there were 260 men, 130 women and 610 children. That made approximately five children for each woman in the train.

The company early divided into two parts, the outfits without cattle taking the lead and the "cow column"

---

[164] *New Orleans Picayune*, nov. 21, 1843, reprinted in the *Quarterly of the Oregon historical society*, I, 399.

traveling in the rear. Later they divided into four sections to facilitate camping arrangements and to make better provision for grazing of the stock.

Upon reaching the Laramie river on july 13, the advance party found the stream too high for fording. They procured two small boats from the forts, lashed them together, and covered them with a platform made of boards from the wagon beds. Upon this platform, they placed their loaded wagons by hand and by means of a rope ferried them across.[165]

Two days were taken for recuperating at the forts. Outfits were repaired and supplies purchased. Peter H. Burnett, first captain of the emigrating company of 1843, and later to become governor of California, gives the following prices of articles at Fort Laramie: Coffee and brown sugar, $1.50 per pint; flour, 25 cents per pound; powder, $1.50 per pound; lead, 75 cents per pound, percussion caps, $1.50 per box; calico (inferior quality), $1 per yard.[166]

The forts on the Laramie as seen by the Oregon emigrants of 1843 are thus described by Johnson and Winter: "Fort Lauramie belongs to the American Fur company, and is built for a protection against the Indians. The occupants of the fort, who have been long there, being mostly French and having married wives of the Sioux, do not now apprehend any danger. The fort is built of dobies, (unburnt bricks). A wall of six feet in thickness and fifteen in height, encloses an area of one hundred and fifty feet square. Within and around the wall, are the buildings, constructed of the same material. These are a trading house, ware houses for storing goods and skins, shops and dwellings for the traders

---

[165] Johnson and Winter, *Route across the Rocky mountains* (reprint of 1932), 14.

[166] P. H. Burnett, *Recollections of an old pioneer* (1880), 113.

and men. In the centre, is a large open area. A portion of the enclosed space is cut off by a partition wall, forming a carell, (enclosure), for the animals belonging to the fort. About one mile below Fort Lauramie, is Fort Platte; which is built of the same materials and in the same manner, and belongs to a private trading company." [167]

Fitzpatrick's division of the Fremont expedition of 1843 visited the Laramie forts some two weeks after the Oregon emigrants had passed. Theodore Talbot, journalist of the party, reports: "In the evening [of august 4] we forded the 'La Rainee' and camped near Fort John [Fort Laramie]. There were several lodges of 'Brulés' and some 'Mine-Konjas' from the Missouri, also camped around the fort. Musquitoes very troublesome.

"SAT. 5. Breakfasted at the fort with Messrs. Bondeau, gentleman in charge, and Galpin, chief clerk. . .

"I went down to Sybille and Adams' post at the mouth of the Laramie river a mile below Fort John. It is called Fort Platte or Bissonette's Fort: it is smaller than the Am. Fur company post but seemingly more active & lively. Many Indians round about it, whose portraits Sir. W. D. Stewart has engaged a painter to remain here and take." [168]

In that summer of 1843 there appeared at the fort a large and rather distinguished party of hunters and health seekers. Sir William Drummond Stewart of Scotland, who for more than ten years had been making hunting excursions into the Rocky mountains, was the most famous member of the group. Jefferson Kennerly Clark and William Clark Kennerly, son and nephew respectively of William Clark of the Lewis and Clark

[167] Johnson and Winter, *op. cit.,* 14.

[168] C. H. Carey (ed.), *The journals of Theodore Talbot,* 34.

expedition, were in the company, as were William Sublette and Baptiste Charbonneau (son of Sacajawea).
Along with the pleasure seekers a group of catholic
missionaries traveled.

Sublette, one of the founders of the first fort on the
Laramie, and for whom that fort was first named, was
one of the health seekers in the party. Having given up
his mountain wanderings to accumulate wealth as a
business man in St. Louis, he found his constitution
weakening from the inroads of tuberculosis. In an effort
to combat the disease and also to enjoy a vacation in his
old haunts, he had joined the Stewart party – in fact
became its leader. A fragmentary journal which he kept
during the first part of the trip has survived. In it, under
date of may 30, 1843, is given an interesting description of the party: "Sir William had 10 carts & one small
2 mule yankee waggon.

"There was some 30 other carts and small 2 horse
wagons in company belonging to individual gentlemen,
some of the armey, some professional gentlemen, come
on the trip for pleasure, some for health, etc. etc. So we
had doctors, lawyers, botanists, bugg ketchers, hunters
and men of nearly all professions, etc. etc. One half or
rather more was hired men belonging to Sir William,
which he had employed on the trip." [169]

Matt Field, prominent actor and newspaper man of
St. Louis and New Orleans accompanied the expedition for his health and wrote interesting accounts of the
company's adventures for the *New Orleans Picayune*
and the *St. Louis Reveille*.

From Fort Platte on july 8, Field wrote to his New
Orleans paper: "Here we are, at this point of our long
travel, in entire safety . . . we are now in the land of

the Cheyennes, and within thirty miles of us is an encampment of some four hundred lodges . . . numbering about one thousand warriors. We are ninety-three strong, well armed and provisioned, and mean to march through them with all ease and confidence. . .

"We are just reviving from a munificent and magnificent jollification that we had upon our ever glorious fourth of july! What do you think of roast beef and plum pudding. . . Rhine wine (three dozen), milk punch, *Minny Warka* (a la Sioux) corn dodgers (a la hunter), all the choice parts of the buffalo, cooked in the best known style, and everything truly and really superb.

"The Stars and Stripes were raised in mid-camp at sunrise, and saluted by three volleys of thirty rifles and three loud cheers." [170]

Just outside of Fort Laramie, says W. C. Kennerly, they came upon some thirty lodges of the Sioux who had come in to trade. Some of the older Indians recognized Jefferson K. Clark from his resemblance to his father, the Red-head chief, and invited him to a special dog feast.[171]

After their six months' excursion the hunting party returned to the states in excellent health and spirits. Field and others afflicted with tuberculosis could not praise highly enough the health-giving virtues of such a trip.

In the summer of 1844 four distinct companies of emigrants and a party of health seekers, to a total of nearly 1,000 persons, passed the Laramie forts.[172] Moses

170 *New Orleans Picayune,* september 6, 1843.

171 James Kennerly papers, Missouri historical society.

172 See W. J. Ghent, *The road to Oregon,* 81-4, for a general summary of the emigration.

(Black) Harris, Elisha Stephens and Andrew W. Sublette, all experienced mountain men, piloted three of the companies. At Fort Laramie the Gilliam party secured the old mountaineer, Joe Walker, to guide it to Fort Bridger.[173]

James Clyman, who had passed the site of Fort Laramie ten years before the fort was founded, was now — ten years after the fort's establishment — trekking to Oregon with the emigrants. In his diary he recorded under date of august 1: "about 4 o'clock in the afternoon we hove in sight of the white battlements of Fort Larrimie and Fort Platte whose white walls, surrounded by a few Sioux Indian lodges, shewed us that human life was not extinct; this being the first we have seen since we left the Kaws, the various emigrants excepted. Crossed the Larrimie river — a clear fine stream about 80 yards wide — only about half of the channel filled with water 2 feet deep. Several persons getting scant of flour, some to be had here (at) superfine at 40 dollars a barrel, Spanish [from New Mexico] at 30.

"2. Clear cool nights & mornings verry warm days. Remained in camp to day trading and waiting for blacksmith and other repairs went down to the fort after writeing to my friend Starr. . . I tried to trade some but found even the products of the country verry high. I purchased a dressed deer skin for 2.50." [174]

John Minto, a member of the Gilliam company, writes: "July 30 we reached Fort Laramie late and camped just west of the line between Indian camps and the fort. . . We had a beautiful camp on the bank of

173 "Reminiscences of W. S. Gilliam," *Transactions of the Oregon pioneer association,* 1903, pp. 204-5. Also, Mrs. Martha E. Gilliam, in *Quarterly of the Oregon historical society,* XVII, 360.

174 James Clyman diary, original MS. in Huntington library. Also C. L. Camp (ed.), *James Clyman, American frontiersman,* 83.

the Laramie, and both weather and scene were delight-
ful. The moon, I think, must have been near the full, to
give us light; at all events we leveled off a space and one
man played the fiddle and we danced into the night." [175]

A correspondent of the *Missouri Republican* writing
from Oregon, Missouri, in june, 1844, reported the
emigration of that year and then proceeded to comment
upon it. "I suppose by next spring a year, we shall hear
but little of emigration to Oregon. . . By next spring
the true character of the Oregon territory will begin to
be known, but not sufficiently, I think, to deter a considerable number from going. But next spring a year,
I think, the mania will run out. At least, I do not per-
ceive how it can be kept up much longer . . . [Ore-
gon] is mountainous and rugged; its plains are dry and
barren; nothing but rain in winter, nothing but sun in
summer. . . In truth, no man of information, in his
right mind, would think of leaving such a country as
this, to wander over a thousand miles of desert and five
hundred of mountain to reach such as that.

"It is wrong in the people of St. Louis to encourage
this spirit of emigration." [176]

But this was a discordant note in the national chorus.
The general voice of the people sang a pean in praise
of expansion. During the year 1844 the refrain was
taken up by the political parties and much fervid ora-
tory was loosed in behalf of the annexation of Texas and
the occupation of Oregon. Following the democratic
victory, President Polk, in his inaugural address, asserted that our title to Oregon was "clear and unques-

[175] John Minto, "Reminiscences of Honorable John Minto, pioneer of 1844,"
in the *Quarterly of the Oregon historical society*, II, 156-158.

[176] Reprinted in the *Publications of the Nebraska state historical society*,
XX, 127-8. The *Reveille* of the next day (june 12) took issue with the *Missouri Republican* article.

tionable" and that our people were preparing to perfect that title by occupation of the land.[177] The fact that Great Britain had a claim to Oregon seemed only to stimulate the ardor of certain Americans who thought of migrating thither. The net result was a great emigration in 1845, one that equaled all that had gone before.

Colonel S. W. Kearny, while leading his First Dragoons over the Oregon trail this year, counted 460 wagons with 850 men, 475 women, and 1,000 children.[178] His figures are somewhat lower than those given by F. G. Young, Oregon historian, who places the total at 3,000.[179] To W. B. Ide, one of the emigrants, the number seemed even larger. He reported that there were 500 wagons and between six and seven thousand souls. "Our team, cattle and wagons," he writes, "stretched out in procession some three miles in length on the broad prairies present a grand spectacle." [180]

---

[177] J. D. Richardson, *A compilation of the messages and papers of the presidents,* IV, 381.

[178] Quoted in *Collections of the Nebraska state historical society,* XVI, 235.

[179] F. G. Young, "The Oregon trail," in *The Quarterly of the Oregon historical society,* I, 370.

[180] "Oregon correspondence, bank of the Nebraska," in *Jefferson Inquirer,* june 26, 1845, found in Missouri state historical society library, Columbia, Missouri. The *Independence Expositor* of may 10, according to the *St. Louis Reveille* of may 16, 1845, computed that the emigration would be not less than 5,000 for the year. The *Reveille* of september 4, 1845, reports a letter written from Fort Platte as saying that 421 wagons of emigrants had passed the fort and 60 were still behind.

The "Oregon song," written for the *Reveille* and appearing in that paper on may 15, 1844, follows:

> To the far – far off Pacific sea,
> Will you go – will you go – dear girl, with me?
> By a gentle brook, in a lonely spot,
> We'll jump from our wagon and build our cot!
>
> Then hip – hurrah for the prairie life!
> Hip – hurrah for the mountain strife!
> And if rifles must crack, if we swords must draw,
> Our country forever, hurrah! hurrah!

In view of the heavy emigration to the far northwest
the *St. Louis Reveille* takes a jibe at the *New Mirror*.
It quotes that organ as having recommended the giving up of Oregon and as having said: "An army of
ten thousand men, with all the baggage and equipments
necessary to give it strength and efficiency, could never
be marched across an unhabited country 2,000 miles in
extent." Then the *Reveille* remarks: "An army of 5,000
men, women and children, frying pans, clothes, horses,
and washing tubs will *debouche* upon Fort Hall, during
the coming september, at any rate." [181]

The company led by Joel Palmer reached the Laramie june 24, 1845, and, as was usual, remained encamped for two days. Emigrants busied themselves with
trading at the fort, shoeing horses and oxen, and repairing their outfits.

On the afternoon of the 25th they gave a grand feast
to the Sioux Indians camped near the forts. Each emigrant family contributed bread, meat, coffee, or sugar
for the repast.

A general council with "talks" preceded the banquet.
One of the fort traders interpreted the chief's speech
and Palmer's response. The pipe of peace was smoked
by the head men and friendly relations were avowed.

William Barlow, another emigrant of this year, tells
of thousands of Indians coming into Fort Laramie when
his company passed, bringing with them tons of jerked
meat and hundreds of buffalo robes to trade at the
forts.[182]

"Here are two forts," writes Joel Palmer. "Fort
Laramie, situated upon the west side of Laramie's fork,
two miles from Platte river, belongs to the North Amer-

---

[181] *St. Louis Reveille,* may 21, 1845.

[182] William Barlow, in the *Quarterly of the Oregon historical society,* XIII,
258.

ican Fur company. The fort is built of adobes. The walls are about two feet thick, and twelve or fourteen feet high, the tops being picketed or spiked. Posts are planted in these walls, and support the timber for the roof. They are then covered with mud. In the centre is an open square, perhaps twenty-five yards each way, along the sides of which are ranged the dwellings, store rooms, smith shop, carpenter's shop, offices, etc., all fronting upon the inner area. There are two principal entrances; one at the north, the other at the south. On the eastern side is an additional wall, connected at its extremities with the first, enclosing ground for stables and *carrell*. This enclosure has a gateway upon its south side, and a passage into the square of the principal enclosure. At a short distance from the fort is a field of about four acres, in which, by way of experiment, corn is planted; but from its present appearance it will probably prove a failure. Fort John [Fort Platte] stands about a mile below Fort Laramie, and is built of the same material as the latter, but is not so extensive. Its present occupants are a company from St. Louis." [183]

The Laramie forts in the year of 1845 received their first visit from military troops of the United States. Colonel Stephen W. Kearny led five companies of the First Dragoons over the Oregon trail to South Pass with the double purpose of guarding the emigrants and impressing the Indians. With some 250 well mounted men, each equipped with carbine, pistol and sabre, he set out from Fort Leavenworth on may 18. Two mountain howitzers and seventeen wagons stocked with sup-

[183] Palmer's *Journal of travels over the Rocky mountains*, in R. G. Thwaites's *Early western travels*, XXX, 60-61. For other accounts of the emigration of 1845 at Fort Laramie, see also the *Narrative of Samuel Hancock*, 19; J. E. Howell, "Diary of an emigrant of 1845," in *The Washington historical quarterly*, I, 139-158.

plies lumbered along in the rear of the column. Fifty
head of sheep and twenty-five beef cattle were driven
along to supplement the food supply. Twenty-seven
days of marching, during which they passed most of the
Oregon emigrants, brought them to the Laramie.[184] The
two forts vied for the distinction of having the Dragoons camped in their vicinity. The boon of good grass
on the Laramie river bottoms, three miles above Fort
Laramie, determined the choice of the post on that
stream.

This fort, wrote Captain Philip St. George Cooke of
the Dragoons, "swarmed with women and children,
whose language – like their complexions – is various
and mixed, Indian, French, English, and Spanish; they
live nearly exclusively on dried buffalo meat, for which
the hunters go at least fifty miles; but they have domestic cattle." [185]

Fortunately for the purposes of the military expedition, some 1200 Sioux were assembled near the fort.
These Colonel Kearny arranged to meet in general
council on the neutral ground between Forts Laramie
and Platte. On high staffs three flags were displayed,
two being the Stars and Stripes and the third, one of
Indian design. On this latter were two crossed bands,
said to represent the winds, with nine stars above the
bands and clasped hands beneath. The people of Fort
Platte had prepared chairs and benches backed with
elk skins, for the council leaders, and had carpeted the
ground with buffalo robes. The Indians seated themselves in a great semi-circle, with women and children,
many deep, making up the rear.

---

184 S. W. Kearny, "Report of a summer campaign to the Rocky mountains,"
etc., in *Sen. ex. docs.*, cong. 29, sess. 1, no. 1, pp. 210-13. See also J. W.
De Peyster, *Personal and military history of Philip Kearny*, 112-15.

185 Philip St. George Cooke, *Scenes and adventures in the army*, 335.

After the peace pipe had gone the rounds, Colonel Kearny addressed the chiefs and braves. He spoke of the love and solicitude of the Great Father at Washington for his red children of the plains, and warned them against the introduction of whisky from Taos. He told them that the emigrant road must remain open and that the whites who traveled it must not be disturbed. Bull Tail, the principal chief, made an appropriate and friendly reply, after which presents of scarlet and blue cloth, red and green blankets, tobacco, knives, looking-glasses, beads, and such things were distributed to the Indians. As an expression of thanks a squaw commenced a chant in which she was joined by many women and some men, the whole producing what Captain Cooke considered "a very fine musical effect." [186] Several shots were fired from the howitzer; the shell that burst upon falling, had an especially terrifying effect. At night rockets were sent into the air, which, the colonel explained, were missives to the Great Spirit, telling that the Sioux had listened to his words.

[186] *Ibid.,* 337-338.

Last Years as a Private Trading-post, 1846-1849

Supreme in the region, Fort Laramie looked toward a large and lucrative trade for the winter of 1845-46. Pierre D. Papin, long experienced in the fur-trade, took charge of the fort in the early fall, replacing Joseph Picotte.[187] When Dr. Elijah White and party, on their way to the states from Oregon, reached the post on september 15, they were hospitably received by Mr. Papin and were sold sufficient dried buffalo meat, flour and groceries to see them through to the Missouri river.[188]

Mr. Papin agreed with the bourgeois at Fort Pierre [South Dakota] that unless there was a good prospect of high water in the Platte, they should join forces in the spring and freight the robes and furs to Fort Pierre and send them thence by boat down the Missouri to St. Louis.[189] Though it was hoped that this could be avoided, such an arrangement would be far better than to boat the robes part way down the Platte and then have to cart them back, as had been done in the previous summer.

Fortunately, the snowfall was rather heavy on the headwaters of the Platte so Papin decided to attempt

---

[187] *South Dakota historical collections,* IX, 211. Papin had been the senior partner in "the French company" that before 1830 built Teton post, on the Missouri river near the mouth of Teton river, in opposition to the American Fur company (*South Dakota historical collections,* I, 334, 374).

[188] *Missouri Democrat* (Fayette, Missouri), december 21, 1845.

[189] From the Pierre Chouteau, Jr., letterbook in Missouri historical society archives. Letter is dated at Fort Pierre, march 11, 1846, and is unsigned.

navigation [190] from Fort Laramie. The product of the winter trade, including that of Bridger and Vasquez, was so large that nine boats were required for its transportation. Two additional boats were to be used by independent traders. The undertaking was so important that Papin assumed personal charge of the venture, leaving Bordeau in control of the fort.

Navigation was never easy on the Platte, but satisfactory progress was made by the little fleet. We get a glimpse of it some distance below the forks of the Platte, about the first of june. Young Francis Parkman "on a tour of curiosity and amusement," is our witness. "The boats," he writes, "eleven in number, deep-laden with the skins, hugged close to the shore, to escape being borne down by the swift current. The rowers, swarthy ignoble Mexicans, turned their brutish faces upwards to look, as I reached the bank. Papin sat in the middle of one of the boats, upon the canvas covering that protected the cargo. He was a stout, robust fellow, with a little gray eye, that had a peculiarly sly twinkle. 'Frederic,' also, stretched his tall raw-boned proportions close by the *bourgeois,* and 'mountain men' completed the group; some lounging in the boats, some strolling on shore; some attired in gayly-painted buffalo robes, like Indian dandies; some with hair saturated with red paint, and plastered with glue to their temples; and one bedaubed with vermilion upon the forehead and each cheek. They were a mongrel race; yet the French blood seemed to predominate: in a few, indeed, might be seen the black snaky eye of the Indian half-breed, and, one and all, they seemed to aim at assimilating themselves to their red associates.

"I shook hands with the *bourgeois,* and delivered the

letter: then the boats swung round into the stream and floated away. They had reason for haste, for already the voyage from Fort Laramie had occupied a full month, and the river was growing daily more shallow. Fifty times a day the boats had been aground; indeed, those who navigate the Platte invariably spend half their time upon sand-bars. Two of these boats, the property of private traders, afterwards separating from the rest, got hopelessly involved in the shallows. . ." [191]

Despite difficulties, the boats safely reached the mouth of the Platte. The *Missouri Republican* of july 7, 1846, reports: "Eight mackinaw boats, laden with buffalo robes, etc., with a company of thirty-six men under the charge of P. D. Papin, arrived at Fort Leavenworth july 2 – from Fort St. John, 'at the junction of the Laramie and Big Platte rivers.' The crews and cargo were there transferred to the steamer *Tributory,* which arrived at St. Louis july 6. The cargo comprised 1100 packs of buffalo robes, 10 packs of beaver, and 3 packs of bear and wolf skins – consigned to P. Chouteau, Jr. and Co. Papin said he had great difficulty in descending the Platte on account of low water. He was obliged to transfer the cargoes from three boats and leave them behind. He thought that two boats which left the fort before he did would be unable to get through, not having men enough to haul them over the shoals." [192]

After passing the boats, Mr. Parkman continued on to Fort Laramie and gives us one of our most interesting and detailed descriptions of the post.

With letters of introduction from the owners of the fort, whom he had met at St. Louis, Parkman was given the best the post afforded. In the absence of Papin, "the

[191] Francis Parkman, *The Oregon trail* (Author's edition, 1901), 70-71.

[192] Reproduced in the *Publications of the Nebraska state historical society,* XX, 159.

legitimate *bourgeois*," Bordeau [193] assumed the honors of host. From the principal gate he led the way across the interior court. "We followed in some admiration," writes Parkman, "to a railing and a flight of steps opposite the entrance. He signed to us that we had better fasten our horses to the railing; then he walked up the steps, tramped along a rude balcony, and, kicking open a door, displayed a large room, rather more elaborately furnished than a barn. For furniture it had a rough bedstead, but no bed; two chairs, a chest of drawers, a tin pail to hold water, and a board to cut tobacco upon. A brass crucifix hung on the wall, and close at hand a recent scalp, with hair full a yard long, was suspended from a nail [This was Papin's apartment, the best in the establishment].

". . . We stepped out to the balcony to take a more leisurely survey of the long looked-for haven at which we had arrived at last. Beneath us was the square area surrounded by little rooms, or rather cells, which opened upon it. These were devoted to various purposes, but served chiefly for the accommodation of the men employed at the fort, or of the equally numerous squaws whom they were allowed to maintain in it. Opposite to us rose the blockhouse above the gateway; it was adorned with the figure of a horse at full speed, daubed upon the boards with red paint, and exhibiting a degree of skill which might rival that displayed by the Indians in executing similar designs upon their robes and lodges. . .

"The little fort is built of bricks dried in the sun, and externally is of an oblong form, with bastions of clay, in the form of ordinary blockhouses, at two of the cor-

---

[193] Parkman, *op. cit.*, 98. Parkman describes Bordeau and tells an incident regarding him, on page 128.

ners. The walls are about fifteen feet high, and surmounted by a slender palisade. The roofs of the apartments within, which are built close against the walls,
serve the purpose of a banquette. Within, the fort is
divided by a partition: on one side is the square area,
surrounded by the store-rooms, offices, and apartments
of the inmates; on the other is the *corral,* a narrow
place, encompassed by the high clay walls, where at
night, or in presence of dangerous Indians, the horses
and mules of the fort are crowded for safe keeping. The
main entrance has two gates, with an arched passage
intervening. A little square window, high above the
ground, opens laterally from an adjoining chamber into
this passage; so that when the inner gate is closed and
barred, a person without may still hold communication
with those within, through this narrow aperture. This
obviates the necessity of admitting suspicious Indians,
for purposes of trading, into the body of the fort; for
when danger is apprehended, the inner gate is shut fast,
and all traffic is carried on by means of the window. . .

"We soon discovered, in the twilight, a band of fifty
or sixty horses approaching the fort. These were the
animals belonging to the establishment; who, having
been sent out to feed, under the care of armed guards,
in the meadows below, were now being driven into the
corral for the night. A gate opened into this enclosure:
by the side of it stood one of the guards, an old Canadian, with gray bushy eyebrows, and a dragoon-pistol
stuck into his belt; while his comrade, mounted on
horseback, his rifle laid across the saddle in front, and
his long hair blowing before his swarthy face, rode at
the rear of the disorderly troop, urging them up the
ascent. In a moment the narrow *corral* was thronged

with the half-wild horses, kicking, biting, and crowding restlessly together.

"The discordant jingling of a bell, rung by a Canadian in the area, summoned us to supper. The repast was served on a rough table in one of the lower apartments of the fort, and consisted of cakes of bread and dried buffalo meat – an excellent thing for strengthening the teeth. At this meal were seated the *bourgeois* and superior dignitaries of the establishment, among whom Henry Chatillon was worthily included. No sooner was it finished, than the table was spread a second time (the luxury of bread being now, however, omitted), for the benefit of certain hunters and trappers of an inferior standing; while the ordinary Canadian *engagés* were regaled on dried meat in one of their lodging rooms." [194]

Although Fort Platte had been abandoned, independent traders had not given up the field wholly to the owners of Fort Laramie. Bisonette and Sybille, with a number of employees, were still trading among the Indians. In august, 1846, Parkman visited their lodges on the head of Horse creek which enters the North Platte some 35 miles below Fort Laramie.[195]

Richard's Fort Bernard, eight miles below Fort Laramie, though a crude structure and only partially completed, was attracting some trade from the Indians and the emigrants. From it had been sent, in the spring of 1846, two mackinaw boats laden with buffalo robes.[196] In the summer of that year two sides only of this quadrangular fort were completed. Parkman visited the principal apartment and describes it thus:

---

[194] Parkman, *op. cit.,* 98-102.

[195] *Ibid.,* 285.

[196] Bryant, *Rocky Mountain Adventures,* 83, 107. One of the Richard brothers accompanied the boats while the other remained behind in charge of the post.

"This was a room ten feet square. The walls and floor were of black mud, and the roof of rough timber; there was a huge fireplace made of four flat rocks, picked up on the prairie. An Indian bow and otter-skin quiver, several gaudy articles of Rocky mountain finery, an Indian medicine-bag, and a pipe and tobacco-pouch, garnished the walls, and rifles rested in a corner. There was no furniture except a sort of rough settle, covered with buffalo robes, upon which lolled a tall half-breed with his hair glued in masses upon each temple, and saturated with vermilion. Two or three more 'mountain men' sat cross-legged on the floor."

Richard, the proprietor, he pictured as "a little swarthy, black-eyed Frenchman" whose dress "was rather singular; his black curling hair was parted in the middle of his head, and fell below his shoulders; he wore a tight frock of smoked deer-skin, gayly ornamented with figures worked in dyed porcupine quills. His moccasins and leggins were also gaudily adorned in the same manner; and the latter had in addition a line of long fringes, reaching down the seams." [197]

In addition there were traders from New Mexico. For years the American Fur company had felt a strong antipathy for these foreign intruders. On march 11, 1846, the company leader at Fort Pierre had written to his superiors at St. Louis saying that it was necessary that they have "four or five hundred bushels of corn next winter at Fort John to oppose the Taos peddlers who are a great annoyance and get a good many robes with that article. I have agreed with Mr. Papin that he should bring up next fall the carts now at Kansas with a light load of corn." [198]

[197] Parkman, *op. cit.,* 93.
[198] Pierre Chouteau Letterbook (MS.) Missouri historical society.

Edwin Bryant saw a group of these Mexican traders with their large herd of pack mules at Fort Bernard in june. They had brought up flour, corn and, no doubt, "Taos Lightning" over the 400 mile trail, to trade to the Indians and the emigrants. Bryant and some of his California-bound companions exchanged their wagons and oxen for some of these mules.[199]

Trade wagons traveled the 300 miles to Fort Laramie from Fort Pierre in the summer of 1846, but we cannot say whether or not they brought corn to compete with the Mexican traders.[200] Nor do we know whether Papin brought up corn from Kansas upon his return journey.

The emigration that passed Fort Laramie in 1846 numbered about half that of the preceding year. Among these homeseekers were such prominent persons as ex-Governor L. W. Boggs and his family from Missouri; W. H. Russell, later to be Father of the Pony Express; and Edwin Bryant, journalist of this year's migration.[201]

At the Laramie river the advance wagons found a raft made of logs tied together with buffalo hide on which they were able to ferry their wagons across the stream.[202]

Mr. Bryant visited Fort Laramie and recorded for us his observations. "On three sides of the court, next to the walls," he writes, "are various offices, store-rooms, and mechanical shops. The other side is occupied by the main building of the fort, two stories in height." He noted two brass swivels defending the gate.

Attempts had been made at growing corn, wheat and potatoes, he learned, but these experiments had met

---

199 *Bryant, op. cit.,* 106, 112.

200 Parkman, *op. cit.,* 279.

201 Edwin Bryant, *Rocky mountain adventures.* See also *Niles Register,* LXX, 211 (june 6, 1846).

202 Luella Dickenson, *Reminiscences of a trip across the Plains in 1846* (1904), 16.

with little success. The Indians were averse to all agriculture and had on one or two occasions destroyed the
growing corn and vegetables. But the Fur company
employees were raising some cattle and poultry and
provided milk and butter for their own use. Mr. Bryant
was invited to dine at the fort, the dinner consisting of
boiled beef, biscuit and milk. Bordeau, the thirty-year-
old principal of the establishment, explained that this
was their usual fare, when they had flour. But in the
absence of bread they lived on fresh buffalo meat, veni-
son, salt beef and milk.[203]

One of the companies of this year, the Donner party,
was destined to be remembered because of its fate. On
reaching Fort Bridger it took the Hastings Cutoff south
of Great Salt Lake. Being compelled to make a new
road it was so delayed that it was caught in the snows
of the high Sierras. Of the eighty-one in the party, only
forty-five survived the terrible ordeals of that fateful
winter.[204]

There was much excitement and preparation for war
among the Sioux in the summer of 1846. "The Whirl-
wind," Oglala chief, was leader in these plans, which
were directed against the Shoshones (Snakes). Inasmuch as war would interfere greatly with the trade,
Bordeau exerted himself in behalf of peace. He gave
presents to the chief and impressed upon him the losses
that resulted from war. Whisky obtained at Fort Bernard by some of the cooperating bands caused jealous-
ies and rivalries to develop which disrupted the campaign against the Snakes.[205]

The Indians must have devoted themselves more to

---

[203] Bryant, *op. cit.,* 109.

[204] C. F. McGlashan, *History of the Donner party,* gives a good general
account.

[205] Parkman, *The Oregon trail,* 113, 129-130.

buffalo hunting than to war during the winter, for the Fort Laramie traders were able to procure from them 1100 packs of robes. There was, however, at least one Indian battle – between the Sioux and the Pawnees at the forks of the Platte in late january, 1847 – in which 32 Pawnees and one Sioux were killed.[206]

The snowfall having been light and the chances unpromising for navigation of the Platte, it was decided to send the buffalo skins overland to Fort Pierre. In middle april, 1847, the wagons were loaded with 600 bales of robes, 10 robes to the bale, and set out for the fort on the Missouri.

Shortly thereafter, Charles Beaumont with nine men, left the region with three ox-drawn wagons loaded with robes, to follow the Oregon trail back to Missouri. These robes were probably the property of independent traders. Beaumont met the band of Mormons on may 4[207] and reached the Missouri river after about a month's travel. He reported that Papin would bring in 1100 packs of buffalo robes.[208]

The wagons had not returned to Laramie from Pierre with supplies and trade goods for the fort when emigrants began to reach that point on the first of june.[209]

By this time the opposition of Richard's Fort Bernard had been effectively disposed of. Who was responsible for this we have been unable to learn. Richard had left his trading post in july, 1846, to go to Taos for supplies. He escorted to the Pueblo on the Arkansas, a little party of Mormons from Mississippi who were seeking winter quarters. They had come west on the Oregon trail as far as his Fort Bernard without know-

---

[206] *Publications of the Nebraska state historical society,* XX, 172.

[207] Journal history (Mormon church archives, Salt Lake City) under date of may 4, 1847. See also *William Clayton's journal,* 128.

[208] *Publications of the Nebraska state historical society,* XX, 172.

[209] *William Clayton's journal,* 211.

ing they were ahead of Brigham Young and the main body of the Saints.[210]

In his absence, apparently, some one set fire to his establishment. When the first emigrants came by in may, 1847, they found that the post had been burned.[211]

The summer of 1847 saw a new element in the emigration that moved past Fort Laramie. A new motive force – religion – was actuating a certain group of west-bound settlers. The Mormons, having been driven from Missouri and more recently from Nauvoo, Illinois, because of religious differences with their neighbors, were trekking westward to find a new Zion beyond the frontier.

They had done some little scouting beyond the Missouri in 1846, but it was not until the following spring that the Pioneer Band of Mormons moved up the Platte and over the mountains to the Salt Lake valley.[212] In Brigham Young they had a vigorous and capable leader. Exerting both temporal and spiritual authority over his followers, he was accorded unquestioning obedience and was able to organize and direct what was, perhaps, the most orderly and efficient migration that ever trekked the trail. A part of his plan was provision for the keeping of adequate records. From these records we get the ground plan and learn the measured dimensions of Fort Laramie and Fort Platte.

Brigham Young had set out from Winter Quarters,

[210] Hafen and Young, "The Mormon settlement at Pueblo, Colorado, during the Mexican war," in *Colorado magazine,* IX, 121-36.

[211] Journal of Thomas Bullock, clerk of Brigham Young's pioneer band. (In Mormon church historian's office, Salt Lake City).

[212] In 1846 Bishop George Miller had gone up the Platte as far as Grand Island to explore. When the Mormon battalion was called into service in the Mexican war and the Mormons decided to winter on the Missouri river, Miller moved north to the Nebraska river and wintered there. Letter of december 28, 1933, from Andrew Jensen, Mormon church historian to F. M. Young. Data also in the journal history, Mormon church archives.

near present Omaha, on april 14, 1847, and joined the
Pioneer Band on the Elkhorn river. The camp consisted of 143 men, 3 women and 2 children.[213] They
traveled in 72 wagons and had 93 horses, 52 mules, 66
oxen, 19 cows, 17 dogs and some chickens.[214]

They traveled along the north bank of the Platte, on
a route thereafter to be called the Mormon trail. It was
the short and logical route from their starting point, a
little above present Omaha. On june 1, they reached
and camped at a point opposite the mouth of the Laramie. The next day Brigham Young and other leaders of
the party crossed the Platte in their leather boat, ex-
amined the ruins of Fort Platte and visited Fort Laramie. "We were shown up a flight of stairs, into a large
room," writes Thomas Bullock, clerk of the Mormon
camp, "where we found seats, bedstead, desk, a fiddle,
and some pictures. Mr. Bordeaux the principal man in
the fort answered all questions that were put to him." [215]

William Clayton, journalist of the Mormon caravan,
writes: "We went across the square to the trading house
which lies on the north side of the western entrance.
The trader opened his store and President Young entered into conversation with him. They trade solely with
the Sioux. The Crows come here for nothing but to
steal. A few weeks ago a party came down and stole
twenty-five horses, all that they had at the fort, although
they were within 300 yards of the fort at the time and a
guard around them. The Sioux will not steal on their
own land. A pair of moccasins are worth a dollar, a
lariat a dollar, a pound of tobacco a dollar and a half,
and a gallon of whisky $32.00.[216] They have no sugar,

---

213 Andrew Jensen, *Church chronology*, 33.
214 *William Clayton's journal*, 76.
215 Bullock's journal, *op. cit.*
216 Bullock gives other prices as follows: "Sheeting, shirting, calicoes and

coffee or spices as their spring stores have not yet arrived. They have lately sent to Fort Pierre, 600 bales of
robes with ten robes in each bale. Their wagons have
been gone forty-five days, etc. The blacksmith shop lies
on the south side of the western entrance. There are
dwellings inside the fort beside that of Mr. Bordeau's.
The south end is divided off and occupied for stables,
etc. There are many souls at this fort, mostly French,
half-breeds, and a few Sioux Indians. Elder Pratt measured the river and found it forty-one yards. He also
took the latitude which was 42 degrees, 12 feet, 13
inches." [217]

Dr. Luke Johnson, of the Mormon party, attended
some sick persons at the fort and was paid for his services in moccasins, skins, etc. The Mormons set up their
portable blacksmith shops and did considerable repair
work on their wagons while encamped near the fort.[218]

Bullock and Clayton, with a tape line, took the meas-
urements of Fort Laramie and Fort Platte and made
sketches of the ground plans, which are reproduced
herewith.[219] Says Andrew Jensen, Mormon church his-

---

cottons are 1.00 per yard. Butcher knife 1.00, robes from 3 to 5.00, buck skins
2 to 3.00, moccasins 1.00, cows from 15 to 25.00, horses and ponies 40, flour
25 per pound."

[217] *William Clayton's journal,* 210, 211.

[218] Biography of Lorenzo D. Young, pioneer of 1847 (MS.) p. 108. L. D.
Young was himself a blacksmith.

[219] Bullock's description of Fort Platte is more detailed than that of Fort
Laramie. He writes that the deserted post measured "144 by 103.2 outside,
the door on the east side 9f. 9 in., height of walls 11 feet – the doorway on s.
side 10.6 wide – all the walls were about 30 inches thick; around the inside
of the walls were 15 rooms; the one on the s. w. corner appeared to have
been a store – these small rooms 16x15 surrounded a yard 61 f. 9 in. by 56 f. –
on the chimney piece of the 2nd room on the west side were paintings of a
horse and a buffalo but little defaced – on the north side was the yard for
horses 98 f. 9 in. by 47 feet inside having on the n. w. corner a square tower
with holes to shoot thro' on the sides – which was 9 f. 3 in. square – on the
n. e. corner, was an attached building 29 f. 4 in. by 19 f. 6 in. outside dimensions – see the lower plat on next page – the Oregon trail runs one rod from

torian, "There were 18 rooms [in Fort Laramie], name-
ly, six on the east, six on the west, three on the north and
three on the south. These rooms were occupied as stores,
blacksmith shops, and dwellings." [220]

The Mormons hired the Fort Laramie flat boat for
$18, and on june third and fourth ferried their wagons
across the Platte, the divisions vying with each other
in speed. The first division took a wagon across every
15 minutes, the second averaged one every 11 minutes.[221]

Close on the heels of the pioneer Mormon party
came large companies of emigrants bound for Oregon
and California. In fact the emigration to the Pacific
coast in 1847 exceeded that of any previous year. It is
estimated that between 4,000 and 5,000 made their way
to Oregon and 1,000 to California.[222] In addition some
2,000 Mormons followed their Pioneer Band to the
Salt Lake valley this season. To all of these emigrants
Fort Laramie was the great way station on the route,
the recruiting and supply depot on the long, weary
trail.[223]

Several eastbound parties of this year visited at the
fort. Early in august, General S. W. Kearny, bringing
Colonel J. C. Fremont to the East for his courtmartial
trial, passed the post.[224] On september 25, Commodore

the s. w. angle of the fort — running the River road, under the bluffs. The
building was made with unburnt bricks & had been white-washed."

[220] Article by Andrew Jensen in the *Salt Lake Tribune*, june 2, 1934.

[221] *William Clayton's Journal*, 212-13.

[222] F. G. Young, "The Oregon trail," in *Quarterly of the Oregon historical
society*, I, 370, and W. J. Ghent, *The road to Oregon*, 91. *Niles Register* of
august 14, 1847, quotes the *St. Joseph Gazette* as stating that 433 wagons
had passed Independence the preceding spring with emigrants for Oregon
and California and says that the aggregate was 1,300 wagons, which if they
averaged five persons each, would make the number of emigrants 6,500. See
also *Publications of the Nebraska state historical society*, XX, 171.

[223] Some of the Mormon companies stopped in the vicinity of Fort Laramie
to make tar for greasing their wagons.

[224] Journal of Nathaniel V. Jones in Mormon church archives, Salt Lake

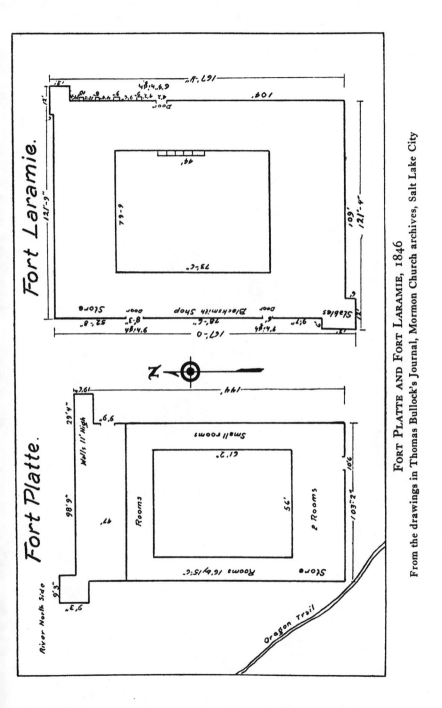

FORT PLATTE AND FORT LARAMIE, 1846

From the drawings in Thomas Bullock's Journal, Mormon Church archives, Salt Lake City

Stockton, also on his way from California, arrived at the fort. Here he met and dined with Brigham Young, who, with others of his leaders, was returning to the Missouri river to direct the Mormon emigration to the Salt Lake valley.[225] A number of horses belonging to Young's party had been stolen by the Indians above Fort Laramie. Young attempted through Bordeau to effect their return, but without success.

One Mormon party had preceded and another followed their leader toward the Missouri.[226] The rear party comprised 32 soldiers of the Mormon battalion that left Salt Lake City on october 18 with a small stock of provisions. They had been unable to get supplies at Fort Bridger and so reached Fort Laramie in november almost destitute. Here there was no flour to spare, but a few crackers and some dried buffalo meat were purchased. Twelve miles below the fort a trader was found who sold them 100 pounds of flour for $25. These supplies enabled the party to reach the Missouri in safety on december 17.[227]

Another party in need of help reached the fort early in february, 1848. It consisted of two mountain men – Joe Meek and George Ebberts – and five companions. They were on their way from Oregon to the states carrying dispatches for the government. Meek told his friends at the fort of the Cayuse uprising and the murder of Dr. and Mrs. Whitman and others at the Whitman mission. The party was hospitably received at the

City. Jones was a soldier of the Mormon battalion in Kearny's escort. See also the Journal of Jesse W. Crosby in Mormon church archives.

[225] *Journal history,* Mormon church archives. Commodore Stockton arrived at St. Louis november 4, upwards of a hundred days on the road. *Publications of the Nebraska state historical society,* XX, 175.

[226] *William Clayton's Journal* and Daniel Tyler's diary, Mormon church archives.

[227] Daniel Tyler's journal in Mormon church archives.

fort by Papillion, and was provided with fresh mules for continuing the journey.[228]

We have found scant record of affairs at Fort Laramie during the winter of 1847-48 and the following spring. The robes from the post appear to have been sent in wagons across country to Fort Pierre during april.[229]

Independent traders with Taos Lightning appear still to have been in the field, but government agents were on their heels. In the spring of 1848, Thomas Fitzpatrick, one time part owner of Fort Laramie but now Indian agent for the upper Platte and Arkansas, confiscated some kegs of liquor owned by Richards and dumped it into the Platte.[230]

The Mormon emigration almost monopolized the trail in 1848. Some 4,000 converts journeyed to the Salt Lake valley while but 1,700 made their way to Oregon and about 150 to California.[231] The usual respite from travel was enjoyed by practically all companies upon arrival at the great way station of Fort Laramie. The activity of Willard Richard's company was doubtless typical of some of the late parties. Blacksmithing and general repair work engaged part of the men, some did trading at the fort, others went fishing. Many of the women busied themselves with washing and baking while others gathered chokecherries and currants.[232]

[228] Frances F. Victor, *The river of the West,* 437. It is likely that the person in charge of the fort was P. D. Papin, and that Mrs. Victor rendered the name "Papillion."

[229] Letter from Fort Pierre april 21, 1848, in *South Dakota historical collections,* IX, 229.

[230] Hafen and Ghent, *Broken hand,* 205, 208.

[231] Figures from the Mormon church historian's office, and Hafen and Ghent, *Broken hand,* 209.

[232] *Journal history* (august 21, 1848), Mormon church archives.

Brigham Young now conceived the idea that the migration of his people could be best effected by making Fort Laramie the half-way station. From some distance west of the fort he wrote on august 28 to Mormon leaders he had left on the Missouri: "We have a proposition to make unto you, which is this. As teams that have been inured to the low country approach the mountains, they become diseased, and die, and as we believe that teams that have been acclimated to the mountain air, can come to Fort Laramie, and return to the valley in a healthy condition, we propose that when the Saints have done their spring work, they can remove themselves to Fort Laramie, at which place we will meet them with our teams, exchange the loads and again separate, the low land teams returning to Pottowattamie county and our teams with the Saints to pursue their journey to the valley." [233] This general plan was used rather extensively for several years.

A reorganization of the firm Pierre Chouteau Jr. and company, still popularly called the American Fur company, was effected in 1848. Six shares, comprising half of the stock of the company, were given to new partners in the field. One share each went to Alex Culbertson, James Kipp, William Laidlaw, Andrew Drips, Frederick Labone and one other to be selected. Culbertson was placed in charge of the western and upper Missouri departments that included Fort Laramie. [234]

Mr. Papin had declined to return to Fort Laramie and so Andrew Drips was placed in charge. "This post," says the letter from the company to Drips, "will require

---

[233] *Ibid.*, august 28, 1848.

[234] Letter from Chouteau, Jr. and company to Andrew Drips, dated at St. Louis, august 18, 1848. This letter we saw through the kindness of Miss Drumm of the Missouri historical society.

a good and careful manager and a person well acquainted with land transportation; we have thought you would fill it to advantage." [235]

In august, 1848, J. V. Hamilton set out from St. Louis for Council Bluffs with 16 men, taking the goods intended for Fort Laramie and for Fort Bridger. He was instructed to carry as much corn as possible to the Laramie. Culbertson followed up the Platte in september.[236]

Major Drips took charge of the fort during the winter of 1848-9 and conducted a profitable trade. On march 10 he dispatched a messenger over the 300-mile road to Fort Pierre for horses or oxen and carts to use in transporting the robes to the Missouri river.[237] During the winter, Laidlaw, one of the partners, had brought forty horses and mules up the Missouri to Fort Pierre and these helped materially in bringing the robes from Fort Laramie and from White river [South Dakota].[238]

Drips left Fort Laramie in the spring of 1849, presumably to conduct the furs to St. Louis, and left Bruce Husband behind, in charge of the fort. A sale of the post to the government was contemplated and certain repair work was to be done to put the property in saleable condition. Of developments, Husband writes:

Fort John, 24 may 1849

"Andrew Drips, Esq., Kansas

MY DEAR SIR: I take the present opportunity of writing you a few lines to acquaint you with the state of matters here. After you left

[235] *Ibid.*

[236] *Ibid.* Culbertson passed Fort Childs on the Platte october 1. *Daily Missouri Republican,* october 31, 1848.

[237] Letter of James Kipp to Major Drips, dated at Fort Pierre, april 14, 1849. (In the Drips papers, Missouri historical society).

[238] *Ibid.* Also letter of M. D. Hodgkiss to Drips, dated at Fort Pierre, january 30, 1849. (Drips papers, Missouri historical society).

we were dull enough for a few days, until Robinson arrived from Mo. When I set him and Burke at whitewashing the rooms, repairing chimneys etc. We had just got through this most necessary job when the first emigration parties arrived, keeping Burke and in fact all of us employed crossing their wagons [over the river], etc. etc. Yesterday three Mormons arrived here from Salt Lake, they were plundered by the Crows at the crossing of the Platte. I bought a few (4) horses from them which were in very bad order, but I get them cheap. I cut down our tongue and made a canoe for them with which they will leave this place tomorrow. It is a great pity you left no robes here as I could sell inferior robes very freely to emigrants at 3 and 4 dollars each; as it is, no robes, no blacksmith to work, and no oxen or horses (all of which would be more than ordinarily profitable) to make anything out of the emigration excepting ferryage, which last will cease when Laramie falls. We might make a little by the shop etc., but every party that has passed informs me and in fact everyone here, that the five men who are with the Sioux at Ash Hollow, scare people from having anything to do with us; Mr. Robidoux is particularly mentioned as having told that we were all damned rascals and cheats at this place. I am not aware of having given anyone cause to say this of me and I shall make him aware of my opinion of his conduct if I ever see him. Everything is going on well here.

"I would write you more fully, but there is nothing of very great interest only this (a fortune in two or three years can be made by taking seven or eight thousand dollars worth of good serviceable merchandise into Salt Lake valley next autumn or even next spring). If you think of anything like this or would feel inclined to assist me therein, I am on hand certainly.

"Mr. Williams, who will hand you this, wishes to make arrangements to furnish horses to the company here. He will explain his views to you, etc.

Meantime I remain, yours most respectfully

BRUCE HUSBAND

"P.S. I don't think I shall go back to St. Louis or even to the states again.   B. H." [239]

The summer of 1849 was to see the end of Fort Laramie as a trading post. For fifteen years, as a log stockade and adobe fort, it had presided in the country of the

---

[239] This letter is among the Drips papers, Missouri historical society.

upper North Platte. It had seen the fur-trade of the Far West reach its heydey and enter its decline. Now, with changed conditions the post itself was to be changed. Though emigrant caravans would continue to creep by, and in increasing numbers, the trafficker in buffalo robes would give place to the soldier. The fort on the Laramie was to be the extended military arm of the government of the United States.

Military Post

Fort Laramie Becomes a Military
Post, 1849

For some years the government had considered establishing military forts along the Oregon trail to protect emigrant travel. Fremont, following his expedition of 1842, had reported that "a combination of advantages renders the neighborhood of Fort Laramie the most suitable place, on the line of the Platte, for the establishment of a military post. It is connected with the mouth of the Platte and the upper Missouri by excellent roads, which are in frequent use, and would not in any way interfere with the range of the buffalo, on which the neighboring Indians mainly depend for support." [240]

In his first annual message to congress (december 2, 1845) President Polk emphasized the need of adequate protection for our emigrants bound for Oregon. "I recommend," he said, "that a suitable number of stockades and block house forts be erected along the usual route between our frontier settlement on the Missouri and the Rocky mountains, and that an adequate force of mounted riflemen be raised to guard and protect them on their journey." [241]

Senator Benton of Missouri, chairman of the military affairs committee, introduced a bill on december 30 following, which embodied the president's suggestion.

[240] J. C. Fremont, *Narrative of the exploring expedition to the Rocky mountains in the year 1842 and to Oregon and north California in the years 1843-44,* 47.

[241] J. D. Richardson, *A compilation of the messages and papers of the presidents,* IV, 396.

The next day representative Brinkerhoff introduced
a similar bill in the house.[242] In due course and after
adoption of minor amendments, "An Act to provide for
raising a regiment of Mounted Riflemen, and for establishing military stations on the route to Oregon" was
enacted on may 19, 1846.

The law provided that the regiment of Mounted
Riflemen comprise ten companies. An appropriation of
$76,500 was allowed for mounting and equipping the
troops. The last section of the law reads:

"AND BE IT FURTHER ENACTED, That a sum not exceeding $3,000, out of any moneys in the treasury not
otherwise appropriated be, and the same hereby is, appropriated, to defray the expenses of each military station or defense which the president may deem necessary
on the line of communication with Oregon, and a sum
not exceeding $2,000 for compensation to the Indian
tribes which may own or possess the ground on which
the said station may be erected, and for each station." [243]

The Mormons, retreating westward from Nauvoo in
1846, sent a representative to Washington to obtain a
contract to build such forts on the Oregon trail while
on their westward trek. Instead, they were solicited for
500 soldiers. The result was the enlistment of the Mormon battalion of the Mexican war, that followed
Kearny to New Mexico and then to California.[244] The
demands of the war caused a temporary postponement
of the project for building forts on the Oregon trail.

But early in may, 1847, a requisition was made on
the state of Missouri for a battalion of mounted volunteers to establish the contemplated forts. Five com-

---

[242] *Congressional Globe,* cong. 29, sess. 1, 122.

[243] *U. S. statutes at large,* IX, 13.

[244] Daniel Tyler, *A concise history of the Mormon battalion in the Mexican war.*

panies (25 officers and 452 men) were raised, but not in time to accomplish much that season.[245] They took up quarters on the Missouri river about 100 miles above Fort Leavenworth. In 1848 this battalion, known as the Missouri Mounted Volunteers, established the first of the posts on the trail, Fort Kearny, near the head of Grand Island, on the Platte. In november of that year they were mustered out, being relieved by the regiment of Mounted Riflemen.[246]

The army officers sought advice as to the most desirable location for the next military post. Thomas Fitzpatrick, veteran trapper and guide, and now Indian agent for the upper Platte and Arkansas, replied to Colonel Wharton's inquiry as follows: "My opinion is that a post at or in the vicinity of Laramie is much wanted. It would be nearly in the vicinity of the buffalo range, where all the most formidable Indian tribes are fast approaching, and near where there will eventually (as the game decreases) be a great struggle for the ascendency."[247]

Francis Parkman, after telling how insolent the Sioux were becoming and how on one occasion, they broke in pieces the cups from which they had been feasted by the emigrants, concludes: "A military force and military law are urgently called for in that perilous region; and unless troops are speedily stationed at Fort Laramie, or elsewhere in the neighborhood, both emigrants and other travellers will be exposed to most imminent risks."[248]

United States Adjutant-general R. Jones sent orders

[245] Annual report of the secretary of war, *Exec. Doc.* 1, cong. 30, sess 1, 79.

[246] *Publications of the Nebraska state historical society*, XX, 189.

[247] Fitzpatrick's letter of january 11, 1847, found in Hafen and Ghent, *Broken hand*, 193.

[248] Francis Parkman, *The Oregon and California trail*. (Author's edition, 1901), 109.

to Brevet-major-general D. E. Twiggs at St. Louis as follows:

"Adjutant-general's office, Washington, march 23, 1849

"GENERAL: To carry out the provisions of the 6th section of the Act of may 19, 1846, relative to establishing the military posts on the Oregon route, and to afford protection to emigrants to that country and California, known to be numerous, it now becomes necessary to establish the second station, as directed by the secretary of war, june 1, 1847, at or near Fort Laramie, a trading station belonging to the American Fur company. The secretary of war, accordingly directs that you take the necessary measures for this purpose, agreeably to the instructions above cited, a copy of which is herewith enclosed, for your information, etc.

"Lieut. Woodbury of the corps of engineers has, for the two last years, been employed on the Missouri frontiers with reference to the subject of the Oregon posts, and you are desired to authorize him to purchase the buildings of Fort Laramie, the second station, should he deem it necessary to do so." [249]

General Twiggs, on april 6, gave orders relative to the movement of troops and supplies for the establishment of the proposed fort. Three days later additional orders (No. 23) were issued, as follows: "There will be a post established at or near Fort Laramie. Its garrison will consist of companies A and E, Mounted Riflemen, and company G, 6th infantry, under the command of Maj. W. F. Sanderson, Mounted Riflemen. . .

"Major Sanderson will leave Fort Leavenworth by the 10th of may, with company E, Mounted Riflemen (rationed for two months), and such quarter master's

[249] Copies of these orders obtained from the Bancroft library, university of California.

stores (tools, etc.) as may be necessary until the arrival of the remainder of his command, and will proceed to locate a post in the vicinity of Fort Laramie, agreeably to the special instructions that will be given him. The remainder of the garrison for this post (companies A, Mounted Riflemen, and G, 6th infantry) will follow on the 1st of june, with the year's supplies already ordered for their post. The trains carrying supplies to the post near Fort Hall, and that in the vicinity of Fort Laramie, will immediately return to Fort Leavenworth." [250]

The train of about 400 wagons carrying supplies for the military posts at Fort Laramie and Fort Hall were to leave Fort Leavenworth on june 1.[251]

Major Winslow F. Sanderson, who was to establish and command the military post on the Laramie, had preceded it. He had been made captain of the Mounted Riflemen on may 27, 1846, and had received the commission of Brevet-major on august 20, 1847, for "gallant and meritorious conduct in the battles of Contreras and Churubusco" in the Mexican war.[252]

With company E, Mounted Riflemen, he reached the Laramie on june 16, 1849. His activity there is recounted in his report to Adjutant-general R. Jones:

"Fort Laramie, june 27, 1849

"SIR: I have the honor to inform you that I arrived at this fort, on the morning of the 16th instant, nothing having occurred on our way to interrupt our march; since that time I have, accompanied by Lieutenant Woodbury of the engineer department, made a thorough reconnoisance of the country in the neighborhood of this place, having passed up the ridge or mountain road, as far as the Boisie (or Big Timber creek) and returning by the river road.

---

250 *Ibid.*

251 Letter of a "subscriber" from Fort Leavenworth, dated may 25, 1849, appearing in the *Missouri Republican,* june 2, 1849.

252 F. B. Hietman, *Historical register and dictionary of the United States army,* 859.

"This was found to be the most eligible for a military post, and was purchased at my request, on the 26th instant by Lieutenant Woodbury, at a cost of four thousand dollars from Mr. Bruce Husband, agent of the American Fur company, who was duly authorized to dispose of the same for that amount.[253]

"Pine timber suitable for all building purposes is found in abundance within twelve miles, on the north side of the Platte.

"The best of limestone is also found about the same distance, on the south side of the same river.

"The Laramie is a rapid and beautiful stream, and will furnish an abundance of good water for the command.

"There is plenty of grass for making hay within convenient distance of the post.

"Good, dry wood is found in abundance and easily to be obtained.

"The entire command (except eight men for stable purposes) are already employed in cutting and hauling timber, burning lime and coal, cutting and making hay. The saw-mill will soon be in active operation: everything is being pushed forward as rapidly as circumstances will permit.

I am, Sir, very respectfully, your obedient servant,
W. F. SANDERSON, Major Com'd'g, at Fort Laramie." [254]

Company E comprised five officers and 58 men. Besides Major Sanderson, the officers included: Major S. P. Moore, surgeon; Captain Thomas Duncan, Mounted Rifles, commanding company; First Lieutenant Daniel P. Woodbury, engineer corps; and First Lieutenant Thomas G. Rhett, Mounted Rifles, post-adjutant and quartermaster.

Company C, Mounted Rifles (two officers and sixty men), under command of Captain Benjamin S. Roberts, joined the post july 26; company G, Sixth infantry (two

---

[253] The four thousand dollars was in payment for the buildings and improvements, and did not include the land, which belonged to the Indians, being claimed by the Sioux, Arapahos and Cheyennes. The chiefs of these bands Major Sanderson planned to assemble the following spring and from them effect a purchase of the ground. See Major Sanderson's letter of december 1, 1849, to Major-general R. Jones.

[254] Manuscript copy in Bancroft library, university of California.

officers and fifty-three men), commanded by Second-lieutenant Levi C. Bootes, arrived on august 12, 1849.[255]

These forces immediately joined in the work of preparing additional quarters.

Major Osborne Cross, quartermaster with the Mounted Rifles enroute to Oregon, reached Fort Laramie on june 22, 1849. Two days later he took an inventory of supplies and "turned over to the acting assistant quartermaster at Fort Laramie twenty wagons and 120 mules; also other property for use of the post. . ."[256]

"An Emigrant," writing from Fort Laramie on august 1, 1849, gives impressions of the post: "The old fort is now used for storehouses, stables, etc., and after the completion of the new one, which is to be erected in the immediate vicinity, will doubtless be used for stables solely. . . [The] post is supplied with eight heavy 12-pound howitzers and ammunition enough to send all the red men of the Western Prairies to their happy hunting grounds forthwith. . . The American Fur company, having sold Laramie, intend to erect a trading post at Scott's Bluff, some forty miles below."[257]

A soldier wrote from the fort on august 27: "On the 26th we received by the supply train for this post a mail from the states. Nearly all rec'd letters from friends. . . The health of the post is excellent. . . Game is beginning to be abundant – buffalo, antelope, elk, deer, mountain sheep and prairie chickens; fish are also very abundant. We are very much occupied building our quarters, and stables, and getting in hay for the coming winter. The neighboring Indians continue very quiet, occasionally paying us a visit. About one hundred and

[255] Fort Laramie manuscript (Bancroft library), 35-36.
[256] Report of Major O. Cross, in *Sen. ex. doc.* 1, cong. 31, sess. 2, 159.
[257] *Publications of the Nebraska state historical society*, XX, 207-8.

fifty Comanches have just left us, gave us a dance, and after receiving three days provisions from the government supplies, by order of the commanding officer, left us. . . The agents of the American Fur company at this place are about moving to their new post Scott's Bluffs, fifty miles east on the Platte." [258]

Another soldier at the fort writes on september 18:

"All hands are driving away at our new buildings, and strong hopes are entertained that before the mercury is at zero we shall be round our new hearths.

"We were visited, a few days since, by about two hundred Cheyennes and Sioux, who danced a little, stole a little, eat a great deal, and finally went on their way rejoicing. These Platte Sioux, by the way, are the best Indians on the prairies. Look at their conduct during the past summer. Of the vast emigration, which rolled through their country this year, not a person was molested, not an article stolen. Such good conduct deserves reward." [259]

Colonel Aeneas Mackay, who reached Fort Laramie on his western tour toward the end of july, reports: "We found Major Sanderson of the Rifles in command. . . [The old fort is] enclosed in a square of about 40 yards of adobe wall of 12 ft. height. On the east side are quarters of two stories with a piazza – on the opposite side, the main gate, lookout, flag staff, etc., with shops, store houses, etc., to the height of the wall on their right and left, and on each of the other two sides, ranges of quarters of one story – all opening on a small parade in the centre. It is in a good deal of decay and needs repairs. In these they were employed and in addition had commenced the construction of other quar-

[258] Letter of a "subscriber," appearing in the *Missouri Republican,* october 16, 1849.

[259] *Publications of the Nebraska state historical society,* XX, 214.

ters outside the wall, a part of which they expected to complete this fall and, by crowding, to shelter the whole command this winter.

"They had a saw mill at work, which was producing lumber very rapidly; pine timber of an excellent quality is found 12 miles from the post, which they were sawing into frames, flooring, &c. In the bluffs they find an abundance of stone of which they had already made 2,500 bushels of excellent lime. Near the place of the lime kilns is found red sand stone which will work very well and the teams were hauling a quantity of it to the post for certain building purposes. Opposite the post south of the Laramie, is procured from the bluffs an abundance of white sand stone mixed with lime stone, suitable for the foundation walls of the buildings to be erected, of which they are making use." [260]

The year 1849, that witnessed the conversion of Fort Laramie from a trapper's post into a military fort, saw other and far more important changes in the far West. This was the year of the great gold rush to California, that impressive hejira of modern Argonauts seeking the Golden Fleece. The news of Marshall's discovery at the Sutter mill race in january, 1848, had been carried around the world. From all sections of the globe streams of gold seekers were to converge on the American river, and over the Oregon trail, past Fort Laramie, was to come the stream of largest volume.

Through the winter of 1848-9, stories of California gold were published in every town of the country and repeated at every crossroads. Around thousands of glowing hearths equally glowing plans were laid for the journey to the land of gold. With the earliest signs of spring, eager wealth-seekers moved toward the fron-

---

[260] Extract from Colonel Mackay's report to T. S. Jessup. Kindly supplied by Dr. Newton D. Mereness of Washington, D.C.

tier towns on the Missouri to complete preparations for the overland journey. Men from many nations and of every station in life were to be found in the crowds that thronged the supply stores. Some calmly provided themselves with all necessary equipment and provisions for a journey known to be long and exacting, others assembled a little food and clothing and hurriedly set forth, depending on Providence and their fellow travelers for their unforeseen needs.

The forefront of the advance is reported on may 18 from Fort Kearny on the Platte: "The ice is at last broken, and the inundation of gold diggers is upon us. The first specimen, with a large pick-axe over his shoulder, a long rifle in his hand, and two revolvers and a bowie knife stuck in his belt, made his appearance here a week ago last sunday. He only had time to ask for a drink of buttermilk, a piece of ginger-bread and how 'fur' it was to 'Californy,' and then hallooing to his long-legged, slab-sided cattle drawing a diminutive yellow-top Yankee wagon, he disappeared on the trail toward the gold 'diggins.' Since then wagons have been constantly passing. Up to this morning four hundred and seventy-six wagons have gone past this point; and this is but the advance guard.

"Every state, and I presume almost every town and county in the United States, is now represented in this part of the world. Wagons of all patterns, sizes and descriptions, drawn by bulls, cows, oxen, jack asses, mules and horses, are daily seen rolling along towards the Pacific, guarded by walking arsenals. Arms of all kinds must certainly be scarce in the states, after such a drain as the emigrants must have made upon them. Not a man but has a gun and a revolver or two, and one fellow I saw, actually had not less than three bowie knives stuck in his belt. Many of the parties as originally formed in the states have had dissensions and are broken up, and each fellow is striking out for himself. This mode of life soon brings out a man in his true colors. No one knows a man and he does not know himself, until he is brought out in his true character – in the tented field, or on some such expedition as is now occupying so many of our citizens.

"Such an emigration as is now passing over the plains, has not had its parallel in any age. Composed, as it mostly is of the best material of our land, the country that receives it must necessarily assume a commanding position. Many rascals, however, are along with this crowd, to give it a little wholesome (?) seasoning.

"The last arrival from the frontiers is a solitary foot traveler, who says he has come all the way from Maine, without the assistance of either railroad, stage, steamboat or telegraph wires. He is accompanied by a savage looking bull dog, has a long rifle over his shoulder, on the end of which he carries his baggage, consisting of a small bundle about the size of your hat. He has no provisions but gets along pretty well by sponging on his fellow travelers. . .

"One of the men with the Mormon mail, is just from the 'diggings' in California, and is certainly a happy fellow, for he says that he has as much gold as he wants. He showed a stocking full as a specimen and as you may well suppose, the emigrants opened wide their eyes at the sight of the glittering mass.

Yours, etc., PAWNEE

"MAY 19. The cry is 'still they come.' Yesterday 180 wagons passed here, making in all 656. A cartload of letters starts for the frontiers this morning, and I presume many mothers, wives, and sweethearts will soon be made happy." [261]

George A. Smith, a Mormon leader writing from Iowa, on may 28, says that about 12,000 wagons had crossed the Missouri below Kanesville. "The world is perfectly crazy after gold," he remarks. "It is estimated that 40,000 men are on their way overland in search of the yellow dirt." [262]

By june 10, the Fort Kearny correspondent writes: "The cry is still they come. Five thousand and ninety-two wagons at sun down last night had moved passed this place toward the gold regions of California and about 1660 more, I think, are still behind. The fever, however, in many cases has completely subsided, and the others a few more doses of rain will put them in a fair way of recovery." [263]

"The great California caravan has at length swept past this point," writes "Pawnee" from Fort Kearny on june 23, "and the prairies are beginning to resume their wonted state of quiet and loneliness. Occasionally, however, a solitary wagon may be seen hurrying on like a buffalo on the outskirts of a band, but all the organized, as well as disorganized companies have cut loose from civilization, and are pushing toward the Pacific. . . At a moderate calculation, there are 20,000 persons, and 60,000 animals now upon the road between this point and Fort Hall. This is below the actual number, as the numerous trains of pack mules are thrown in." [264]

Westward the great throng moved, wearing deeper

---

[261] Correspondence from "Pawnee," in *Missouri Republican,* june 14, 1849.
[262] *Journal history,* may 28, 1849.
[263] *Missouri Republican,* july 6, 1849.
[264] *Publications of the Nebraska state historical society,* XX, 206.

and broader the great White-medicine road, convert-
ing the Oregon trail into the California trail.

Captain Howard Stansbury of the Topographical
engineers, on the way to his survey work in the Salt
Lake valley, witnessed the great trek. Under date of
june 12 he writes: "We have been in company with
multitudes of emigrants the whole day. The road has
been lined to a long extent with their wagons, whose
white covers, glittering in the sunlight, resembled, at
a distance, ships upon the ocean." [265]

Major Cross, from above the forks of the Platte, reports: "The banks of the South Platte seemed to be
lined with large trains moving on both sides of the river
and over the divide which separates the North and
South Forks. They could be seen as far as the eye extended. To look at them it would seem impossible that
grazing could be found for such an immense number
of cattle." [266]

By may 22 the first goldseekers had reached Fort
Laramie. Their health was reported good and their
teams in satisfactory condition.[267] Of the mighty throng
in their rear no such favorable report could be given
however. Not only were the usual hazards of overland
migration taking their levies, but the dread Asiatic
cholera had attacked the emigrant trains. It struck
without warning, terrifying its victims. A strong man
might be well in the morning and be buried by night-
fall. From the great cities of the country it followed

---

[265] Howard Stansbury, *Exploration and survey of the valley of the Great Salt Lake of Utah,* etc., (Washington, 1853), 24.

[266] *House ex. doc.* 1, cong. 31, sess. 2, 149.

[267] *Journal history* in Mormon church archives, under date of june 22, 1849. From the report of three men who left Salt Lake City may 6 and reached Council Bluffs june 22.

westbound emigrants up the Platte to the vicinity of Fort Laramie. An express from Salt Lake City that passed the fort on may 22, encountered the first victims on the South Platte. One company had lost fourteen men and were so disabled that they had to lie by.[268] From thence to the Missouri the express carriers noted numerous fresh graves dotting the Oregon trail. It was estimated that the deaths averaged one and one-half per mile for the entire distance from the Missouri river to Fort Laramie.[269]

A. W. Babbitt, who made a hurried trip from Council Bluffs to Salt Lake City and back in the summer of 1849, reported that the "cholera was very bad among the emigrants on the south side of the Platte river, between the head of Grand Island and Fort Laramie, but had entirely disappeared west of that point. The cholera was more fatal among the Indians than among the whites." [270] On his west bound trip with the mail Mr. Babbitt counted 6,000 wagons below Fort Laramie and 4,000 between that post and the Mormon metropolis.

Writes Wilford Woodruff, another Mormon leader: "It is said that some 35,000 gold diggers had passed over that route this season besides the Saints, and some 60,000 head of animals." [271]

The deaths of men and of animals and the breaking down of overloaded wagons necessitated the abandonment of all kinds of equipment and supplies. Such wreckage was strewn along the trail for hundreds of

[268] *Journal history*, Mormon church archives, under date of june 22, 1849.

[269] *Publications of the Nebraska state historical society*, XX, 209.

[270] *Journal history*, under date of october 1, 1849. This is from Babbitt's letter published in the *St. Louis Union*. Babbitt, returning east, was a Mormon delegate to Washington.

[271] *Journal history*, october 13, 1849.

miles, especially west of Fort Laramie, where the road became rougher, the grass scarcer.

One emigrant writes from Green River of western Wyoming on august 19, 1849: "From Laramie grass began to fail for our stock, and the utmost diligence had to be used to sustain them. From thence after the first fifty miles, dead cattle and fragments of wagons come in sight, and as far as here, I have counted about one thousand wagons that have been burnt or otherwise disposed of on the road. . .

"From Deer creek to the summit, the greatest amount of property has been thrown away. Along the banks of the North Platte to where the Sweetwater road turns off, the amount of valuable property thrown away is astonishing – iron, trunks, clothing, etc., lying strewed about to the value of at least fifty thousand dollars in about twenty miles. I have counted about five hundred dead oxen along the road, and only three mules. . .

"The reason of so many wagons having been disposed of, was the apparent necessity of packing, in order to insure quick and certain transit to the mines; and people did not care for the loss of any personal goods, so they reached there." [272]

Captain Stansbury, too, was impressed with the extent and variety of wreckage on the trail, and Major Cross counted fifty dead oxen in one day's march.[273]

Around Fort Laramie itself there was much abandoned equipment such as wagons and furniture, yet a scarcity of animals and certain items of supplies. Amos Steck records in his diary at the fort on june 19: "We

---

[272] "Joaquin," in the *Missouri Republican,* october 25, 1849. Reprinted in the *Publications of the Nebraska state historical society,* XX, 212-213.

[273] Stansbury, *op. cit.,* 57, and *House ex. doc.* 1, cong. 31, sess. 2, 168.

endeavored to purchase some ox shoes and was asked
$1. for two foot, and nails for sale at that, though there
was a blacksmith there and a copious abundance of iron.
Such imposition we would not stand. Camped one mile
beyond the fort." [274]

To the great host of weary travelers Fort Laramie
was a refuge. "Its neat, white washed walls," writes one
traveler, "presented a welcome sight to us, after being
so long from anything like a civilized building, and
the motley crowd of emigrants, with their array of
wagons, cattle, horses, and mules, gave a pleasant appearance of life and animation." [275]

The earliest of the forty-niners had found the post
still in the hands of the fur company. After the spring
shipment of furs the post was left almost deserted of its
regular occupants, but the throngs of emigrants soon
made it a place of spirited activity. As one writer reports, it was constantly "surrounded with emigrants
who were gratifying their long pent up curiosity" [276]
by visiting once more a white habitation, examining the
famous outpost of civilization toward which for long
days they had been slowly creeping.

William Kelly found it "a miserable, cracked, dilapidated, adobe quadrangular enclosure, with a wall
about twelve feet high, three sides of which were
shedded down as stores and workshops, the fourth or
front having a two-story erection, with a projecting
balcony for hurling projectiles or hot water on the foe,
propped all around on the outside with beams of timber, which an enemy had only to kick away and down
would come the whole structure. It stands, or rather

[274] Amos Steck diary; MS. in library of the State historical society of
Colorado.
[275] A. Delano, *Life on the plains,* 76.
[276] Diary of Joseph Warren Wood; MS. in the Huntington library.

leans upon a naked plain by the side of a rapid little river. . .

"I found Mr. Husband, the manager, or governor, as he is styled, a most obliging, intelligent, and communicative person. He offered us apartments to sleep in, but we did not deem it prudent to make a change in our living in that respect, lest it should afterwards affect our health. We, however, made use of the forge to tighten our wheel-tires, and make other small repairs connected with the waggon and harness. There were some Indians of the Sioux tribe about the fort trading while we were there; the trading colloquy between whom and Mr. Husband was most amusing; each praising their own and depreciating the value of the other's ware; rattling away with great volubility, and 'suiting the action to the word.' It requires great patience to carry on this system of dealing, the smallest bargain consuming as much time as the largest transaction; and it matters not how well soever the articles may suit the Indian, or how much he may desire to secure it, he will never give way to precipitancy, yielding up his final acquiescence with an affectation of reluctance." [277]

At the fort provision was made for the deposit of letters,[278] these to be carried eastward by some military or private express and be placed in a post office of frontier Missouri. Thousands of precious letters, many of them bearing tragic messages, were thus started on their way from the famous fort on the Laramie.

After Fort Laramie became a military post (june 26, 1849) it was even more than before, a helpful way station on the long trail. Writes a soldier at the fort in late

[277] William Kelly, *Across the Rocky mountains from New York to California*, 113-14.

[278] Delano, *op. cit.,* 76, says that a charge of 25c for each letter was in payment of carriage.

august: "Nearly all the parties remain here a few days to reset wagon tires, exchange and purchase cattle, mail letters for the states, and replenish their supply of provisions from the commissary, who is permitted 'to sell to those actually in want.' " [279]

Of the emigrant throng that surged past Fort Laramie all were not reckless irresponsibles. One of the many mothers who survived the hardships of the journey writes of reaching South Pass, the continental divide: "I had looked forward for weeks to the step that should take me past that point. In the morning of that day I had taken my last look at the waters that flowed eastward, to mingle with the streams and wash the shores where childhood and early youth had been spent; where all I loved, save O, so small a number, lived; and now I stood on the almost imperceptible elevation that, when passed, would separate me from all these, perhaps forever. Through what toils and dangers we had come to reach that point; and, as I stood looking my farewell, a strong desire seized me to mark the spot in some way, and record at least one word of grateful acknowledgement. Yes, I would make a little heap of stones, and mark on one of them, or on a stick, the word 'Ebenezer' . . . 'Then Samuel took a stone, and set it between Mizpeh and Shen, and called the name of it Ebenezer, saying, Hitherto hath the Lord helped us.'

"Nobody would notice or understand it; but my Heavenly Father would see the little monument in the mountain wilderness, and accept the humble thanks it recorded. So I turned to gather stones. But no stone could I find, not even pebbles enough to make a heap – and no stick either, not a bush or a shrub or a tree within reach. So I stood still upon the spot till the two wagons

[279] Correspondence in *Missouri Republican,* october 16, 1849.

and the little company had passed out of hearing; and when I left not a visible sign marked the place." [280]

After the passing of the summer flood of gold seekers, life about the fort became comparatively quiet. Some belated emigrants straggled in to the post, infrequently military mail arrived and departed, and occasional expresses stopped on trips across the plains.

On november 14, a party of Mormon missionaries traveling east from Salt Lake City reached the post. One of them writes: "On our arrival at Fort Laramie we obtained supplies for our selves and horses. Those of our number who had passed this fort the present summer were astonished at the great improvements which have been made here in a few months time. There is an air of quietness and contentment, of neatness and taste, which in connection with the kind of reception given by the polite and gentlemanly commander, Major Sanderson, made us feel as if we had found an oasis in the desert." Another member of the party reports: "Major Sanderson and his officers received us kindly and supplied us with such articles as we needed at the original cost. And while buying flour at $2.60 per cwt. and sugar at 6 cents a pound, and other things in proportion, I remembered that twenty-five months before I had paid in the same place 25 cents a pound for flour and $1.00 a pound for sugar and coffee." [281]

Some of the flour purchased by this party was added to the feed and water given the horses; and with the animals thus sustained, the missionaries made the winter trip to the states in safety, crossing the Missouri on the ice to reach Kanesville, Iowa, december 11.

The buildings erected at the fort during the fall of

---

[280] Sarah Royce, *A frontier lady. Recollections of the gold rush and early California*, 26-27.

[281] *Journal history*, october 19, december 11, 1849.

1849, as reported by the chief engineer of the army, were the following: "a two-story block of officers quarters [later known as 'Bedlam'], containing 16 rooms; a block of soldiers quarters, intended for one company, but which will be occupied by two during the coming winter; a permanent bakery and two stables for one company each." [282] The officers' quarters, however, appear not to have been finished until the next year.[283]

These improvements at the post and the presence of the soldiers put new life into Fort Laramie. It was to begin its forty years of service as a military post on the western frontier.

---

[282] Annual report of Brevet-brigadier-general Joseph G. Totten (november 9, 1849), in *Sen. ex. doc.* 1, cong. 31, sess. 1, 225.

[283] Totten's annual report of 1850, in *Sen. ex. doc.* 1, cong. 31, sess. 2, 363.

America on Wheels, 1850-1851

With mild weather and no extraordinary events, the winter of 1849-50 passed rather quietly at Fort Laramie. In the rooms of the old adobe fort and in the newly built quarters the soldiers were comfortably housed. Before the winter was over some of the soldiers were attacked with scurvy and with the coming of spring they awaited anxiously for the wild onion to grow with which a cure could be effected.[284]

Traders in the vicinity carried on some barter with the Indians for buffalo robes, but on the whole this traffic was meagre and unprofitable. The Indians were afraid of the cholera and had fled from the Oregon trail, the Cheyennes having gone south to the South Platte and the Sioux north of the North Platte.[285]

A number of belated forty-niners who spent the winter near the fort, wore out their welcome. "Cheyenne," a correspondent of the *Missouri Republican,* wrote from Fort Laramie on april 9: "The emigrants who passed the winter here (may Heaven never send us any more, for the winter), are getting ready and in about two weeks will be on the road to California. I presume," he continues, "by the first of june we shall again be inundated with the gold seeking gentry from the states, with their six-pounders, gold rockers, saw mills, etc. If some of them would bring along a ready made steam-

---

[284] George Keller, *A trip across the plains* (Photostat copy in Huntington library), chapter IV.

[285] Correspondence of "Cheyenne" from Fort Laramie under date of april 9, 1850, and appearing in the *Missouri Republican* of june 1, 1850.

boat it might be of use to them when they reach California – at least it would be about as valuable as most of the trash which was brought on the plains last year. If an emigrant has enough provisions and comfortable clothing, he cannot shave down too close in all other articles." [286]

By early may California-bound emigrants were arriving at the fort. Some replenished their supplies of flour and hard bread by purchases at the commissariat; others were encouraged to wait until they reached Fort Hall to lay in additional provisions.[287] A party of Mormon missionaries that left Salt Lake City on april 19, encountered the first California-bound emigrants eleven miles west of South Pass on may 15.[288] These were probably the company that wintered at Fort Laramie. The missionaries met some ox teams on may 21 that had wintered at the fort.

Thomas Woodward, who reached the Laramie on may 30, writes: "The[re] is 2 companys of United States troops here. It consists of 8 or 10 buildings, some of them built with adobes or sun burnt brick. The rest is slabs on frames." [289] James Abbey, one of a party that reached the fort june 1, records: "It is a great trading post and has about twenty houses enclosed by a wall." [290] A party from Birmingham, Iowa, that had traveled up the north bank of the Platte, reached Laramie on june 1. While the wagons were being ferried over the Platte at one dollar each, some of the party visited the fort. One of these, Leander V. Loomis, was agreeably sur-

[286] *Ibid.*

[287] Keller, *op. cit.* Keller reached the fort may 4, 1850.

[288] L.D.S. *Journal history.* Also, Jesse W. Crosby, history and journal, may 15; MS. in Mormon church archives, Salt Lake City.

[289] Woodward's diary in *Wisconsin magazine of history*, XVII, 356.

[290] James Abbey, *California, a trip across the Plains in the spring of 1850*, etc. (Photostat in Huntington library.)

prised. "Insted of 6 or 8 little log huts, we found 30 or 40 buildings, and some of them of a pretty fine style, some first rate fraim buildings two-storys high, and quite large, . . .

"the fort was enclosed by a wall about 11 feet high, made of adoby's or spanish brick; in the fort were plassed 2 brass cannon of a pretty good size – about 9 pounders. The parade ground was situated joining the fort, which was a beautiful level spread over by nature with small gravel. Their stabling joined the parade ground; this was a long row of buildings, or two long buildings, being some 3 or 4 hundred feet long. Evry thing about these stables were kept in splinded order; they were very neat and clean. As luck always turns to our hand, it happened that the day we passed they were Drilling the soldiers. We saw them all dressed in uniform, and martched on the parade ground and drilled for some time; they looked splendid, I tell you; neat as new pins." [291]

There were 150 soldiers at the fort in early june and more were expected soon.[292]

The ferry over the Platte was owned by the government and was managed by the officers at Fort Laramie. On the 9th of june the boat was sunk "by some Californians who were on a spree." [293] They were crossing horses, contrary to orders, and had over-loaded the boat. The rope broke, the boat filled with water and drifted down the stream.[294] Impatient emigrants now tried to

---

[291] L. V. Loomis, *A journal of the Birmingham emigrating company*, etc., 30-31.

[292] Journal of Silas Newcomb. (Photostat in Huntington library).

[293] Jerome Dutton, "Across the Plains in 1850," in *Annals of Iowa*, IX, 447 ff. Newcomb, *op. cit.*, had crossed the ferry on june 7. A party from Salt Lake City that reached the fort june 10, reported that the ferryboat had gone down the river.

[294] T. M. Marshall (ed.), "The road to California: letters of Joseph Price," in *Mississippi valley historical review*, XI, 252.

ferry the river in their wagon boxes. Mr. Dutton reported that seven men were drowned in such attempts.

Others who had followed the Mormon trail on the north bank of the Platte, continued farther on the same side of the stream, hoping to effect a crossing farther up. Within two weeks after the sinking of the ferryboat, another had been constructed and was in operation.[295]

One of the most interesting parties to follow the trail to California in 1850 was led by the Hon. Henry J. Coke. This eccentric Englishman wrote a most engaging account of the journey. On reaching the fort he writes: "The first sight of stone buildings was very exhilarating. The Yankee flags, the lines of tents, and the attempts at cultivation, were undeniable proofs that the first stage of our journey was at an end." [296] Although he carried with him a letter of introduction, the officers of the fort were none too cordial at first. But he was invited to dinner and at the officers mess sat with Colonel Sumner, Major Thompson, Captain Dyer, Van Vliet, and Stillett. "The conversation," he reports, "ran upon general topics, and we were struck with the intelligence and information of the officers. In other respects, small blame to them, they were entirely Yankee – perhaps, a little more gentlemanlike and more hospitable than the generality of their countrymen."

While spending two weeks at the fort, buying mules, preparing equipment and laying in supplies, he found time to engage in a chase. "Captain Rhete mounted us on a couple of chargers and took out his greyhounds to show us a hunt. We saw one or two wolves, but not near enough to run. We had a short gallop after a badger,

[295] A. W. Harlan journal, in *Annals of Iowa,* XI, 43.

[296] Henry J. Coke, *A ride over the Rocky mountains to Oregon and California* (London, 1852), 149.

which we killed, but not till Rhete had used his pistol, and pinned him to the ground with a large knife. . .

"Wolves, like policemen, are numerous enough, unless you particularly want to find one. Almost every night we have one or two prowling about the camp."

With the great migration to California and with stories afloat of fortunes being made on the Pacific coast, it was natural for soldiers to long to be free to join the rush. From time to time individuals deserted. Some were caught and returned to the post, others succeeded in getting beyond reach. Mr. Coke reports on august 26: "Yesterday, eighteen men deserted from the fort, and have taken the best horses in the troop. A party left today to retake them, but the odds are greatly in favor of the deserters, especially if the capturing party take it into their heads to shoot their officer, and join the fugitives in the attempt to make their fortunes in California." [297]

The cholera again raged on the trail in 1850. Jesse W. Crosby, of the eastbound Mormon missionary party, passed the whole of the emigration and was impressed with the heavy toll taken by the disease. A little below Fort Laramie he encountered the first victims. In his journal we read:

"JUNE 12, 1850.   Met with two cases of cholera, both fatal; reports of sickness and death before us; great press of wagons insomuch that we seldom have the road. . .

"[JUNE 17]   seldom pass a train but what has lost from one to six men . . . one company of men all died; some women left alone with teams. . .

"[JUNE 21]   Cholera still bad, nearly every wagon had lost some; one wagon of 3 men had lost two; one

---

[297] *Ibid.,* 151-157.

woman said she had lost her father, mother and sister; herself and another sister remained alone." [298]

Early in june the scourge had struck the emigrants in Plum creek valley. A correspondent counted 40 graves in 60 miles. On june 7 he saw "three wagons with only one man able to sit up; originally twelve; six dead and buried; four dying of cholera. . . Sixteen out of seveneteen of one train were sick; another buried seven, and had five or six sick, one dying. In two instances the correspondent passed trains where all but one had died. He saw five graves beside one tent standing and another struck. Thinks 250 had died within the last fifteen days." [299] A doctor, R. H. D., reports: "On the north side of the Platte (Council Bluffs road) where emigration was less and water better, not a single case occurred." [300]

The disease made its inroads at the fort as well as along the trail. John Steele writes at Laramie on june 22, 1850: "This forenoon three men were buried from the fort. Seven others are sick." [301]

Coke, the Englishman, spent a week or two at the fort, considering himself fortunate to be within reach of medical aid. He writes under date of june 28: "Most of us are suffering from severe dysentery; I for one have swallowed nearly an apothecary's shop full of paregoric, opium pills, and cholera powders. The sickness is possibly owing to the change of diet and general mode of living. It is fortunate that we are so near medical advice; such severe attacks in the prairies would no doubt have left one of us by the roadside." [302]

[298] Crosby's journal, *op. cit.,* Mormon church archives.

[299] *Publications of the Nebraska state historical society,* XX, 224.

[300] *Ibid.,* 229.

[301] John Steele, *Across the Plains in 1850* (ed. by Joseph Shafer).

[302] Coke, *op. cit.,* 158.

The cholera scourge along the trail practically ended at Fort Laramie. West of this point the health of emigrants was markedly improved. Writes the correspondent "Cheyenne," from this post on july 8: "Sickness had been severe as far as Laramie, but beyond there was little mortality." He goes on to explain that of the 700 "who now lie buried between here and the Missouri," nine-tenths died of carelessness and lack of experience and cleanliness. He states that of the several detachments of troops who passed along the road during the season not a man was lost, owing to the strict attention to diet, water and camp regulations. Emigrants would drink stagnant water from pools and holes dug in the sand in preference to the running water of the Platte because it might be cleaner and cooler. "The graves encircling these pools show the consequences." [303]

Though health conditions improved west of Fort Laramie, as much could not be said for travel conditions. A more marked ascent, rougher roads and scantier grass affected the weakening animals. Exhaustion and death of stock induced many emigrants to discard furniture and supplies and even to forsake their wagons. Wreckage similar to that strewn along the road in 1849 again marked the trail in 1850. Franklin Langworthy writes from the Sweetwater region: "Large numbers are leaving their wagons, and packing upon their animals. Horses, mules, and even oxen, are used for packing. The wagons are generally broken in pieces by their owners, and used for fuel before they leave the ground. The number of vehicles that share this fate it would be impossible to calculate. Thousands of fine trunks, boxes and barrels, are burnt for cooking purposes. Property that cost one hundred dollars in the states, is none too

---

[303] Correspondence in *Missouri Republican* reproduced in *Publications of the Nebraska state historical society,* XX, 225.

much to make one comfortable fire in an evening. The whole way begins to be strewn with property of every description, which has been thrown away by the owners.

"The number of carcasses of dead animals increases as we proceed. From the upper crossing to this place, I think an average of those lying near the road would be one each half-mile. The effluvia is quite annoying, and with it the atmosphere seems everywhere to be charged." [304]

Writes another emigrant, "We frequently cook our suppers with the spokes of a better wagon than half the farmers in St. Louis county own.

". . . you can buy a good rifle for three or four dollars. Hundreds are broken up and thrown away." [305]

The westbound throng of 1850 was even larger than that of the famous "rush" year, 1849. The register at Fort Laramie on august 14 recorded 39,506 men, 2,421 women, 609 children, 23,172 horses, 7,548 mules, 36,116 oxen, 7,323 cows, 2,106 sheep, 9,927 wagons; deaths enroute, 316. It was stated that not more than four-fifths of the travelers registered, so the total emigration was estimated at about 55,000.[306] The Mormon influx to the Utah region was estimated at about 5,000 for the season;[307] while 8,000 to 10,000 were reported bound for Oregon.[308]

---

[304] Franklin Langworthy, *Scenery of the plains, mountains and mines* (ed. Paul C. Phillips), p. 60.

[305] *Publications of the Nebraska state historical society*, XX, 227.

[306] Correspondence from Fort Laramie august 26, 1850, reprinted in the *Publications of the Nebraska state historical society*, XX, 230. There is probably an error in the figure reported for the number of children.

[307] *Ibid.*, 230. In the *Journal history*, june 12, an estimate of 700 Mormon wagons is given. On august 14, 850 wagons are reported.

[308] "Cheyenne," correspondent at Fort Laramie, august 9, in *Publications of Nebraska state historical society*, XX, 225.

Among the emigrants of this year was a wheelbarrow man who attracted considerable attention. Interviewed at Fort Kearny he responded: "Na, na, mun, I ken ye'll all brak doon in the mountains, sa I'll gang along mysel." [309] The Scotchman reached Salt Lake City with his one-wheeled wagon but at this point was induced to continue with a better equipped company, so he "left his faithful hand-carriage by the side of the road and on he came a whistling," arriving in Colona, California, at the end of july. [310] "Suingkiss," an Indian near Fort Laramie, exhibited his impression of the emigration of 1850 by painting on a buffalo robe a mass of men, women, children, horses, oxen and wagons all running as for a wager. "Near the center of them the wheelbarrow man was under full headway." [311]

At Fort Laramie some blacksmithing and repair facilities were afforded emigrants, but these were hardly equal to the demands. Accordingly, Assistant-quartermaster Van Vliet wrote to General Jessup on july 25, making the following request: "I beg to state that I consider it necessary that a sum of five thousand dollars ($5,000) be appropriated for the purpose of erecting suitable work shops for the use of the emigrants who annually go over this route toward California and Oregon. This is the most important point on the entire route, & some 650 miles from the frontiers of Missouri. By the time the emigrants reach here they generally find that they have many alterations to make before entering the mountains, & government should offer them every facility of doing so. A suitable blacksmith shop with two forges, & wagon makers shop, are all that

---

309 *Ibid.,* XX, 222.
310 *Weekly Tribune* (Liberty, Missouri), november 8, 1850, quoting from the *Alta California,* august 6, 1850.
311 *Weekly Tribune,* february 10, 1851.

would be required, & could readily be built of adobes for the sum of $5,000 & perhaps less. No additional or yearly expense would be necessary as the coal & timber that would be required would be paid for by the emigrants whom I have always found anxious to pay for such services as have been rendered them.

"I beg, General, that you will give your earliest attention to this subject, for should my application be favorably received it will be necessary to commence operations this fall in order to meet the wants of the emigration of next season." [312]

A number of old-time mountain men came to the Fort Laramie region in the summer of 1850 to trade with the goldseekers. "They are as keen on a trade," writes one emigrant, "as any Yankee wooden nutmeg or clock peddler you may meet with in the states. I will give you some of their prices: sugar 25 cents per lb., bacon sides, 18c., hams, 25c., flour, $18. per cwt., loaf bread 50c., whiskey one dollar a quart, brandy $18. per gallon." [313] Among these traders were Kit Carson, William Bent and Tim Goodell, one-time fur trappers, who had come up from New Mexico and the Arkansas river. Carson had brought along thirty horses and mules to trade.[314] John S. Tutt wrote to John Dougherty from Fort Laramie on july 1, 1850: "I have sold $1200 worth of Indian goods at 50% – no transportation – to Jim Metcalf, all cash. Kit Carson and Bill Bent have just left. All the Arkansas men were here, scattered from Ash Hollow to North Fork ford." [315]

Some building was done at the fort in 1850 but there

---

312 Letter from the war department files, Washington, D.C., supplied through the kindness of Dr. Newton D. Mereness.

313 James Abbey, *A trip across the Plains in the spring of 1850* (Photostat copy in Huntington library), under date of june 1, 1850.

314 *Publications of the Nebraska state historical society*, XX, 225.

315 Dougherty papers (Missouri historical society), july 1, 1850.

was less progress in this direction than had been anticipated. The chief engineer of the army, Joseph G. Totten, reported on november 30: "a two-story bldg. for
soldiers' quarters – for a co. of 100 men – is now under
way, and will probably be prepared for occupation, but
not finished, this fall.

"A powder magazine 17′ x 27′ inside, of which the
stone walls are now up, will doubtless be finished before
winter.

"The frame bldg. erected last year, containing four
sets of officers' quarters – 3 rooms in each set – has been
floored, lathed and plastered, and is now nearly finished.
200,000 brick have been burnt, of which about 150,000
will remain for the operations of next year.

"The results of the year at both posts [Fort Kearny
and Fort Laramie] have been decidedly less than those
anticipated a year ago. At both places the horse-power
saw mills which are mainly relied upon for the produc-
tion of lumber, were broken, and continued idle many
months, until the machinery necessary for their repair
could be obtained from St. Louis. The difficulty of obtaining and retaining efficient workmen goes on increasing.

"Many of those hired leave for California, and all
become tired of the deprivations necessarily experienced so far from the settlements.

"During the season of emigration the mounted troops
are to be kept hereafter more upon the road, and less
assistance will be obtained from them.

"The officers of engineers hitherto in charge of these
works have been ordered to other duties, and the works
themselves turned over to the quartermaster's dept." [316]

---

[316] Annual report of the chief engineer, U.S. army, in *Sen. ex. doc.* 1,
cong. 31, sess. 2, p. 363.

Reverend Richard Vaux came to Fort Laramie in the summer of 1850. He not only served as chaplain at the post, but became also its first school teacher. He has the honor of being the first clergyman to have a charge in the region that was to be Wyoming.[317]

Experiments in raising garden vegetables, corn and potatoes, were carried on at Fort Laramie with fair success in the summer of 1850.[318] The chief difficulty was in keeping laborers at the fort. They would succumb to the gold fever and set out for California. Assistant-quartermaster Van Vliet finally resorted to the employment of Mexicans. He writes to General Jessup from the fort on july 23: "I have the honor to inform you that I have employed an agent to proceed to Taos, New Mexico for the purpose of hiring ten or twelve Mexicans to carry on the farming operations at this post & also for herding or any other labor that may be deemed necessary. I have been obliged to take this step as it is only by irrigation that the land in this vicinity can be cultivated & I have no one who understands it, and besides, so long as this California emigration continues it will be impossible to keep Americans, as the experience of the present season has shown.

"The Mexicans can be engaged for a year, work cheaper & are much better than any other people for the use that I wish to make of them. . . This morning some sixteen Riflemen overpowered the horse guard & taking each a horse, & completely armed, started for California. A command of twenty-five men is in pursuit of the deserters & will doubtless overtake them &

---

317 Joel J. Breed, The early development of the Wyoming country, PH.D. thesis, MS., university of California.

318 *Publications of the Nebraska state historical society*, XX, 231.

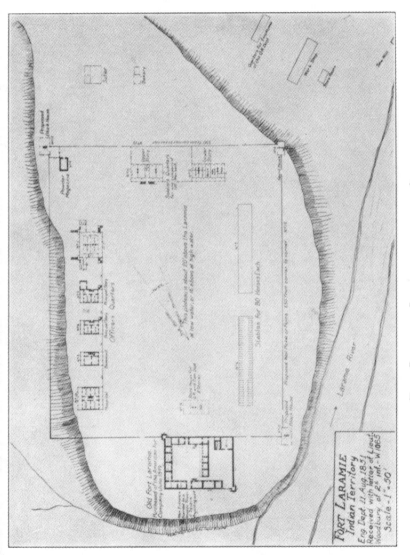

FORT LARAMIE, INDIAN TERRITORY, 1851

bring them back, unless they too, decide upon visiting California." [319]

The small amount of foodstuffs produced at the fort formed but an inconsequential portion of the provisions needed. Supplies for the establishment were freighted from the Missouri river. This was the beginning of an important industry for the plains – the freighting of supplies to a rapidly increasing number of western government forts. Contracts were let by the government for this transportation service. On july 9, 1850, David Waldo left Fort Leavenworth with a train of nineteen wagons loaded with 97,592 pounds of supplies for Fort Laramie. The freight rate was $7.74 per hundred pounds. [320]

Official mail service by way of Fort Laramie to Salt Lake City was inaugurated in the summer of 1850. Samuel H. Woodson was awarded a contract for transportation of the United States mail from Independence, Missouri, to the Mormon capital, monthly each way on a thirty-day schedule, for $19,500 per year. No mail stations were maintained and one team or set of pack animals was used for the entire trip. [321] The service was irregular and the schedule seldom maintained, especially in the winter time, but it did help in placing the fort in closer touch with the outside world.

The winter of 1850-51 was severe. Captain Van Vliet, who set out from the fort for the states in november was driven back by a snow storm and remained until spring. William H. Arnolls, who had brought the mail to Fort Laramie by wagon, had to resort to pack mules. Near South Pass he found the snow five feet deep and

319 Letter from the army archives in Washington, kindly supplied by Dr. N. D. Mereness.

320 Joel J. Breed, *op. cit.*

321 L. R. Hafen, *The overland mail*, 56-7.

was compelled to camp from january 25 to february 22. Continuing the journey, he reached Salt Lake City, march 12.[322] Ephraim K. Hanks led a party which set out with the mail from Salt Lake early in january, 1851. From Fort Bridger they took a route to the south of South Pass and reached Fort Laramie after traveling through the snow for thirty-six days. [323]

In late april Captain Van Vliet again set out for the Missouri, reaching Fort Leavenworth after seventeen and one-half days of travel. At the Little Blue, on may 2, he met the year's first west moving emigrant train. Thereafter companies were encountered daily. The majority of these were bound for Utah, only a few being headed for Oregon or California. [324] The gold fever had somewhat subsided [1851], and of those going to California a large proportion now went by ocean steamer.

The Mormon emigration was augmented this year through the aid provided by the Perpetual Emigration Fund. This fund, built up by contributions, was employed in helping poor converts to emigrate to Utah. Those helped were to repay the loan, the money thus becoming a revolving fund to aid migration to Utah.[325]

Eastbound travelers reported to the *Frontier Guardian* (a Mormon paper, published at Kanesville, Iowa), information about the western emigration met on the trail. Phineas Young and General Brown were met five miles east of Salt Lake; A. W. Babbitt and company, fifty miles farther east; President Hyde and his com-

[322] *Journal history,* march 12, 1851. Mormon church archives.

[323] *Journal history* and *Publications of the Nebraska state historical society,* XX, 231.

[324] *Publications of the Nebraska state historical society,* XX, 233.

[325] See G. O. Larson, Perpetual emigration fund company (M.A. thesis, university of Utah).

pany, thirty-three miles west of Fort Laramie; a company of Oregon and California emigrants, twenty-six miles west of the fort; Captain George A. Smith and his company, four miles west of the fort; Stevens' company, five miles east of the fort; Captain Cumming's company of 100 wagons, ten miles west of Ash Hollow; Shurtliff's company of 50 wagons, five miles in the rear of Cumming's train; "Captain John Brown with the emigrating poor [Perpetual Emigration Fund beneficiaries], twenty-two miles east of Ash Hollow"; Wilkin's merchandise train of ten wagons with a Scotch company in the rear, near Brown's company; "also Gordon's. Next day they met Father Allred's company the other side [west] of Cold Springs, and Elder Orson Pratt's company at the springs. Mr. Shelton, one of the company from Oregon, met six hundred and seven wagons between Willamette valley and this place [Kanesville], for Oregon; also seventy-two wagons from the junction of the roads, the latter bound for California." [326] The total emigration of 1851 has been estimated at approximately 20,000.[327] Fortunately, cholera was not epidemic on the trail this year and the health of emigrants was generally good.[328]

The U.S. mail line, running from Independence, Missouri, to Salt Lake City was divided into two sections in 1851, with Fort Laramie as the division point. The mails from each end of the line were to meet at the fort on the 15th of the month.[329] But as winter came on, the schedule was not maintained. Wrote Governor Brig-

[326] Copied in the Mormon *Journal history* under date of august 19, 1851.
[327] N. J. Breed, The early development of the Wyoming country, (MS., university of California).
[328] *Publications of the Nebraska state historical society*, XX, 234.
[329] L. R. Hafen, *The overland mail*, 58.

ham Young on february 28, 1852, to the Utah delegate in congress: "So little confidence have we in the present mail arrangements that we feel considerable dubiety of your receiving this or any other communication from us." [330]

In his report to the secretary of war, General Scott appears to have recommended the abandonment of the military forts on the Oregon trail. This suggestion found little or no support on the western frontier. J. Dougherty, for one, wrote a rather strong protest to the Missouri congressmen, in which he said: "The people in Oregon have a right to expect this road will be protected by the government, that emigrants may reach there in safety and join them in filling up and settling that country, and the emigrants themselves have a right to expect not only protection but aid from the government along this difficult and dangerous route; Forts Laramie and Kearny have every year since their establishment rendered important assistance and protection to hundreds of our people on their way to Oregon and California. Some of them had lost their horses and oxen, their wagons broken down, and others again were sick, unable to travel, some had broken limbs and some entirely destitute of anything like provisions, all of these unfortunate individuals met with instant relief at these posts from the hands of the officers stationed there, but what, let me ask, would have been the situation of such unlucky pilgrims without the aid of these posts, you can imagine.

"A few Dragoons could and would protect any party of emigrants travelling in company with them, but others in the rear or in advance 50 or 100 miles might be cut to pieces before the Dragoons would hear of

[330] *Ibid.,* 59.

it. . . I say it would be unwise, unjust and unpopular
to call back the troops, and abandon the forts in question. My word for it, if it is done our members of congress, and the members from several western states will
be called to an account by their people at home, particularly in our own state where 'The Great I did' is
watching with an eagle's eye to find something which
will enable him to pounce down upon the Whig members who he says have stolen their way into the capital
at Washington." [331]

The protests and the general opposition were effective
in preventing the abandonment of the forts.

---

[331] Written from Liberty, Clay county, Missouri, january 29, 1852. MS. in
the Kansas state historical society collections.

The Great Fort Laramie Treaty Council, 1851

The conversion of Fort Laramie into a military post and the unprecedented rush of covered wagon emigrants across the plains emphasized the importance of relations with the Indians. So long as the caravans were small and their members few, the Indians were not greatly disturbed, but when the wagons came to form an almost endless chain, the red men were alarmed. Their game was driven from the Platte river trail, and for miles along its course grass was cropped close by the emigrants' cattle and horses. It had been the established policy of the United States to make some reimbursement to Indians for losses of game and grass caused by white invasion. That steps be taken to placate the indignant Indians was becoming more and more urgent. The safety of emigrant trains and the maintenance of peace were at stake.

For years there had been government agencies established among the tribes along the Missouri, the lower Platte and the Kansas, but not until 1847 was an official representative placed among the nomad tribes of the high plains. For these Indians – principally the Cheyenne, Arapaho and Sioux – an excellent government representative was chosen. Thomas Fitzpatrick, for more than twenty years a trapper and guide in the far West, received the appointment as the first agent to the tribes.[332]

---

[332] Hafen and Ghent, *Broken hand, the life of Thomas Fitzpatrick*, 186.

He early began laying plans for a general treaty with the Indians under his jurisdiction. He wanted to provide against outbreaks and to secure the pledged word of the Indians to keep the peace. In the summer of 1849 he went to Washington and presented the proposal to the Indian office. The commissioner of Indian Affairs and the secretary of the interior indorsed his plan and recommended it in their annual reports. Senator Atchison of Missouri introduced a bill in congress on march 18, 1850, proposing an expenditure of $200,000 for the purpose. When it failed of enactment at that session, Fitzpatrick was greatly disappointed and made a strong appeal in his annual report of september, 1850.

"I regret exceedingly," he writes, "that the whole arrangement has not been completed the last summer, as I am confident that the Indians of that country will never be found in better training, or their dispositions more pliable, or better suited to enter into amicable arrangements with the government, than they are at the present time."

He urged compensation for the Indians' losses.

"The immense emigration," he says, "traveling through that country [along the Oregon trail] for the past two years has desolated and impoverished it to an enormous extent." Thus far the Indians had remained peaceful. "Under these circumstances," he concludes, "would it not be just, as well as economical policy for the government at this time to show some little liberality, if not justice, to their passive submission?" [333]

Congress acceded, and in february, appropriated $100,000 for the holding of a treaty council. D. D. Mitchell, superintendent of Indian Affairs at St. Louis, and agent Fitzpatrick were designated commissioners

---

[333] Annual report of the commissioner of Indian Affairs for 1850.

for the government. They chose Fort Laramie as the place of meeting and september 1, 1851, as the date. During the summer, the agent journeyed up the Arkansas and north to the Platte, visiting his wards, spreading the news and issuing a call for the council. Upon reaching Fort Laramie on july 25, he sent out runners in various directions to notify the different bands of the contemplated gathering.[334]

On september first, superintendent Mitchell arrived at the fort. With him came Colonel Samuel Cooper of the regular army; Colonel A. B. Chambers, editor of the *Missouri Republican;* Robert Campbell, whom we recall as one of the founders of the original fort and who was at this time a leading merchant of St. Louis; and B. Gratz Brown, later to become a governor of Missouri, but now a newspaper reporter at the meeting.

The wagon train that was to bring the presents and supplies for distribution at the council was late in starting from the Missouri frontier and could not arrive at the treaty grounds before the middle of september. This was unfortunate, for Indians were ever responsive to issues of presents, and the commissioners relied on the distribution of supplies to promote good feeling and insure success for the treaty making. In the meantime, however, the council could convene and begin negotiations.

For days preceding the appointed date Indians had been gathering in to the fort. The first arrivals, Sioux, Cheyennes and Arapahos, being friendly, mingled freely. The real test would come when their hereditary enemies, the Snakes and Crows, came in. As an insurance for peace under such circumstances, some two hundred white soldiers were at hand.

---

[334] Hafen and Ghent, *op. cit.,* 227.

When word came that the Snakes, led by Chief Washakie, were approaching, excitement spread among the
Indian bands. All would be tension, for some insignificant act might precipitate a fight. Private P. G.
Lowe, who was stationed with the Dragoons to the west
of the fort, pictures the arrival of the mountain Indians.

"About noon one bright day, a long line of dust was
seen from our camp, looking west, towards Laramie
Peak. Soon a long line of Indians came moving slowly
down in battle array, arms ready for use and every man
apparently expectant, the women and children and baggage bringing up the rear well guarded. It turned out
that Major Bridger, the interpreter, had reported to
headquarters the approach of the Snakes, and he had
been directed to lead them down near to our camp. All
the head men of the Sioux and Cheyennes had given
assurance that they should not be molested, so down they
came, moving very slowly and cautiously, the chief
alone a short distance in advance. They were dressed in
their best, riding fine war horses, and made a grandly
savage appearance. In the absence of Major Chilton
down at the post, seeing all this caution on the part of
the Snakes, Lieutenant Hastings had 'boots and saddles'
sounded so as to be ready whatever happened. Just below us was a large Sioux camp, and the people were
showing great interest and some excitement at the approach of their hereditary enemies, and a few squaws
howled in anguish for lost friends who had died in
battle with these same cautiously moving warriors.
When the Snakes reached the brow of the hill overlook-
ing the beautiful Laramie, less than a mile away, and
the chief commenced the descent, a Sioux sprang upon
his horse, bow and arrows in hand, and rushed towards
him. A Frenchman, an interpreter, had been watching

this Sioux, expecting trouble, and he, too, mounted his horse and was instantly in pursuit. The Snake column stopped and sent up a wild shout of defiance, the chief moved a few steps farther and raised his gun ready to fire just as the intrepid Frenchman reached the reckless Sioux, pulled him from his horse, disarmed and stood over him. Then ensued a harangue between interpreters and chiefs. The wild Sioux, who sought to revenge himself on the Snake chief who had killed his father some time before, was led back to camp while the Snakes held their ground. Their position was a good one; every man had a good gun, plenty of ammunition, besides bows and arrows. Not one out of a hundred Sioux [had guns, and the Snakes, though not one to five of the Sioux,] would have defended themselves successfully, and the battle would have been the most bloody ever known amongst the wild tribes." [335]

Lowe met Bridger at the treaty council, became attached to him, and thus reports the old scout in a subsequent conversation:

"Well, you seen that fool Sioux make the run, didn't you?" "Yes sir," "Well, —," referring to the brave interpreter, whom he knew well, "saved that fellow from hell; my chief would 'er killed him quick, and then the fool Sioux would 'er got their backs up, and there wouldn't have been room to camp 'round here for dead Sioux. You Dragoons acted nice, but you wouldn't have had no show if the fight had commenced – no making peace then. And I tell you another thing: the Sioux ain't goin' to try it again. They see how the Snakes are armed. I got them guns for 'um, and they are good ones. It'll be a proud day for the Snakes if any of these prairie tribes pitch into 'um, and they are not a bit afraid. Uncle

[335] P. G. Lowe, *Five years a Dragoon*, 79-81.

Sam told 'um to come down here and they'd be safe,
but they ain't takin' his word for it altogether." [336]

The Snakes set up their lodges near the tents of the
Dragoons and peace prevailed. But difficulties of another nature rose at once. The thousands of Indian
ponies added to the hundreds of soldiers' horses rapidly
cropped the grass for miles around the fort. The matter
of forage was considered and in view of the probable
duration of the council, it was decided that another
place where grass was more abundant must be found.
The bottomlands about the mouth of Horse creek,
thirty-six miles below the fort, were reported upon
favorably, and to this place it was decided to remove the
council. News of the decision spread quickly through
the camps and preparations were made for a general
trek on the 4th.

For the commissioners much planning was necessary.
Not only must provisions for two or three weeks be
taken from the fort to the treaty grounds, but some
presents and supplies must be available for distribution
to the Indians. There must be tobacco to smoke, sugar
and coffee to give out, and a few blankets, knives, beads
and trinkets to distribute. "Without these," wrote B. G.
Brown, a secretary of the conference, "no man living –
not even the president of the United States – would have
any influence with them, nor could he get them into
council or keep them together a day. . . Provisions are
the great and most important item. I have yet to see the
first Indian, whether chief or notorious brave, that is
not hungry or wanting something to eat." [337]

---

[336] *Ibid.*, 82.

[337] An excellent description of the treaty council was written by Mr. Brown
and was published in the *Missouri Republican* in october and november,
1851. This account is the chief source for the story in this chapter. The late
Dr. Grace R. Hebard, of the university of Wyoming, kindly lent us her copy
of the Brown correspondence.

It was an interesting cavalcade that moved down the Platte on the well-worn and dusty Oregon trail. Two companies of troops were in the lead; then followed the white dignitaries riding in carriages prepared for the occasion. Heavy wagons creaking under their loads of supplies followed behind, while all about were Indian villages on the move. Chiefs rode with some decorum, while braves and boys dashed about, displaying their horsemanship and working off their surplus energy.

Upon the squaws and girls had fallen the burden of camp moving. After taking down the lodges, they had attached horses to their travois – prairie buggies – and on these placed their lodge skins, camp equipage, and small children. Some of these buggies were provided with a wicker framework and with skin covering for shelter. Even the dogs were harnessed to small travois which carried light articles.

As each band or village got under way, the horses and dogs assumed a regular order of march. Should some foreigner break into the line ahead of a dog, the aggrieved canine would set up a piteous howl until he was again in his proper line of succession. The cavalcade stretched out for several miles and about it a cloud of dust rose thick and stifling.

In the afternoon of the second day the council ground was reached. The Platte with its two affluents – Horse creek on the south and Spring creek on the north – provided a broad area of bottom lands with good grazing.

Each tribe was assigned a suitable place and soon the respective villages were set up in accustomed form. Care had been taken to place the troops between the camps of the Snakes and the Plains tribes. Although there were but 270 soldiers at hand, while the Indian bands totaled more than 10,000, these troops would have a wholesome and quieting effect, especially for the control of any minor difficulties that might arise. But in general, the hope of peace must depend on good will. This seemed to grow as the tribes mingled.

It was not only a peace council that assembled at the mouth of Horse creek, but a great exhibition tournament as well. The program commenced on the day following arrival at the treaty ground. A formal call upon the commissioners was first in order. We have a description of it from the pen of Mr. Brown:

"On saturday, a large band of the Sioux chiefs, braves and men, nearly a thousand in number, well mounted, came down the Platte. They marched in solid column, about four abreast, shouting and singing. As they passed over the hill into the plain they presented an imposing and interesting sight. In the centre rode their principal chiefs, who carried an old American flag, which they say was given them by Gen. Clark, in the early days of his superintendency. They marched into camp. The chiefs and braves dismounted, and formed a circle – Col. Mitchell gave them some tobacco, and vermillion, and informed them that he would expect them to meet him in council on monday morning, at the firing of the cannon.

"Later in the day, several hundred Cheyennes, also mounted, rode over the hill, in manner similar to the Sioux, came into camp, and were treated with the same presents."

The 7th being sunday, the Indians were informed that it was the white man's Medicine Day and that the council would not convene until the morning following. The Sioux and Cheyenne women took advantage of this respite to prepare a place for the council to meet. With remarkable dexterity they erected in the center of the encampment a kind of amphitheatre, out of lodge covers and poles, with an arbor in the center for the commissioners, interpreters and head men. The tribes devoted the day to visiting. In the afternoon the Oglala Sioux were hosts to the Snakes, Arapahos and Cheyennes at a great dog feast. The banquet was followed by dancing. Feasts and dances were given in most of the other villages and the drumming of the tom toms and the chanting of the revelers continued through the night. The white commissioners slept poorly but felt well, for while the continuing merriment disturbed slumber, it proclaimed good will and augured success for the council.

With the break of day on monday, the Indian villages were astir. In front of the superintendent's tent a flag staff had been improvised by lashing three lodge poles together, and from this standard the Stars and Stripes fluttered out to the morning sun. At nine o'clock the cannon thundered forth its signal for assembling, and from all directions the Indian nations moved toward the council circle. The chiefs and braves who were to take part were in the lead on foot; behind them came the young men mounted or on foot, and in the rear came the squaws and children. We are indebted to Mr. Brown for an eyewitness description:

"When the whole body commenced moving to the common centre, a sight was presented of most thrilling interest. Each nation approached with its own peculiar song or demonstration, and such a combination of rude, wild, and fantastic manners and dresses, never was witnessed. It is not probable that an opportunity will again be presented of seeing so many tribes assembled together displaying all the peculiarities of features, dress, equipments, and horses, and everything else, exhibiting their wild notions of elegance and propriety.

"They came out this morning, not armed or painted for war, but decked out in all their best regalia, pomp, paint and display of peace. The chiefs and braves were dressed with punctilious attention to imposing effect. The 'bucks' (young men) were out on horse or afoot, in all the foppery and display of prairie dandies. In their efforts to be elegant, fashionable and exquisite, it must be confessed that the prairie dandy, after his manner, displays quite as much sense and taste as his city prototype, with this advantage. The Indian does not conceal his features with a superabundance of hair. In their bearings, and efforts to show pride of dress and tinsel, they are on a par.

"The squaws were out in all the richness and embellishments of their toggery. Their displays, according to their stations and wealth of their husbands or fathers, marked their ability to dress, and their distingue in genteel Indian society. The belles (there are Indian as well as civilized belles) were out in all they could raise of finery and costume, and the way they flaunted, tittered, talked and made efforts to show off to the best advantage before the bucks, justly entitled them to the civilized appelation we have given them. We concluded that coquetry was not of foreign origin. Even more than ordinary care had been bestowed on the dress of the children. They were evidently on their best behavior. . . Some were decked out in all the variety of finery that skins of wild animals, beads, porcupine quills, and various colored cloths could suggest. Others were in more simple costume, a string of beads round the neck, and a string round the loins."

The council ground was a circle. Sheds made of poles and lodge skins formed two-thirds of the circumference, while one-third, facing the east, was left open. Only the head men of the various nations took positions within the circle prepared for the council. The warriors found places in the rear of their respective chiefs, and behind these, many deep, stood the women and children.

When all was in readiness, Supt. Mitchell arose and addressed the council. Interpreters for the different tribes made known his message. He was there on important business and wanted everything done in good faith. As evidence of sincerity they would smoke together the pipe of peace, but only those whose hearts were free from deceit were to touch the pipe.

The ceremony commenced. A large calumet of red pipestone, equipped with a three-foot stem and ornamented with bright colored beads and hair was brought forth. The bowl was filled with a mixture of tobacco and kinnikinnick. The Sioux interpreter lighted the pipe and passed it to Supt. Mitchell. He took a few puffs and passed it to agent Fitzpatrick, from whom it went to the chiefs about the circle. Each Indian had his own peculiar form for smoking. Some, on taking the pipe, extended it to the four points of the compass, then up to the Great Spirit and down to the Bad. A ceremony observed by nearly everyone as a solemn protestation of truthfulness was to extend his right hand to the bowl and draw it back along the stem to his throat. By some, this movement was repeated several times.

At the close of the ceremony Supt. Mitchell addressed the council. He was pleased with the manifestations of good faith. He and Fitzpatrick had been sent by the Great Father at Washington to make peace with the assembled tribes. It was true that the buffalo were becoming scarce and that the emigrants' horses and cattle were eating up the grass. For these injuries the Great Father expected to make compensation. The white men wanted unmolested passage over the roads leading to the West; they wanted the right to build military posts for their protection. The limits of the territory of each tribe should be defined, and a lasting peace established between the various nations. The Great Father wanted each nation to choose a chief who would have control over and be responsible for his nation. If the tribes would agree to these terms of peace he would give them an annuity of $50,000 for fifty years, this sum to be expended for goods, merchandise and provisions. He is anxious for a visit from representatives of each of the tribes and wants chiefs chosen to accompany father Fitzpatrick to the white man's capital city. A train of ox-wagons is on the way with supplies and presents for all.

Fitzpatrick then spoke briefly. He advised the Indians to talk the matter over among themselves and to mingle freely together.

A number of chiefs expressed pleasure at the prospect of peace and friendliness, and the council adjourned. Feasts and dances again became the order of the day and night.

Tuesday passed rather quietly. There was to be no joint meeting, but the tribes held councils of their own to consider the commissioners' proposals. In the afternoon a band of about one hundred young Cheyenne soldiers gave an exhibition of military maneuvers. They were painted, and dressed in war costume and were armed with guns, lances, or bows and arrows. The manes and tails of their horses were colored and on the sides of each mount were painted symbols of the owner's coups – his record of horses stolen, enemies slain, and scalps taken.

In their demonstration they would fire their guns,

shoot their arrows, give a yell, and charge. Squaws and children at a distance kept up a succession of songs and wailings. The white soldiers and visitors were surprised at the precision of the drill, for at times the twisting, turning and mingling of horsemen appeared likely to trample the footmen and produce a general melee. But nothing such occurred. Then followed songs and dances and the counting of coups. For this last feature the Indians formed in a semicircle, while one after another took the center and recounted the feats of his career. Some braves presented twenty-five to thirty coups, each of which was duly counted off by the drummers with a resounding thump on the tom toms.

At nine o'clock on the 10th, the raising of the flag and firing of the cannon announced the opening of the second session. On this day the Crow delegation, conducted by Robert Meldrum, the interpreter, was to arrive, and a party went out to meet them and escort them to the treaty grounds. The favorable impression created by these mountain warriors is well expressed by Mr. Brown:

"This is much the finest delegation of Indians we have yet seen, and although they were just from a journey of nearly eight hundred miles, they made a most splendid appearance. They were all mounted. . . They came down the plain in a solid column, singing their national songs. In front rode the two principal chiefs, each carrying a highly ornamented pipe; behind them the remainder of the party with their arms, and in the rear a few squaws. . . Col. Mitchell met them; the chiefs dismounted, made a short speech in reply to the colonel, smoked all round, and then he assigned them a camp ground near his own, and invited the chiefs and principal men to attend the council that morning."

The Crow chiefs were assigned a place within the council circle and after they were seated, the chiefs of other tribes presented to them the pipe and smoked with them in token of friendship.

This was the day for responses to the white commissioners' proposals. Many Indian chiefs responded, the general expressions being favorable. The most frequent note was one of misgiving for the future. They lamented the passing of the buffalo, deplored the poverty of their people, and hoped that the presents would soon arrive. One quotation will illustrate the Indian responses.

Cut Nose, chief of the Arapahos, spoke thus: "Grand Father, I thank the Great Spirit, the Sun and the Moon, for putting me on this earth. It is a good earth, and I hope there will be no more fighting on it – that the grass will grow and the water fall, and plenty of buffalo. You, Grand Father, are doing well for your children, in coming so far and taking so much trouble about them. I think you will do us all much good; I will go home satisfied. I will sleep sound, and not have to watch my horses in the night, or be afraid for my squaws and children. We have to live on these streams and in the hills, and I would be glad if the whites would pick out a place for themselves and not come into our grounds; but if they must pass through our country, they should give us game for what they drive off. . . We have chosen our chief as you requested us to do, Father. Whatever he does we will support him in it, and we expect, Father, that the whites will support him."

A council with the Crows was the chief feature of the following day. Toward evening there arrived agent Culbertson, Father De Smet and a delegation of Assiniboin, Crow, Minnitaree and Arikara Indians from the upper Missouri. In the preceding spring, De Smet had been asked to come to the Fort Laramie council, for his great knowledge of and influence with, the Indians was appreciated and valued. Leaving St. Louis in june he had traveled by river steamer to Fort Union at the mouth of the Yellowstone. Here he had joined Major Culbertson and with the thirty-two Indian chiefs had traveled overland to Fort Laramie. From the fort to the treaty grounds the catholic father, upon invitation, rode with Col. Robert Campbell in his carriage. The ten thousand Indians assembled here, afforded opportunity not only for promotion of friendship but also for some proselyting by the zealous priest.

The 12th was devoted largely to a discussion of boundaries for the territory of the respective tribes and in delineating these boundaries on a map. Fitzpatrick, Jim Bridger and others familiar with western geography were of especial value in this undertaking.

The day following, fitting preparations were made for the priest's first sunday at the council. Writes Father De Smet: "Some lodges of buffalo hides were arranged and ornamented as a sanctuary, on the plain of the great council. Under this tent I had the happiness of offering the holy sacrifice, in presence of all the gentlemen assisting at the council, of all the half-bloods and whites and of a great concourse of Indians. After my instructions twenty-eight children (half-bloods) and five adults were regenerated in the holy waters of baptism, with all the ceremonies of the church." [338]

During the next few days while the various provisions of the treaty were being discussed and agreed upon, Father De Smet, with an interpreter, visited the various tribes.

"I held daily conferences on religion," he writes,

---

[338] Chittenden and Richardson, *Life and letters of De Smet*, 677.

"sometimes with one band of Indians, sometimes with another. They all listened with great attention and unanimously expressed the wish to be supplied with catholic missionaries.

"Among the Arapahos, I baptized 305 little ones; among the Cheyennes, 253; and among the Brulés and Osage Sioux, 280; in the camp of Painted Bear, fifty-six. The number of the half-bloods that I baptized in the plain of the great council and on the river Platte is sixty-one."

The father thus describes a ceremony of peace and restitution witnessed at the council: "The Shoshones, or Snake Indians, had scarcely quitted the Rocky mountains to repair to the great council, when they were pursued and attacked by a party of Cheyennes, who killed two of their men and carried away their scalps. The Cheyennes must pay, or 'cover the body,' which is a satisfaction required by the savages on such occasions, before they can accept the calumet of peace or smoke it together. On this day the principal braves of the Cheyenne nation and forty warriors of the Shoshones were assembled. Several orations were delivered as preliminaries of peace.

"Then followed a feast, of which all partook. It consisted simply of corn, crushed and thoroughly boiled. The dogs were spared this time, for the Shoshones are an exception to the common rule among the Indians; that is, they never eat dog flesh. The feast over, the Cheyennes brought suitable presents of tobacco, blankets, knives, pieces of red and blue cloth, and deposited them in the centre of the circle. The two scalps were also exposed, and then returned to the brothers of the two wretched victims, who were seated at the head of the circle, between the two chiefs of their nation. The brothers were solemnly assured that the scalp dance did not take place. They wore, however, a very sombre air, and accepting the scalps were deeply affected. However, they embraced the murderers, received the donations, and distributed the larger portion of them to their companions. After this, the usual signs of peace and amity, presents and reciprocal adoptions of children, were interchanged; their orators employed all their eloquence to strengthen the good feeling which appeared to reign in the assembly, and to render it lasting. The next night the Cheyennes visited the lodges of the Shoshones, who were encamped beside my little tent. Songs and dances were prolonged till daylight, and prevented me from sleeping. These amusements among the Indians are perfectly innocent. I have never been able to detect the slightest gesture that could offend modesty." [339]

By the 17th the treaty was ready for signature, being drawn up substantially as originally planned by the white commissioners. Its provisions had been fully discussed and were understood by the chiefs.

It provided for a lasting peace among the signatory tribes and with the whites; recognized the right of the United States to establish roads and military posts in the Indian territory; made depredations by Indians or whites punishable and restitution obligatory; fixed the boundaries of the territory of the respective tribes, but left all the Indian territory open to any tribe for fishing and hunting; provided for the payment by the United States of an annuity of $50,000 in goods for a term of fifty years; declared that violations of the treaty on the

[339] *Ibid.*, 679-80.

part of any tribe would be punishable by withholding a part or all of the annuity from the offender.[340]

The usual signals summoned the council for the formal signing of the treaty. All the chiefs and head men of the various tribes were present, displaying a gravity and dignity appropriate to the occasion. The instrument was read, sentence by sentence, and again fully explained. Then the United States commissioners signed the treaty and the chiefs in turn made their crosses opposite their names on the document. The whole was attested by the white witnesses and the treaty was ready for presentation to the United States senate.

The wagon train had not yet come, but assurance had been received of its early arrival. Notwithstanding the scarcity of provisions, wrote Father De Smet, "The feasts were numerous and well attended. No epoch in Indian annals, probably, shows a greater massacre of the canine race."

The grazing grounds had become a barren plain and stifling clouds of dust rose up with every gust of wind. Camp refuse was everywhere and the stench was becoming unbearable. The military moved two miles down the river to escape some of the filth, but the commissioners felt obliged to hold their ground until all was completed.

On the 20th the long-looked-for caravan pulled into camp and formed a corral. Crowds quickly formed about the dust-covered wagons in eager anticipation. But the distribution was not to take place until the following day. The wagons were unloaded. A $50,000 pile of merchandise and a throng of more than 10,000 Indians!

---

[340] C. J. Kappler, *Indian affairs, laws and treaties*, II, 594-96.

Each tribe was assigned a section of the area encircling the goods. The distribution began by presentation of uniforms to the chiefs. Writes Father De Smet: "The great chiefs were, for the first time in their lives, pantalooned; each was arrayed in a general's uniform, a gilt sword hanging at his side. Their long, coarse hair floated above the military costume, and the whole was crowned by the burlesque solemnity of their painted faces." [341] The Indian footwear was also retained, for nothing could replace the moccasin. A medal, bearing the likeness of the president on one side and clasped hands on the other, together with a document bearing an immense seal and ribbon, were the certificates of character for the chiefs.

Head men of the various tribes were employed as assistants in distributing the merchandise and supplies. The behavior of the crowd was excellent and all the recipients appeared pleased. Throughout the day the work continued and not until the middle of the next day was the distribution completed.

The Indian villages now began to move off in all directions. Gayly bedecked as never before they formed colorful cavalcades as they turned in the direction of their own haunts, or hastened to the reported grazing grounds of the buffalo herds.

The council had been a great success and the resulting treaty gave promise of a lasting peace. As a further guarantee, agent Fitzpatrick took a delegation of eleven chiefs and head men back to Washington. On the way they visited St. Louis, where they were shown the sights of the city and were given a banquet by the catholic university. At Washington they called on President

---

[341] Chittenden and Richardson, *Life and letters of De Smet*, 683.

Fillmore in the White House. While the president, his
wife and daughter and a number of invited guests sat
in the center of the room, the Indians, in full regalia,
squatted about on the carpet. The White Father gave
a brief address and presented medals and flags to the
chiefs. In january, 1852, the delegation left the national
capital and returned to the western plains.[342]

---

[342] Hafen and Ghent, *Broken hand, the life of Thomas Fitzpatrick*, 246-50.

The Emigrant Tide, 1852-1855

The emigration across the plains in 1852 was large. The newspapers in St. Louis and the Missouri river towns reported the outfitting points alive with activity. The number of emigrants "passing out from and through here, has exceeded all the calculations we have ever made," writes a correspondent from Independence on may 1. "The road from here to the Little Blue is lined with wagons." [343]

The emigrants were warned not to load their wagons too heavily, as supplies were procurable at Forts Kearny, Laramie and Bridger. At Fort Laramie the government was reported to have a large supply of provisions which would be furnished to emigrants at the cost to the government.[344] Captain William S. Ketchum, of the Sixth infantry of Fort Laramie, who left the fort with his wife about the time the emigrants began to arrive there, reported that the government had abundant supplies of flour and meat at the fort but could not supply sugar, coffee, etc.[345]

Colonel George E. Blodgett, upon returning to Missouri from the Plains in the fall of 1852, estimated the total emigration of the season as 40,000 people, 8,000 wagons and about 60,000 cattle.[346] Thomas Turnbull, who traveled along the north bank of the Platte to and

---

[343] Reprinted in *Publications of the Nebraska state historical society,* xx, 238.

[344] *Ibid.,* 238.

[345] *Ibid.,* 240. Reprinted from the *Missouri Republican* of august 18, 1852.

[346] *Ibid.,* 240-241. From the *St. Joseph Gazette,* september 8, 1852.

beyond Fort Laramie, reached a point opposite the fort on june 8, 1852, and recorded in his journal:

"At the opposite [west] side of the ferry [across the Platte] there is a blacksmith & waggon makers shop. The garrison & houses are built with spanish brick; number about 12 houses. The garrison is about 2 miles from the ferry. Hundreds of ponies, horses, oxen, mules, & waggons around here . . . some of the compy. went to leave letters at the fort; lots of Indians camp'd on each side of the rivers, Platt & Laramie Fork . . . at the fort hard bread $13 per c. Loaf bread worth 10cts in Chicago, 60cts here. Tobacco 6s pr lb. Vinegar $2 pr gallon. Tea $2 pr lb. Every thing very dear."[347]

Mrs. Lodisa Frizzell, who was with a company that reached Fort Laramie on june 11, 1852, writes her impressions:

"This is quite a place, several fine buildings nestled here among the hills. It looks like a rose in the wilderness. There were several Indian lodges not far from the road and plenty of Indians."[348]

A bridge had been built across the Laramie some distance below the fort, for the use of which a toll of $2.50 per wagon was charged.[349]

Gilbert L. Cole reports: "About 9 o'clock the next morning, we came to Laramie river, near where it empties into the North Platte, which we crossed on a bridge, the first one we had seen on the whole route. At this point a road turns off, leading up to the fort, about one mile distant. Being selected to deliver the mail, I rode out to the fort, which was made up of a parade

347 F. L. Paxson, T. Turnbull's travels from the United States across the Plains to California, in *Proceedings of the state historical society of Wisconsin* for 1913, p. 170-171.

348 Mrs. Fizzell's original manuscript is in the New York public library.

349 Mary Stuart Bailey, "A journal of wife of Dr. Fred Bailey, from Ohio to California" (MS. in the Huntington library), p. 10.

ground protected by earthworks, with the usual stores, quarters, barracks, etc., the sutler and post office being combined. On entering the sutler's, about the first person I saw was the young leader of the Indians, who had lunched at our camp the afternoon before. He was now dressed in the uniform of a soldier, recognizing me as soon as we met with a grunt and a 'How.'

"Delivering the mail, I rode out in another direction to intercept the train. When about one-half mile from the fort I came to a sentinel, pacing his beat all alone. He was just as neat and clean as though doing duty at the general's headquarters, with his spotless white gloves, polished gun, and accoutrements. In a commanding tone of voice, he ordered me to halt. Asking permission to pass, which was readily granted, I rode on a couple of miles, when I met some Indians with their families, who were on the march with ponies, dogs, women, and papooses.

"Long spruce poles were lashed each side of the ponies' necks, the other ends trailing on the ground. The poles, being slatted across were made to hold their plunder or very old people and sometimes the women and children. The dogs, like the ponies, were all packed with a pole or two fastened to their necks; the whole making an interesting picture.

"Overtaking the train about noon, we camped at bitter Cottonwood creek, the location being beautifully described by the author of the novel *Prairie Flower*."[350]

A group of thirty men left one of the California-bound parties of this year at Fort Laramie to prospect for gold in the mountains to the north, agreeing to overtake the main party on the Humboldt river. Eight of them did overtake the main group as promised, report-

[350] Gilbert L. Cole, *In the early days along the Overland trail in Nebraska territory in 1852*, 54-6.

ing the discovery of gold on two streams and asking the
company to return to the site of their find. But the main
body decided to push on to California. The other 22
men were never heard from and were supposed to have
perished.[351]

The season's latest emigrants to leave the Missouri
river were companies of Mormons. They comprised the
last of the Saints from Nauvoo and numbers of recent
converts from England. Altogether the Mormon emigrants of this year numbered about 10,000, larger than
for any other year.[352] A sugar mill to be set up at Salt
Lake City was freighted across the plains by the last of
these companies.[353]

The health of the emigrants of 1852 was generally
good, although there were some cases of chills and fever
and some of cholera.[354] One sidelight on the emigration
is given by Mrs. Margaret W. Iman who journeyed to
the Oregon country in 1852. She writes: "On our trip,
I think I am safe in saying, I carried a little motherless
babe five hundred miles, whose mother had died, and
when we would camp I would go from camp to camp in
search of some good, kind, motherly woman to let it
nurse and no one ever refused when I presented it to
them."[355]

An eastbound Mormon company, made up largely of
74 missionaries (most of whom were going to Europe)

---

351 H. H. Bancroft, *History of Nevada, Colorado and Wyoming*, 695.
Miners in 1876 found old prospect holes and rusted mining equipment on
Battle creek and Whitewood creek which Bancroft thinks may possibly have
been relics of the party that left Fort Laramie in 1852.

352 From figures compiled by Andrew Jensen, Mormon church historian.

353 L.D.S. *Journal history* (Mormon church archives, Salt Lake City),
under date of november 2, 1852.

354 *Publications of the Nebraska state historical society*, XX, 241. Granville
Stuart, *Forty years on the frontier*, I, 43, tells of cholera raging all along the
road, but this is not borne out by the accounts of others.

355 Margaret Windsor Iman, in *Washington historical quarterly*, XVIII, 254.

reached Fort Laramie october 9, 1852. Writes John Brown, one of the company: "Here we purchased supplies of the govt. store; we get them at cost and carriage; sold some weak animals and traded for fresh ones, which aided us much in our journey." [356]

Major Sanderson left the fort for a trip to the states, reaching Missouri in september, 1852. On the way down he met Campbell's train loaded with Indian goods for the red men of the Fort Laramie region.[357] Stephen B. Ross, who arrived at Independence, Missouri, from Utah on october 17, reported that when he passed Fort Laramie the Indians in great numbers were already assembled at the fort awaiting the arrival of their agent, Thomas Fitzpatrick, and the distribution of the goods in conformity with the Fort Laramie treaty of the previous year.[358]

Fewer emigrants traveled the Oregon and California trail in 1853 than during the previous year. There were reported as having passed Fort Kearny up to august 15, 1853, the following: males, 9,909; females, 2,252; children, 3,058; horses, 5,477; mules, 2,190; cattle, 105,792; sheep, 48,495; wagons, 3,708.[359] While the numbers of persons, wagons and horses had materially diminished as compared with the preceding year, the numbers of cattle and sheep had approximately doubled. This had come about through the high prices prevailing in California. Large herds of cattle and sheep were driven westward in response to the economic demand. From the New Mexico region several flocks of sheep were taken to the Pacific coast. Kit Carson, Lucien Maxwell and Uncle Dick Wootton drove flocks to California and

[356] L.D.S. *Journal history*, under date of november 2, 1852.

[357] *Publications of the Nebraska historical society*, XX, 241.

[358] *Journal history*, under date of october 20, 1852.

[359] *Publications of the Nebraska historical society*, XX, 252.

the venture proved profitable. Carson went by way of Fort Laramie with his 6,500 head of sheep. In California he sold them at $5.50 apiece, an advance of about one hundred percent over the New Mexico price.[360] Herds of California-bound cattle and sheep passed Salt Lake City in july and it was rumored there that the drovers and speculators were endeavoring to form an agreement to hold the price of cattle at $100 for four-year-olds, $80 for three-year-olds and $60 for two-year-olds.[361]

George Balshaw, leader of one of the first emigrant parties of the year to reach the Laramie, writes under date of may 17, 1853: "I crossed the Plat river and went over to see the forte. There is a post office, and store and blacksmith shop. A pleasant looking place. Some fine larg stone buildings. Some soulders on guard all the time.

"Dried apples 12 Dollars per bushel, vinigar 2 dollars per gallon. Everything else in proportion." [362]

The trees in the vicinity of Fort Laramie were most welcome to Claire Warner Churchill, who journeyed to Oregon in 1853. On june 21 she wrote in her diary: "We sat under a tree and ate dinner the first time for several months, and how pleasant to sit under a shade once more. It seemed like our old home where we were raised. I am sitting now under a pine tree on the Black Hills. And is it possible that we are in the Black Hills so far from home – the place I have so often read about and looked at on the map. But here we are. I wonder, is it possible? Today we made our first ascent. Yester-

---

360 E. L. Sabin, *Kit Carson days* (1935 edition), 634. See also H. L. Conard, *"Uncle Dick" Wootton,* 249.

361 *Journal history,* under dates of july 9 and 11, 1853.

362 George Balshaw, Journal from Indiana to Oregon, march 22 to september 27, 1853. Typewritten copy in the Huntington library, San Marino, California.

day we crossed Laramie's Fork, a very rapid stream. We swam the cattle across and paid two dollars apiece to get the wagons ferried across." [363]

S. H. Taylor, while enroute to Oregon in 1853, wrote a series of letters to the home-town paper. In one of these, written after having reached the boundary of the Oregon country, he says: "To those who intend going over this road, they should make their calculations to live as nearly as possible as they do at home. The last place to get good whipstocks is on the west side of the Des Moines. There are some, but not the best, on the east side of the Missouri, going up from Kanesville to the upper ferry. Opposite and about 60 rods above the present eastern landing of that ferry, on the west side of the Missouri, is a good place, and the best place to get good hickory for spare ox-bows – three or four of which ought to be taken with every team. A man wants about three dozen common screws; 2 papers 8 oz. and 10 oz. tacks; 2 lbs. shingle and 2 lbs. 6d nails; a saw, hammer, good axe, spade, ½, ¾ and inch augers with one handle, wrench, screw driver and two good pocket knives – one being to lose on the way. So far, a gun is of little use except to fire off, clean out and load up again every three or four days. A family should be supplied with such medicines as they know how to use, especially for such diseases as proceed from a neglected and dirty condition of the skin and overcharging of the bowels with Platte water sand, and colds taken by swimming the Platte for cattle and fuel; and the best of remedies for murrain, alkali, overflowing of the galls, hobnail and other ails of cattle and horses. There is an abundance of a purer and honester article of saleratus in this country than can be got at factories, and a man may get more

---

[363] Claire Warner Churchill, "Girl's diary of Oregon migration, 1853," in *Oregon historical quarterly*, XXIX, 88-89.

or less as he pleases at Kanesville. Salt for cattle is unnecessary after striking the Platte – from that point, for
some reason, they will not eat it. There are about ten
ferries on the road. The aggregate cost on each wagon
is about $25 to $30 – by all but two of which – the Mississippi and Missouri – we swam our cattle without
difficulty. The loss of cattle on the road is just according to the care they have. The loss of sheep, some 15,000
to 20,000 of which are on the way, I am informed by
the most judicious drivers to be not much less than 20
per cent, or one-fifth. If any one wishes to take hens,
they can manage a half dozen or so with little trouble.
There are some in our company, and they ride well,
being let out at evening, and have laid nearly all the
way. There is no trouble in taking a dog, unless a bad
traveler, by seeing to it that he has water supplied to
him on the dry stretches. It is not well to take cows that
will 'come in' on the road; I have seen many such, and
many young calves traveling, but there are great objections, to wit: Good butter cannot be made on the road,
and such as we have is little cared for. A can holding 6
to 20 qts., keeps our sour milk and cream, and makes
our butter by the motion of our wagon. Everything
should be carried in tin cans and bags. Pickles, and, I
presume, pork, can be kept in cans while air tight. The
flesh of poultry, cooked down, is found an excellent
article of food. The dried eggs were a failure with us.
Tin ware should be substituted for earthen, and sheet
for cast iron. Russia is the only sheet iron, that, in a
stove, will last through. An excellent substitute for a
stove when no baking is to be done, is a sheet of iron like
a stove top, to be put over a fire hole in the ground, a
common means of cooking, and one which the traveler
soon learns to make and use. It is just as good as a stove

FORT LARAMIE, 1853

for every purpose but baking. Every one needs flannel underclothing here. In regard to supplies of clothing for the future, every one is convinced that anything not needed for the road, costs a great deal more than it comes to. Take nothing for use after getting through — excepting money, of course, tho' I can assure you, you will have much less of that than you expected, when you get there. No water should be used for drinking or cooking, nor allowed to cattle, unless in a running stream or containing insects; otherwise it is probably alkaline. Everyone ought to have too much sense to use water from the stinking holes dug by some foolish persons in the margins of 'slews' and alkaline marshes. No poison water is found east of here, that I am aware of, except as the alkaline is called poison. We have seen one alkaline spring, on the upper Platte, but the alkali is too apparent to the taste to be dangerous. To this point it is safe to use all running water, or that which contains the young of mosquitoes and frogs. The guide books are full and reliable in their information on the subject. A man wants a guide, of course, and the latest to be got. The *Mormon Guide* is the best as far as it goes. This, as everything the emigrant wants, is to be got at Kanesville." [364]

The Mormon emigrants journeying to Salt Lake City in 1853 were later in setting out from the Missouri river than those traveling to Oregon and California. The first Mormon emigrating company of this year was organized at Six Mile Grove, six miles from Winter Quarters (near present Omaha), on june 1 and reached Fort Laramie july 15.[365]

In Moses Clawson's company practically all the teamsters were inexperienced. Mr. Clawson reports:

[364] *Oregon historical quarterly,* XXII, 147-9.
[365] *Journal history,* under date of july 15, 1853.

"On the 30th of july, 20 teams and wagons, and on the 3rd of august, 17 teams and wagons ran off at a furious rate, many of the company escaping with their lives most miraculously, and to the utmost astonishment of all the company. Although a number of oxen were run over, they escaped with but a few scratches, and only 7 wagons were injured, which were immediately repaired and the company permitted to go ahead with little loss of time." [366]

Joseph W. Young, who had sailed from England with a company of Saints on february 15, 1853, led them across the plains and reached Fort Laramie august 26. He records in his diary: "Arrived at the ford opposite Fort Laramie at 6 P.M. All seemed to rejoice at the sight of a few houses and that we have thus far been so highly favored on our journey. It is six weeks this day since we crossed the Missouri. After resting and herding the cattle the songs of Zion were heard singing through the camp. We were visited by several Indians, all of whom behave themselves courteously and honestly.

"SATURDAY, AUG. 27. Commenced crossing the Platte at 8:30 A.M. by double teams, the second fifty leading. All got through in safety by 11 A.M. At noon we were on our way." [367]

It is to be noted that by late august the water was so low in the North Platte that the emigrants were able to ford the stream.

A description of the fort as seen in 1853 is given by J. Linforth in his interesting book, *From Liverpool to the Great Salt Lake Valley* (p. 92): "Fort Laramie was formerly known as Fort John, and was established and owned by the American Fur company for the protec-

[366] *Ibid.,* august 7, 1853.
[367] J. W. Young's diary (MS. in Mormon church historian's office, Salt Lake City).

tion of their trade. Its walls are built of adobe or sun-burnt brick, being about 15 ft. high, and of a rectangu-lar construction, inclosing a court of about 130 ft. sq. The walls form a portion of a range of houses opening on the inside. In 1849, it was sold to the U. States, and was improved and extended by the erection of addi-tional quarters for the troops, of which about 100 with officers, &c. are generally stationed there. Opposite the fort is old Laramie ferry, considered the best crossing of the Platte river on the route to the South Pass. The proprietors of the ferry have also a blacksmith's shop, and do considerable business in supplying emigrants with horses, mules, grain, outfitting goods, &c. The road on the other side of the Platte crosses the Laramie Fork 1 m. below the fort. Laramie river is a small mountain stream, of pure, clear, cold water, which makes a pleas-ant contrast with the yellow and muddy waters of the Platte."

The experiment in farming at the fort met with some success in 1853. In the fall of this year it was reported: "The yield of vegetables at the farm, near the post, has been pretty fair. The onions turned out extremely well. . . A substantial bridge has been erected over Laramie [river] for the accomodation of emigrants and travelers at reasonable rates; but to guard against high water next spring, the bridge is to be raised about four feet." [368]

The summer of 1853 witnessed some difficulties with the Sioux at Fort Laramie. Alarmed at the heavy white migration over the Oregon trail, the consequent destruc-tion of game and the introduction of new diseases among the tribes, these Indians began to annoy the emigrants and show hostility toward the soldiers. On june 15 the

---

[368] *Publications of the Nebraska state historical society*, XX, 253.

Miniconjou Sioux captured the boat at the North Platte
ferry near the fort. Sergeant Raymond recovered it,
but while he was crossing the river one of the Indians
fired at him and the shot struck near the boat. When
informed of the affair, Lieutenant Richard B. Garnett,
commander of the fort, ordered Lieutenant Hugh B.
Fleming with twenty-three men and an interpreter "to
proceed to the village and demand the individual who
had shot at the sergeant, and in case he was not forth
coming, to take two or three prisoners, by force, if
necessary." [369]

Upon reaching the village about four miles north of
the fort, Lieutenant Fleming demanded the offender.
The request being refused, he marched into the midst
of the village; whereupon the Indians retreated to a
ravine in the rear of their encampment and began to
shoot at Fleming's detachment. The soldiers promptly
returned the fire. In the skirmish three Miniconjous
were killed, three wounded, and two taken prisoners. [370]

Several days later the chief of the band and some of
his men appeared at the fort for a parley. They received
little satisfaction, for the military felt that the soldiers
were in the right and that the Indians deserved discipline. Although these Sioux made no immediate retaliation, they were not reconciled to the treatment received
and harbored a feeling of revenge that was to continue
and would exhibit itself the following year.

When the Indian agent, Thomas Fitzpatrick, reached
the vicinity of Fort Laramie in early september he
found a bitter feeling among the Miniconjou Sioux.
"They stoutly insisted," writes the agent, "upon the im-

369 R. P. Bieber (ed.) *Frontier life in the army, 1854-1861*, by Eugene
Bandel, 23-24, quoting original manuscripts in the old files section, Adjutant-
general's office, war department, Washington, D.C.

370 *Ibid.*, 24.

mediate removal of the post from amongst them, saying that, when first placed there, they were told it was for their protection, 'but now the soldiers of the great father are the first to make the ground bloody.' At length one or two of the head mên went so far as to decline having anything more to do with treaties; but after an explanation from Captain R. Garnett, U.S.A., of the reasons which induced his action, and the provocation which had been given, they became somewhat pacified." [371] They accepted their annuities from the Indian agent.

During this council with the Sioux two companies of rifles under the command of Captain Van Buren, U.S.A., were encamped in the vicinity of the fort and remained there at Fitzpatrick's request until termination of the negotiations.[372]

The U.S. mail service that had been inaugurated between Missouri and Utah in 1850 continued to serve Fort Laramie. The monthly schedule had been maintained with fair regularity during the summer seasons but in the winter had been far from dependable. In the winter of 1852-3 Feramorz Little, sub-contractor on the route from Fort Laramie to Salt Lake City, had great difficulty in making his trips. He and his Indian companion, after leaving the fort in november, struggled through deep snow in the South Pass country for a month. Unable to reach Salt Lake valley over the ice of Weber river, they finally left their horses, cached the bulk of the mail, and continued on foot, dragging the letter-mail over the snow of the Wasatch mountains for forty miles to its destination.[373] The december mail that had started eastward from the Mormon capital was

---

[371] Commissioner of Indian Affairs, annual report, 1853, in *Sen. ex. doc.* I, cong. 33, sess. 1, 366-7.

[372] *Ibid.*

[373] L. R. Hafen, *The overland mail*, 60.

forced to return because of the snow.[374] With the coming of spring regular service was resumed.

The following winter again brought its difficulties and we find citizens of Salt Lake City reporting in the summer of 1854 that sacks of mail, containing newspapers, books and letters, some of which had been mailed in 1852, were just arriving in Utah by ox team. "From all we can learn," it was said, "they have been accumulating a long time past, at different points, from Independence to near Fort Laramie." [375]

A party of Mormon missionaries bound for Europe and under the leadership of F. D. Richards, left Salt Lake City march 29, 1854. "We traveled by the Mormon mail as far as Fort Laramie," writes one of the party. "We expected to find relays en route, but the wolves and severe winter had destroyed them. Notwithstanding this – rough, snowy, and stormy weather likewise – we had an expeditious and agreeable journey. From Fort Laramie to the states we had a change of weather and circumstances. We had frequent relays of grain-fed animals, who were well whipped and loudly cursed by drivers whose conduct was a disgrace to their race, and with it all, less expedition." [376] The carriage of the mail in the summer of 1854 was given to another contractor, W. M. F. Magraw, who began his term with greatly improved service.[377]

The emigration to California and Oregon was rather small in 1854,[378] but that to Utah maintained its usual proportions. Nearly 3,000 proselytes from Europe made their way this season to their new Zion. Cholera and

---

[374] *Incidents in Utah history*, 19.

[375] *Journal history*, august 17, 1854.

[376] *Journal history*, march 2, 1856. Letter of William H. Kimball.

[377] *Ibid.*, august 3, 1854.

[378] *Publications of the Nebraska state historical society*, XX, 256.

scurvy raged in most of the Mormon trains, the Scandinavian company and the Church Train [poor Saints being aided by the Perpetual Emigration Fund] suffering most.[379]

The last Mormon company of the season was led by Robert Campbell [not to be confused with the one that built Fort Laramie]. The record kept of its organization and procedure gives something of the flavor of the time and place:

"Camp ground, state of Missouri, 14 july, 1854.

"At a council meeting this evening Elder Empey presiding, IT WAS RESOLVED:

"THAT Bro. Robert Campbell be president of the company.

"THAT Bro. Richard Cook be his first councillor and Bro. J. Woodard be his second counselor.

"THAT Bro. Brewerton be captain of the guard.

"THAT Bro. Chas. Brererton be wagon master and Bro. Wm. Kendall to assist him.

"THAT Bro. Richard be captain of the first ten.

"THAT Bro. Thos. Fisher be captain of the second ten.

"THAT Bro. Balliff be captain of the third ten.

"THAT Bro. Thos. Sutherland be clerk and historian of this company.

"THAT no gun shall be fired within 50 yards of the camp under a penalty of one night's guard.

"THAT the captain of each ten shall awaken the head of every family at 4 o'clock in the morning and be ready to roll out at seven, if circumstances will admit.

"THAT all go to bed at 9 o'clock in the evening.

"THAT every man from 16 to 60 years of age be eligible to stand guard. . . Bro. Campbell spoke of the necessity of appointing a committee of three to enquire into the amount of provisions in each wagon. Bro. Empey remarked that no man should take his gun out of his wagon without leave from his captain and also that every man should be careful in taking off the cap in putting his gun in his wagon

---

[379] Notes from Andrew Jensen, Mormon church historian. See *Journal history* of august 26, 1854, for additional data on the emigrating companies.

and also to have buckskin attached so as to put it on the pillar under the cock.

"Bro. Fisher, replied that he made enquiry and found each wagon according to his estimation well supplied, except Bro. Weltshire, Bro. White and Sis. Hiskins, and they calculated on buying some at Ft. Laramie and had money in their possession for the purpose. The wagons have not been overloaded.

"RESOLVED, that all the men in camp from 16 to 60 years of age be called out this evening and see what defence they can make with fire arms.

"RESOLVED, that Bro. Thos. Fisher be captain of the English brethren and Bro. Bailiff of the foreign brethren.

"RESOLVED, that the foreign brethren start in the morning and go as far as Indian creek.

"RESOLVED, that Bro. Fisher, our wagon master, and the rest of the carpenters in camp go to the wood and bring as much wood as will make 4 axletrees. Bro. Campbell gave instructions that the captain of each ten should see that there was a strong rope in his company to hitch to the wagons to take them across creeks and difficult places where the cattle cannot bring it. . . Bro. Campbell held a council meeting this evening when it was resolved that we rise at half past three o'clock and roll out at 6 o'clock.

"THAT Bro. Cook, Fisher and Kendall call on Bro. Fraith and council him to lighten his luggage." [380]

On august 17 these emigrants met a company of thirty-three wagons returning to the states from Fort Laramie, having been there with provisions for the government.[381] Six days later ten more wagons eastward bound from the fort were encountered. On the 27th some mountaineers were met carrying dispatches from the fort telling of the Gratton massacre [to be discussed in the following chapter].

Upon reaching the vicinity of Fort Laramie this company was threatened with Indian attack. The Gratton massacre had occurred about two weeks before, and the Indians were in hostile mood. When first encoun-

[380] *Journal history,* under date of october 28, 1854.
[381] *Ibid.*

tered the Indians "brandished their firearms." When the train stopped the chief and six braves came into the camp. "They were treated kindly," says the chronicler. "Having received plenty to eat and drink, they made signs that they wished to go to sleep. Bro. Campbell gave his tent to them. . .

[SEPT. 1] "We did not move far until we met the Indians on every side of us. They were all on horseback and well armed. They blockaded the road in front of us, but every man in camp carried his rifle loaded on his shoulder and we drove right through them. Bro. Campbell exchanged hands with them after which he made a call on every wagon to give them a portion of sugar which was at once given. They kept following us until dinner time and stated they were going to war with another nation. . .

[SEPT. 6] "We met a company of men, mules and ox teams going to the states. We also met the Indian agent who advised us to be on the lookout as all the Indians had left Ft. Laramie and had gone, no one knew where. He himself was obliged to make his escape from them." [382]

Traveling past the scene of the massacre the company reached Fort Laramie september 15. "There are only 42 soldiers stationed here at present," writes the journalist. "Provisions seemed scanty with them. They would not sell flour under $20.00 per bag of 100 lbs. There is a post office and settler's [sutler's] store at the fort." [383]

Several stations had been established in the Fort Laramie region for trade with the emigrants. The historian of the Robert Campbell train tells of reaching

[382] *Ibid.* The Indian agent was now John W. Whitfield. Fitzpatrick, his predecessor, after having survived Indian battles and dangers in the West for over thirty years, died of pneumonia in a hotel in Washington, D.C., february 7, 1854.

[383] *Ibid.*

one on september 10. It was located twenty-one miles
up the North Platte from Chimney Rock. The keeper
did blacksmithing and kept oxen and horses to trade.
On september 13 he reports: "After a drive of 16 miles
one ox gave out today and was changed with the settler
for a buffalo skin. This settler keeps large herds of oxen
and some horses to sell or exchange. Some of the brethren bought and exchanged oxen. The prices are higher
than in the states.

"SEPT. 14. We traveled 8 miles to Bordeau's station.[384] There are mountaineers settled here and they do
blacksmithing and trade oxen and horses. It was at this
place that the Indians killed the 29 soldiers with their
officer [Grattan massacre]."

About twelve miles above Fort Laramie they reached
another trading post and blacksmith shop.

Earlier in the summer of 1854, Fort Laramie had
been enlivened by the arrival of Sir George Gore, titled
sportsman from Ireland. In his elaborate outfit were
included six wagons, twenty-one carts, twelve yoke of
cattle, one hundred twelve horses, fourteen dogs and
forty servants.[385] He made the fort headquarters for his
hunting excursions. On the first of these he went into
North Park, at the headwaters of the North Platte, and
continued westward over the continental divide to leave
his name on the Gore range and the Gore pass of present
north-central Colorado.

While spending the winter at Fort Laramie, Gore
became acquainted with the old mountain man, Jim
Bridger, and employed him as guide. The association
of these two characters, so diverse and yet so attracted

---

[384] Bordeau's trading post had been rebuilt.

[385] C. G. Coutant, *History of Wyoming*, 324. R. E. Strahorn, *Handbook
of Wyoming*, 220-221. H. H. Bancroft, *History of Nevada, Colorado and
Wyoming*, 695; and *Historical society of Montana contributions*, I, 144.

to each other, is celebrated in western lore. Sir George frequently read to Bridger and elicited comment from the old trapper. Gore's "favourite author was Shakespeare, which Bridger 'reckin'd was too highfalutin' for him; moreover he remarked, 'thet he rather calcerlated that thar big Dutchman, Mr. Full-stuff, was a leetle too fond of lager beer,' and thought it would have been better for the old man if he had 'stuck to bourbon whisky straight.'

"Bridger seemed very much interested in the adventures of Baron Munchausen [whom he came to rival], but admitted after Sir George had finished reading them, that 'he be dog'oned ef he swallered everything that thar Baron Munchausen said,' and thought he was 'a darned liar,' yet he acknowledged that some of his own adventures among the Blackfeet would be equally marvellous 'if writ down in a book.' " [386]

In 1855 Gore turned north to the Powder and Tongue rivers and after another year of adventure embarked on the upper Missouri and returned to civilization.

During the winter of 1854-55 there was some danger from Indians in the Fort Laramie region. Horse stealing and other depredations were reported during the early spring. Indians shared with the weather the blame for interruptions in the mail service to and from the fort. But the summer emigration over the trail appears not to have been affected by the Indian danger.

By far the larger portion of the emigrants that traveled past Fort Laramie in 1855 were bound for Utah. A few, however, journeyed on to Oregon or California. John L. Smith, a Mormon missionary who traveled eastward over the trail this year, writes from Fort Kearny on june 10, 1855: "We left Fort Laramie

---

[386] Henry Inman, *The old Santa Fe trail*, 332.

on the 31st of may and came down the south side of the Platte. Since leaving there we have passed over four thousand head of cattle, some 85 wagons, 250 men, bound for California. Besides these we have seen 2 or 3 companies on the north side of the Platte." [387]

The Mormons made rather extensive preparations for the emigration of 1855. For some years past their large numbers of proselytes from Europe had been coming by way of New Orleans and on the river steamers up the Mississippi and Missouri. But the heavy toll taken by cholera had induced president Brigham Young to order a change of route. "I wish you to ship no more to New Orleans, but ship to Philadelphia, Boston, and New York, giving preference in the order named." [388]

Elder Erastus Snow was placed at St. Louis in charge of the emigration. Information and instructions sent out by him included the following: "My assent will not be given for any Saint to leave the Missouri river, unless so organized in a company of at least fifty effectual well armed men, and that too under the command of a man appointed by me; one who will carry out my instructions.

"Behold here is wisdom! 'He that hath ears to hear, let him hear.' Every male capable of bearing arms, should provide himself with a good rifle, or other effectual fire arms, and ammunition.

"I will furnish at the point of outfit, for such as desire it, wagons, oxen, cows, guns, flour, bacon, &c.

"Choice wagons made to order and delivered at the point of outfit, with bows, projections, &c., will be about $78; without projections, $75. Oxen, with yokes and

[387] *Journal history,* june 10, 1855.

[388] Young's instructions to F. D. Richards, president of the Mormon mission in Europe. L.D.S. *Journal history,* february 17, 1855.

chains, from $70 to $85 per yoke; cows from $16 to $25 each.

"My experience, derived by six journeys over the plain enables me to know what kind of teams and outfits are wanted for the plains. . .

"One wagon, 2 yoke oxen and 2 cows will be sufficient (if that is the extent of their means) for a family of eight or ten persons, with the addition of a tent for every two or three families. Of course, with that amount of teams only the necessary baggage, provisions and utensils can be taken, and then the persons ride but little.

"Those who have a surplus of means after paying their tithing and making provisions for their own outfit, should contribute to the Perpetual Emigrating Fund, according to their means and faith, so that other long tried and faithful Saints who lack means, may receive aid through that channel." [389]

Andrew Jensen, Mormon church historian, places the Mormon emigration to Utah at 4,684 for the year 1855 and gives the figure 3,167 as that for the preceding year.[390]

A point on the Missouri that came to be known as Mormon Grove was chosen as the Mormon outfitting place for 1855, and about it the town of Atchison quickly developed. After seeing the last of the Mormon emigrants take the road, Erastus Snow set out on august 3 for Utah, traveling in a carriage drawn by four mules. Upon completing his trip he reports:

"We passed and met a great number of government trains going to and coming from Forts Laramie and Kearney.

"The Sioux were all off the road except a few of the

[389] *Journal history.*
[390] Data from Mr. Jensen.

Oglallahs about Ward and Guerrier's [at Sant Point, seven miles above Fort Laramie]. Saw a few Pawnees on Little Blue. The Cheyennes were at Laramie receiving their annuities. Saw a few Arrappahoes at Platte bridge. Traders all along the road were badly frightened, and all from below were moving to Laramie or to the states, and those above, as far as the Devil's Gate, were preparing to move down when the next escort came up.

"Mr. Kerr and others recently from this city [Salt Lake], were stopping at Seminoe's Fort [at Devil's Gate] waiting for the escort.

"Seven companies of regulars, 5 of infantry, and 2 of Dragoons were at Kearney preparing for a sixty days campaign, and about the same number at and about Laramie. It was understood that the expedition would be directed towards the Missouri where the Sioux warriors were supposed to be gathering.

"The agent [Twiss] from Laramie had sent for them to come in and settle, and have a talk and receive their annuities, but they had not come, and it was thought they would not. The troops awaited the arrival of General Harney who was soon expected from Leavenworth.

"Beyond Laramie we had plenty of rain, but this side the country was dry, water scarce, and feed but indifferent." [391]

Throughout 1855 there had been considerable interruption in the mail service, but emigrant trains had experienced little disturbance, even though a military expedition (to be discussed in the following chapter) was operating against the Indians. The emigrants passed the Harney battlefield after the fight had taken place.[392]

---

391 *Deseret News* (Salt Lake City), v, no. 269.

392 *Journal history,* november 7 and 26, 1855.

The Grattan and the Harney
Massacres, 1854-1855

Since the establishment of the military post on the
Laramie in 1849 the troops had had constant dealings
with the Indians of the region and relations had been
generally peaceful. Antipathy resulting from the large
white migrations had been in part assuaged by the great
treaty council of 1851 and the annuities it provided.
Although emigrants on the trail had been subjected to
annoyance by inquisitive and thieving Indians, they had
been little threatened with real danger. Fort Laramie,
with its small garrison of infantry, was looked to by
west-moving Americans less as a military post affording protection than as a supply depot and an outpost
representing civilization.

This general condition, especially as it pertains to
soldiers and Indians, suddenly changed by an unfortunate occurrence in the late summer of 1854. The Indians had gathered in the Fort Laramie vicinity to receive their annuities from Indian agent Whitfield. Some
of the goods had been sent up the Platte river trail and
were stored at the American Fur company post five
miles below the fort. The agent himself had traveled
west along the Arkansas river to meet others of his
wards on that stream and on the South Platte and was
now approaching the North Platte region from the
south.[393]

393 *Annual report of the commissioner of Indian Affairs* (1854), pp. 89-98.

Three tribes of the Sioux nation were encamped along the North Platte, a little southeast of Fort Laramie – the Oglala village near the American Fur company trading house, the Miniconjous next below, and the Brulés farthest down and near Bordeau's trading post (eight miles below the fort).[394]

All the emigrant trains except one or two bound for Utah had passed. On august 18 a Mormon caravan composed of Scandinavian proselytes under the leadership of Hans Peter Olsen passed the Brulé encampment.[395] A cow from the emigrant herd was killed by one of the Indians. Just how this occurred is a matter of conjecture. According to some accounts the cow was lame, fell behind the main herd, wandered into the Indian camp and was killed by an Indian who thought the animal had been deserted.[396] Another version asserts that "a Miniconjou Sioux, anxious for revenge against the whites, shot an arrow at an emigrant and, failing to hit him, let fly another arrow and killed the emigrant's cow." [397] The Mormon account deserves consideration: "At Sarpy's Point, eight miles east of Laramie, while a company of Saints were passing a camp of Indians, about 1000 strong, a cow belonging to the company became frightened and ran into the Indian camp, where she was left; some of them killed and ate her." [398]

Upon reaching Fort Laramie the company reported its loss to the post commander, Brevet-second-lieutenant

[394] *House ex. docs.*, cong. 33, sess. 2, no. 63, p. 20-22.

[395] Letter of Andrew Jensen, Mormon church historian, dated february 3, 1934.

[396] Report of James Bordeau and others, appearing in the *Annual report of the commissioner of Indian Affairs* (1854), p 93. Other versions similar in character, appear in L. F. Crawford, *Rekindling camp fires*, p. 55; and H. D. Hunter, *History of Fort Leavenworth*, p. 110.

[397] R. P. Bieber (ed.), *Frontier life in the army, 1854-1861*, p. 25. This version is based primarily on the contemporary military reports.

[398] L.D.S. *Journal history*, under date of august 19, 1854.

Hugh B. Fleming. On the same day the chief of the Brulé Sioux, Martoh-Ioway (Bear-that-scatters), who had been a signer of the Fort Laramie treaty of 1851,[399] came to the post and reported the affair. He doubtless realized that, in conformity with the terms of the treaty, claim for the animal would have to be satisfied before his band would receive its annuities.[400] He indicated a willingness to give up the offender, a Miniconjou Sioux, temporarily lodged with the Brulés.

Lieutenant Fleming, it will be remembered, was the officer who had led the detachment of soldiers that had a skirmish with the Miniconjou Sioux the year before, following the capture of the North Platte ferry boat by the Indians. Now, apparently, the Indians needed further discipline, for the Mormon cow was but one of a number of animals belonging to the emigrants and traders that had been killed during the summer.[401] Such depredations must cease and the Indians be taught to respect white man property. Accordingly, Fleming "sent Brevet-second-lieutenant L. Grattan, 6th infantry, with the interpreter, Sergeant Faver, Corporal McNulty and twenty [27] privates to receive the offender." [402]

Lieutenant Grattan, recently graduated from West Point and eager to distinguish himself, set out from the fort with his command on the afternoon of august 19. The lieutenant, the interpreter and a few others were mounted; the body of soldiers rode in an army wagon drawn by mules. Two cannon, a twelve pounder and a

---

[399] Statement of J. H. Reed in *House ex. docs.*, cong. 33, sess. 2, no. 63, p. 22. C. J. Kappler, *Indian affairs, laws and treaties*, II, p. 596. On the treaty his name is signed as Mah-toe-wha-you-whey.

[400] See article eight of the treaty in Kappler, *op. cit.*, p. 595.

[401] Fleming's report of august 20, 1854, in *House ex. docs.*, cong. 33, sess. 2, no. 63, p. 2.

[402] *Ibid.*, p. 2.

mountain howitzer, were taken along. When the command reached Gratiot's house (the American Fur company post), five miles below the fort, a halt was made and the men were ordered to load, but not cap. Instructions as to conduct were given.[403] Before reaching Bordeau's trading house, three miles farther down, another halt was made and the howitzers were loaded.

At the trading house Bordeau was called for and was asked to notify the chief of the soldiers' mission. When Martoh-Ioway, commonly called the Bear, appeared, he said that he was unable to get the offending Indian to surrender.[404] Grattan then induced the Oglala chief, The-man-who-is-afraid-of-his-horses, to go into the village to persuade the culprit to give himself up. Upon returning, this chief reported that he had found six Miniconjou in the lodge loading their guns and that they refused to give up the offender. "Last year the soldiers killed three of us" [the ferry boat affair], said the Miniconjou. "And again this year, as we sat by the side of the road, an emigrant shot at us and hit a child in the head. The child still lives. Our chief, the Little Brave, is dead, and we want to die also." [405] Chief Bear

403 Report of Major O. F. Winship, Assistant-adjutant-general, in *House ex. docs.*, cong. 33, sess. 2, no. 63, p. 5. Obridge Allen, who accompanied the soldiers as far as Bordeau's house, stated that Lieutenant Grattan instructed the men "to obey only his orders or those of the sergeant; said he, 'When I give the order, you may fire as much as you d——d please.' He told them he didn't believe a gun would be fired, but he 'hoped to God they would have a fight.'" *Ibid.*, 20.

404 The Miniconjou is reported to have said: "I am alone. Last fall the settlers killed my two brothers. This spring my only relative died (an uncle). I have a gun with plenty of powder and balls, a bow and quiver full of arrows and the soldiers will have to kill and then take me." Letter of Capt. L. B. Dougherty, written to his father, Major John B. Dougherty, from Fort Laramie, august 29, 1854. A manuscript copy of this letter was found in the Kansas City public library.

405 Bieber, *op. cit.*, 26, quoting the Oglala chief's deposition, found in the old files of the war department.

was now sent to the Miniconjou lodge but was also unsuccessful in effecting a surrender.

Lieutenant Grattan, writes Major Winship, was now "compelled to seek and take by force, if need be, the offender, or submit to the mortification of retiring without having accomplished the object of his mission; and rather than do this, he resolved boldly to enter the Brulé camp and take the Indian at all hazards, having previously informed himself of the precise locality of the offender. This was nearly in the center of the camp and not far from the lodge of the Bear." [406]

The Brulé camp was semi-circular in form, with its convex side to the river. Immediately in the rear of the camp was an abrupt depression partially overgrown with bushes.[407] As the negotiations were under way this brush-covered depression was being occupied by Indian warriors.

Grattan's move into the center of the village would appear to have been, under the circumstances, a foolhardy act. Although he knew that in the difficulties of the previous year Lieutenant Fleming had taken a similar position and that the Indians had been routed, an older and wiser leader would have sensed that the conditions now faced were quite different.

What happened from this point on cannot be determined with accuracy of detail, for none of the soldiers survived and reports from the Indians and traders are conflicting. It appears that upon reaching the center of the village Grattan placed his men and howitzers facing the Miniconjou's lodge and opened another parley. He was greatly handicapped by the interpreter, Lucien Auguste. This man was not only disliked by the Indians, but he had a special grievance in that two of his animals

---

[406] Winship's report, *op. cit.,* 5-6.

[407] *Ibid.,* 5.

had recently been stolen by the Indians. But most tragic, he was intoxicated while on this important mission. In passing the upper villages he is reported to have called out to the Indians, daring them to make good their threats to wipe out the whites, "adding that he was coming with thirty men and a cannon, and that this time he would eat their hearts raw." [408] With his attitude and in his condition it is apparent that difficulties would be aggravated as communication continued.

Bordeau asserts that he told Grattan that Auguste would make trouble. "During this time," says Bordeau, "his interpreter was in the camp, bantering the Indians and irritating them. I told him that he would make trouble, and that if he would put him in my house, I would settle the difficulty in thirty minutes. He said he would stop him. He had told him several times to stop but he did not mind him.

"As soon as he [Grattan] halted he was immediately surrounded by Indians, and one of the chiefs came running to me and said, 'My friend, come on; the interpreter is going to get us into a fight, and they are going to fight if you don't come.' I got on a horse to go, but finding the stirrups too long I turned back, and the chief came to me a second time urging me to go. I started with him, but when I got within 150 yards I saw that it was too late – the excitement was too great. At this moment the first gun was fired. . ." [409]

Matters reached a crisis. "One report says," according to Col. Hoffman, "that just at the close of the interview Lieutenant Grattan took out his watch and said, 'It is getting late, and I can't wait any longer;' to which the Bear replied, 'I have done all I could; and since you

---

[408] *House ex. docs.*, no. 63, *op. cit.*, 16, statement of Paul Carrey.
[409] *Ibid.*, 25. Bordeau's statement.

will have him, now push on and take him,' or something
to that effect, and then turned to walk away. As he did
so, he was shot by the soldiers, and wounded in three
places. I am inclined to think this report is true." [410]

Perhaps the fullest account of the affair and by the
person in the best position to see what happened is that
given by Obridge Allen, whom Colonel W. Hoffman
refers to as "a man of character and veracity." [411] Allen
had accompanied the troops from Fort Laramie to Bordeau's post. His horse having been borrowed, he took
a position on top of Bordeau's house and from this vantage point tells of happenings in the village, some 300
yards away:

"The party [Grattan's] was halted about thirty yards
from two lodges which were pitched on the edge of a
small slough which runs through the camp, in one of
which the offender lived. The two cannon were placed

[410] *Ibid.*, 18. Colonel Hoffman's report. A correspondent of the *Missouri
Republican* reports that the Bear finally said, "I can not take the man; you
take him; you shoot him; there he stands." The Indian stood at his lodge
door, about sixty yards off, leaning upon his gun with a bow and arrows
in his hand. Grattan gave some command, and one soldier fired, then
another, and the fight was on. This correspondent believed that the whole
censure should be against the authority that removed an efficient and re-
spected officer from command of the fort and left an inexperienced second
lieutenant in charge. "Had Lieutenant Garnett been here, or Captain
Ketchum, the difficulty would have been readily settled without the loss of
a drop of blood." Reprinted in *Publications of the Nebraska state historical
society*, xx, 266-267. Brevet-lieutenant-colonel E. J. Steptoe defended Lieutenant Grattan against the charge of rashness. He quoted J. H. Reid, a
soldier whom Steptoe had left at Fort Laramie, as saying that the Miniconjou
Indian fired first. Grattan "then ordered his musketry to fire. The Indians,
who had gathered about him to the number of fifteen hundred, perhaps, fell
flat on their faces, and the balls passed over, as did also the whole charge
of the pieces which were fired immediately afterwards. The whole party
was then destroyed before either the cannon or the muskets could be re-
loaded. They were all killed with knives and arrows. Lieutenant Grattan
had dismounted and given his horse to one of the men, while he worked as
gunner, and was found where he fell, by the side of his piece." Doc. no. 63,
op. cit., p. 3.
[411] *Ibid.*, 19.

near each other, the largest on the right, and the infantry were divided into two parts, half on the right of the cannon and half on the left. The cannon were loaded at Bordeau's house. The men all sat down on the ground.

"The council lasted about three quarters of an hour and during this time I saw many Indians collecting and mounting their horses near the river, and the women and children were leaving the village. At length, I saw the soldiers stand up and bring their pieces down as if to fire, and at that moment I heard, I thought, the report of Indian guns, followed immediately by that of muskets. The two cannon were fired directly after. I then saw the limber of the gun turned and start to leave the camp, followed by the wagon. A man was trying to get into the wagon. At the same time the soldiers all commenced to retreat, pursued by the Indians. The limber was overtaken in a quarter of a mile, and the wagon reached the first point of the bluffs which crosses the road, near a half a mile, before it was overtaken. The footmen, about eighteen in number – some who had been with the cannon, without arms – reached the road between the two bluffs which cross it, about a mile, where they were all killed by Indians who followed them, and, as I supposed, by those who came from the Oglala camp above. I saw a great many coming from there over the second point of bluffs. Three or four men were killed near the cannon. The interpreter, who was mounted, and a soldier who was on the lieutenant's horse, were overtaken by some Indians who came from near the river below Bordeau's house, passing close to it, near the wagon where they were killed. The soldiers were loading and firing as they retreated. . .

"When the firing took place, there were only about fifty Indians in front of the troops. The others were either concealed in the slough, or were getting ready near the river, which was three or four hundred yards distant." [412]

All the soldiers except one were killed and this one was so badly wounded that he died within two or three days. The principal Indian casualty was the chief of the Brulés. He was severely wounded and died within a week. It was reported that one or two others were wounded, but none killed. [413]

The frenzied Indians wreaked vengeance on the bodies of the soldiers. Heads were crushed, throats cut, legs amputated and other mutilations perpetrated. Lieutenant Grattan, bristling with twenty-four arrows, was later identified by his watch. [414]

As the fighting began, Bordeau had barricaded his doors and prepared to defend his post. Maddened warriors who proposed its destruction were dissuaded by friendly Indians and traders with Indian wives. But Bordeau was discreet enough to give over without hesitation the supplies the Sioux demanded. [415]

Then to the American Fur company the vengeful Indians went, broke into the warehouses and helped themselves to the annuity goods stored there. They raided corrals and pastures along the Platte, and pillaged the government farm north of the fort. [416] The more militant and reckless among the Indians de-

[412] *Ibid.,* 21-22. Allen's statement.

[413] Statement of Paul Carrey, in doc. no. 63, *op. cit.* Carrey says he was told that the Bear prepared the trap for the soldiers and had told the Indians to prepare for a fight, that he himself (the Bear) killed Grattan. If the Bear did kill Lieutenant Grattan, this may account for the chief's being shot three times.

[414] *Missouri Republican,* september 13, 1854, in *Publications of the Nebraska state historical society,* XX, p. 259. Bieber, *op. cit.,* p. 27. See also Dougherty's letter, *op. cit.*

[415] Allen's statement in doc. no. 63, *op. cit.*

[416] Winship report, *op. cit.* Dougherty's letter, *op. cit.*

manded an attack on Fort Laramie, but calmer counsels prevailed. L. B. Dougherty wrote from the fort on the 29th: "I have never seen such a general stampede in any country. We have been kept in a terrible state of suspense by reports of their charging on the fort. They boasted of killing more than half of the command. Several traders have come to the fort, 'lock, stock and barrel.' Others have gone with the Cheyennes for protection. The old American Fur company fort [the adobe structure sold to the government in 1849] is fixed up for the last resort. A small block house is being erected which held by ten men, will add greatly to the strength of the Post and protect the frame buildings from being fired." [417]

On the day following the massacre, Lieutenant Fleming sent a report and an appeal for reenforcements to Fort Leavenworth.[418] He could not safely leave the fort, so when appealed to by Bordeau, directed the latter to take care of himself as best he could and also requested him to recover the bodies of the slain soldiers.[419]

Burial was effected, but in a shallow grave. When a Mormon emigrant company passed the site less than a month afterward, they saw ample reminders of the tragedy. From Bordeau's Station the historian of the company writes on september 14. "It was at this place that the Indians killed the 29 soldiers with their officer; they are buried close by the road. I have visited the grave and some of the men's heads are not even covered. It was the settlers that buried them, as the remainder of the soldiers could not leave the fort, being few in number. There was also a man's face lying on the bank

417 Dougherty's letter, *op. cit.*

418 Fleming's report of august 20, in doc. no. 63, *op. cit.*

419 Fleming's letter of august 20, printed in the *Missouri Republican* of september 13, 1854.

with the teeth firm in the jaw bone and the flesh appeared recently taken off. Several military gloves were lying on the grass close by."

Upon reaching Fort Laramie the next day he records: "There are only 42 soldiers stationed here at present. Provisions seemed scanty with them. They would not sell flour under $20 per bag of 100 pounds." [420]

Indian agent John W. Whitfield, accompanied by Major O. F. Winship, who was making a trip of inspection to western military posts, arrived at Fort Laramie shortly after the massacre. He was shocked at what had occurred and felt that had he been present the tragedy would have been avoided. He reported:

"I regret that the demand for the offender had not been postponed until my arrival. If it had been, I could have settled the whole affair without the least trouble. To have prevented a collision, I have no doubt but that the Sioux would have paid any number of horses, for I was told, by several reliable gentlemen, that they offered to pay for the cow; and if the [Indian] intercourse law is to be obeyed, nothing more could be required. Indians consider themselves disgraced for life if arrested and confined. This feeling is general among all Indians, but more especially the wild tribes; consequently, they prefer to die to being taken and confined. In this case, it is evident that that was the feeling of the Indian who committed the depredation; and if the lieutenant had understood the character of Indians, I doubt whether he would have done as he did. Why Lieutenant Grattan took the position he did, in the midst of the village, surrounded by at least fifteen hundred warriors, perhaps never will be known; for it is evident that he must have

---

[420] Record kept by Thomas Sutherland, historian of Robert Campbell's company, and found in the L.D.S. *Journal history.*

known, before he went into the village, that a fight
would be the result if he fired a gun. . .

"No doubt Lieutenant Grattan's want of knowledge
of the Indian character, and the rash language used by
a drunken interpreter, was the cause of the unfortunate
affair. The Sioux, or the bands in the Platte agency,
have heretofore been regarded as the most peaceable
and friendly Indians on the prairies to the whites. This
is the only case I have ever heard of their disturbing
the stock of any train during this season, and if the Mormon had gone into the village he could have got his cow
without any trouble; but he took fright and left the
cow. The Indians killed and ate it. This is the history,
in a few words, of the commencement of the whole
affair.

"The forts at present located in the Indian country
are most emphatically poor affairs. They can give no
protection to any person beyond the reach of their own
guns. Infantry in the Indian country, so far as protecting the roads is concerned, are about the same use as so
many stumps would be. Emigrants are compelled to
protect themselves, and buy their way with sugar and
coffee." [421]

After the massacre, and the raiding that immediately
followed it, the Sioux left the Fort Laramie region.
Agent Whitfield, in traveling up from Fort St. Vrain,
had met some of them south of the fort. The greater
number moved off to the north.

Most of the North Platte Cheyennes and Arapahos
remained at the fort after the departure of the Sioux,
awaiting the coming and the distribution of their annuities. When the agent arrived with his 15,000 pounds
of Indian goods and held a council with these Indians,

---

[421] *Annual report of the commissioner of Indian Affairs* (1854), 97-98.

he found them none too friendly. The speaker for the Cheyennes spoke his mind. "He commenced," says Whitfield, "by stating that the travel over the Platte road by emigrants should be stopped; that next year I must bring four thousand dollars in money; balance of their annuity in guns and ammunition, and one thousand white women for wives." Continuing, the agent reports: "During the same day I distributed the goods to them, and before sunset not one was to be seen." [422]

Nor did the agent himself remain long in the region. He began his return journey down the Platte at once and reached Westport on september 26.

In the meantime Lieutenant Fleming had written to his superiors on september 30: "Should a sufficient force be sent out immediately by the government to punish the offenders in an effectual manner, no hostility from other surrounding tribes may be expected. But should this not be done, then great sacrifice of life may be expected; as all the surrounding tribes, stimulated by neglect of this bloody massacre, will join hand in hand and rush on to the slaughter.

"I have recommended that all traders in the country be prohibited from trading guns or ammunition on any pretense whatever, and the Indian agent, General Whitfield, has accordingly prohibited this kind of trade with the Indians until further orders." [423]

In response to Lieutenant Fleming's appeal, companies B and D of the Sixth infantry, numbering 111 men, under the command of Major and Brevet-lieutenant-colonel William Hoffman set out for the West. These troops reached Fort Laramie on november 12 and Colonel Hoffman assumed command of the post. [424]

[422] *Ibid.*, 94.

[423] In doc. no. 63, *op. cit.*

[424] Coutant, *History of Wyoming*, p. 324.

The uneasiness and the fear of attack that had pervaded the fort since the massacre was relieved, but the Indian danger was by no means removed.

During succeeding months a number of Indian depredations were committed in the Fort Laramie region. On november 13, 1854, a party of Brulé, seeking to avenge the death of the Bear, attacked the Salt Lake mail stage, some 22 miles below the fort, killed the three employees, wounded and robbed the only passenger, and carried off $10,000 in gold.[425] A son-in-law of the Bear headed a party that stole the mail mules from Fort Kearny.[426]

Colonel Hoffman wrote from Fort Laramie on november 29, giving the numbers and locations of the Sioux bands and recommending that three commands be sent against the Sioux – one from Fort Pierre on the Missouri, one from Fort Kearny on the lower Platte, and one from Fort Laramie. A single command might be eluded by the Indians during a whole season, he warned. He reported having received word that a thousand lodges of Brulés, Miniconjous and others were camped on the L'eau qui-court (Running Water) and were saying that they would keep up the war all winter and in the spring would meet the troops sent against them.[427]

Alfred J. Vaughan, Indian agent on the upper Missouri, wrote with consternation from Fort Pierre on november 21 that the Brulé, Miniconjou and a few allies "openly bid defiance to the threats of the govern-

---

[425] R. P. Bieber (ed.), *Frontier life in the army, 1854-1861*, p. 28, referring to Colonel Hoffman's letter of november 19, in the old files of the war department, and to other sources.

[426] *House ex. docs.*, cong. 33, sess. 2, no. 36, p. 5. Colonel Hoffman's letter of november 29, 1854.

[427] *Ibid.*, 5.

ment, and go so far as to say that they do not fear the result should soldiers come to fight them."

He reported that in returning from the Yellowstone he met Unc-pa-pas and Blackfoot Sioux who told him that "they did not want any of their father's presents; that they preferred scalps and stealing horses to anything he could give them." And when the agent gave some presents to the Yanctonies, "Red Calf drew from his scabbard a huge knife and cut each one of the sacks, and scattered the contents furiously in every direction." Then the agent concludes: "Something should be done to show the power of the government, and that speedily, otherwise there is no knowing the result. Every man's life in the country is in jeopardy." [428]

John Dougherty, early Indian trader and one-time Indian agent, added his suggestions: "It is highly important that a decisive blow should be given them [the hostile Sioux] at the very onset. This would have the effect to deter all other neighboring tribes from joining in with the Sioux against us. . . A prompt and decisive blow on the Sioux in effect would be worth to us, for years to come, millions of dollars and many strong armies." [429]

The communications of Hoffman, Vaughan and Dougherty, cited above, were submitted by Jefferson Davis, secretary of war, to President Pierce and by him transmitted to congress on january 16, 1855. The president also renewed the recommendation of his last annual message for an increased regular army and, for the present emergency, he suggested the employment of volunteer troops. Unless, he said, "a force can be early brought into the field, adequate to the suppression of

---

[428] *Ibid.*, 6. Letter of agent Vaughan.
[429] *Ibid.*, 7.

existing hostilities, the combination of predatory bands will be extended, and the difficulty of restoring order and security greatly magnified." [430]

General Winfield Scott, commanding general of the army, had already recommended that "a signal punishment" be given the hostile Indians. And the war department on october 26, 1854, had informed Colonel William S. Harney of the Second Dragoons, who was then on leave in Paris, that he would be placed in charge of the Sioux expedition if available, in season. [431] Harney returned to the United States and on march 22, 1855, received the appointment. He was instructed to establish a military post at or near Fort Pierre on the upper Missouri and to collect supplies and make preparations for operations from forts Kearny and Laramie. He was "to avoid, if possible, all partial operations until a sufficient number of troops has been collected to render the campaign short and decisive." [432] He was ordered to St. Louis at once and was to begin his movements as soon as practicable.

The war department ordered two companies of the Sixth infantry from Jefferson Barracks (St. Louis) to Fort Riley, Kansas, while two companies of the Second infantry from Fort Riley and four companies of the same regiment from Carlisle Barracks were to ascend the Missouri and establish a post at or near Fort Pierre. The remaining four companies of the Sixth infantry at Jefferson Barracks and the light battery of the Fourth artillery at Fort Leavenworth were ordered to reinforce forts Laramie and Kearny. [433]

---

430 *Ibid.*, 1. Message of President Pierce.

431 Bieber, *op. cit.*, 28-29, citing manuscript records in the old files of the war department.

432 *Ibid.*, 29.

433 *Ibid.*, 30.

Upon arrival at St. Louis on april 1 Harney began preparations for the campaigns. With the small number of cavalry assigned him he feared he could conduct "partial operations" only, but on so reporting to the war department he was informed that active operations must be undertaken during the current season. Accordingly, he left St. Louis by boat on july 12, and reached Fort Leavenworth six days later. He moved his troops out of this post on august 4, and in sixteen days reached Fort Kearny, his progress having been retarded by storms and mud. Additional troops from Fort Riley joined him here, so that when he set out from Fort Kearny on august 24 he was in command of some 600 men.[434] His determination to make a demonstration against the Sioux was voiced in a communication to the war department, and as he left Fort Kearny he is reported to have said, "By God, I'm for battle – no peace." [435]

In the meantime, certain bands of the Sioux had given additional evidence of their hostility. Through the winter they had made every effort to procure horses, ammunition and iron for arrow points. Ward and Guerrier, old-time traders, from their post at Sandy Point, seven miles northwest of Fort Laramie, wrote on february 14, 1855: "A part of our horses and mules, about sixty-five head, were driven off yesterday by the Sioux Indians. . . We do not consider any property safe on this river, or lives either, any longer, as the Sioux, we think, have commenced their war on the traders, as well as the soldiers." [436]

---

[434] *Ibid.*, 31.

[435] *Ibid.*, 31. Publications of the Nebraska State Historical Society, xx, quoting Missouri newspapers. J. P. Dunn, *Massacres of the mountains*, p. 233.

[436] Letter of Messrs. J. M. Horner & company of Salt Lake City, and appearing in the *Deseret News* of that city, march 5, 1855.

Thomas S. Williams, traveling east from Salt Lake City, reported from Fort Laramie on april 20: "I arrived here yesterday all well, and found all our mules here, as Ward and Gurier had rescued them from the Indians by paying for them, costing ten dollars per head. . . Three or four days before I got to Devil's Gate [a few miles west of Independence Rock, on the Sweetwater], a large war party of Indians had driven off all of Semino's horses,[437] and all of Pappan's and the mail mules, making a clean sweep of all the animals at that point. Also, the very morning we got to the bridge on the Platte river, they had taken 75 head from Racheau and the traders at that point. I saved myself by traveling nights, which I shall do all the way down." [438]

A correspondent writes from Fort Laramie on may 9: "It is known that the Minecajoux Sioux are guilty of all the late robberies. This week they stole four of Major Johnson's escort mules, not far from the fort, on the Salt Lake side . Some squaws have brought in a report that two war parties, one hundred strong each, are coming down on Laramie to steal. All the traders agree that the government ought to whip the Sioux – in fact, that it is absolutely necessary." [439]

On june 22 Robert Gibson, leader of a wagon train from Missouri, met some Sioux near the Deer creek crossing below North Platte bridge. While he was shaking hands with one Indian, another shot him through the heart.[440] Several days later, according to report, an emigrant party was attacked at the same locality by

[437] Semino had a trading post at or near Devil's Gate.

[438] *Deseret News*, v, 77. *St. Louis Luminary*, june 16, 1855.

[439] *Missouri Republican*, june 11, 1855, quoted in L.D.S. *Journal history* under date of june 16, 1855.

[440] Bieber, *op. cit.*, 28, citing war department records and Missouri newspapers.

eighteen Indians, who lanced a man and a woman and drove off sixteen head of horses.[441]

Despite the depredations and reports of depredations, the overland emigration of 1855 was but slightly affected, as indicated in the preceding chapter. Nearly five thousand Mormons trekked to Utah and other emigrants made their way safely to California and to Oregon. Indeed, certain wild stories of Indian outrages that were circulated were without foundation. Major Rose, who made a trip from Salt Lake City to the Missouri river in the summer of 1855 reported that he did not hear of nor see a hostile Indian on the plains and denied the correctness of reports of outrages, especially of that one which said a train had been intercepted and one hundred persons murdered. John Ray, who left Salt Lake City on may 8, reported meeting only friendly Indians on his trip across the plains.[442]

Certain of the Sioux who had been strong for war in the fall of 1854, were more inclined to peace by the summer of 1855. News of the punitive expedition to be directed against them had no doubt been an important factor in effecting this change of spirit.

The newly appointed Indian agent, Thomas S. Twiss, arrived at Fort Laramie august 10, 1855. Information gathered by him from all available sources convinced him that most of the Indians were for peace. He decided to separate the peaceful from the hostile, and to place the former under his own protection. Accordingly, he declared the North Platte to be the boundary between friend and foe and sent runners to bring the bands in for councils. The Brulés met him at Bordeau's trading post, eight miles below Fort Laramie, on august 19 and the

[441] J. P. Dunn, *Massacres of the mountains*, p. 233-4.

[442] L.D.S. *Journal history*, june 30, 1855.

Oglalas had a council with him at Ward and Guerrier's, seven or eight miles above the fort, ten days later. In both of these councils Twiss explained that friendly Indians must demonstrate their friendship by moving to the south side of the river and by driving all hostiles from their midst. These bands appear to have taken his advice and were placed well to the south of the North Platte river.[443]

In the meantime, Harney made his way up the Oregon trail, reaching Ash Hollow on september 2, 1855. Having learned that Little Thunder and his band of Brulés were encamped on Blue Water creek, six miles from the left bank of the North Platte, he made preparations for an attack. He ordered Lieutenant-colonel Philip St. George Cooke of the Second Dragoons, with four mounted companies, to set out at three o'clock the next morning and make a circuit to the rear of the villages to cut off retreat.

Having given Cooke time to reach his position, General Harney, at 4:30 A.M., moved his five companies of infantry across the North Platte and toward the Indian villages that were scattered along Blue Water creek. As the infantry approached, a Sioux delegation came to parley with the General, but he refused to receive them and continued his march. Then Little Thunder, carrying a white flag, again approached the troops and Harney halted his men.[444] The Brulé chief entreated for his people, protesting friendship for the whites. Harney reports: "I stated the causes of the dissatisfaction which the government felt toward the Brulés, and closed the interview by telling him that his people had

---

[443] Letter of agent Twiss, written from Fort Laramie october 1, 1855, found in the *Annual report of the commissioner of Indian Affairs,* 1855, p. 80.

[444] R. P. Bieber (ed.) *Frontier life in the army, 1854-1861,* 34, citing manuscript records in the war department files.

depredated upon and insulted our citizens whilst moving quietly through our country; that they had massacred our troops under most aggravated circumstances, and that now the day of retribution had come; that I did not wish to harm him, personally, as he professed to be a friend of the whites; but that he must either deliver up the young men, whom he acknowledged he could not control, or they must suffer the consequences of their past misconduct, and take the chances of battle. Not being able, of course, however willing he might have been, to deliver up all the butchers of our people, Little Thunder returned to his band to warn them of my decision, and to prepare them for the contest that must follow.

"Immediately after his disappearance from view I ordered the infantry to advance. . ." [445] And the battle, or massacre, was on.

Eugene Bandel, a soldier in the infantry, reports: "We attacked them with our rifles, while their arrows or the bullets from their poor flintlocks could not reach us. They were forced to flee. But they ran straight into the arms of our dragoons, who followed them as they turned back towards us." [446]

Another infantryman reports: "I never saw a more beautiful thing in my life. When the infantry saw the Dragoons coming down in such beautiful style, they gave a yell, which resounded far and wide. The Indians threw away everything they had in the world. . . We, of necessity, killed a great many women and children. We took forty women and children prisoners, a good many horses, buffalo meat enough to supply a whole company for some time. I do not suppose the Indians

[445] *Senate ex. docs.*, cong. 34, sess. 1, no. 1, part 1, p. 49-50. This report was written september 5, 1855.

[446] Bieber, *op. cit.*, 84.

in this country ever had such a perfect clearing out as upon this occasion. They will have cause to remember Gen. Harney for some time." [447]

"There was much slaughter in the pursuit," writes Colonel Cooke, "which extended from five to eight miles. . . Very few, if any, of the enemy should have escaped if I could have handled the reserve. . . I will remark that in the pursuit, women, if recognized, were generally passed by my men, but that in some cases certainly these women discharged arrows at them." [448]

Harney reports that the "results of this affair were, 86 killed, 5 wounded, about 70 women and children captured, 50 mules and ponies taken, besides an indefinite number killed and disabled. The amount of provisions and camp equipage must have comprised nearly all the enemy possessed; for teams have been constantly engaged in bringing into camp everything of any value to the troops, and much has been destroyed on the ground.

"The casualties of the command amount to 4 killed, 4 severely wounded, 3 slightly wounded, and one missing, supposed to be killed or captured by the enemy."[449]

News of the engagement – the battle of Blue Water, the battle of Ash Hollow, or the Harney massacre, as it is variously called – reached agent Twiss, encamped with the friendly Sioux on the Laramie river, some thirty-five miles above the fort, on september 7. He immediately assembled the chiefs and principal men of the

[447] Correspondence from Ash Hollow of september 5, 1855, in the *Daily Missouri Republican* of september 27, 1855. Reprinted in the *Publications of the Nebraska state historical society*, XX, p. 280.

[448] *Sen. ex. docs.,* cong. 34, sess. 3, no. 58, p. 4.

[449] Harney's report, *Sen. ex. docs.,* cong. 34, sess. 1, no. 1, part 1, p. 50. An account of the engagement, by General Richard C. Drum, and a study of the battlefield (accompanied by a map), appear in *Collections of the Nebraska state historical society*, XVI, 143-164.

villages and "gave them all the particulars of the battle, and the loss sustained by Little Thunder's band in killed, wounded and prisoners. They replied that 'Gen. Harney had done right; Little Thunder had been told by me, through friendly runners sent by them, to keep off from the emigrant trail, and to come over to the south side and take me by the hand, if he was friendly to the United States. By remaining on the north side of the Platte he showed himself an enemy to the whites.' " [450]

General Harney established a temporary post, called Fort Grattan, at the mouth of Ash Hollow, garrisoned it with a company of the Sixth infantry and then continued up the Platte to Fort Laramie. Here he received a delegation of Sioux chiefs from the bands that had placed themselves under the protection of agent Twiss. General Harney treated them coldly. Only by surrendering the Indians who had murdered the mail party, by restoring stolen animals, and by pledging a cessation of depredations could they hope for peace, he informed them. "They begged piteously to be spared –" he wrote, "only suffered to live – and offered to comply with all my demands." [451]

Harney's austerity towards these Indians was probably invoked in part by the growing schism between the war department and the Indian Bureau in reference to the conduct of Indian affairs. G. W. Manypenny, commissioner of Indian Affairs, and Alfred Cummings, superintendent at St. Louis, had opposed the military expedition led by Harney.[452] And though agent Twiss

---

[450] Twiss's letter of october 1, 1855, in the *Annual report of the commissioner of Indian Affairs* (1855), p. 81.

[451] Bieber, *op. cit.,* p. 36, quoting Harney's letter of september 26, 1855, in the war department files.

[452] A. W. Hoopes, "Thomas S. Twiss, Indian agent on the upper Platte, 1855-1861," in *Mississippi valley historical review,* XX, 355.

at first appeared to approve the General's actions, he was soon at variance with him.

Considering it advisable to continue his demonstration against hostiles, General Harney set out from Fort Laramie on september 29 to further penetrate the Sioux country. Provided with scouts and hunters, he led his command of some 450 men, toward Fort Pierre on the Missouri. Without encountering hostile bands, he reached his destination on october 19.[453] Delegations from the principal tribes soon came in, imploring for peace. He concluded that further military operations were unnecessary and so appointed a general peace council for march 1 at Fort Pierre.

In the meantime at Fort Laramie, agent Twiss and the military authorities had developed antagonisms. The agent felt that he should have a leading part in peace negotiations, while General Harney thought that dealings would be more effective if conducted by the military alone. Accordingly, Twiss prevented representatives of the Brulé and Oglala Sioux from attending a preliminary council in february, 1856. In retaliation, General Harney ordered Colonel Hoffman, commander of Fort Laramie, to restrict Twiss to intercourse with the Cheyennes and Arapahos and to "inform him he was to have nothing to do with the Sioux." [454] Twiss's conflict with Ward and Guerrier over the latter's intercourse with the Indians, and the traders' appeal to Colonel Hoffman had only added fuel to the flame.[455] Then, on march 6, Harney forbade Twiss to have dealings with the Arapahos and Cheyennes. Thereupon the

[453] Letter of General Harney written from Fort Pierre, october 19, 1855. Reprinted in *South Dakota historical collections*, I, 397.

[454] A. W. Hoopes, *op. cit.*, 358, quoting Harney's letter of february 28, 1856, found in the old files of the war department.

[455] *Ibid.*, 359.

agent set out for Washington and presented his case to commissioner Manypenny. Here he was upheld. With additional instructions he returned to his post, resumed his official position and was duly recognized by Colonel Hoffman.[456]

General Harney's council with the Indians at Fort Pierre, which convened march 1, lasted for five days. At its conclusion the nine tribes represented signed the agreement dictated by the military. All perpetrators of murders and outrages on the whites were to be delivered up for trial, stolen property was to be restored, travelers on the trails were not to be disturbed, and chiefs must be chosen and be responsible for the good conduct of their respective bands. The United States agreed to protect the Sioux from white impositions, to restore the Sioux annuities, and to provide agricultural implements to Indians desiring them.[457] Thus ended the Sioux Expedition.

---

[456] *Ibid.,* 360-361.
[457] *House ex. docs.,* cong. 34, sess. 1, no. 130, pp. 1-39.

From Handcart to Pony Express, 1856-1860

In addition to the usual covered wagon trains that for more than a decade had lumbered past Fort Laramie on the Oregon trail, there came in 1856 a new type of emigrant transport into the West. This was the humble handcart, now first employed on a wholesale scale by the Mormons.

The handcart plan was conceived by Brigham Young, famous Mormon leader, and was carried through under his direction. During the 'fifties the Mormons were actively proselyting in Europe and their many converts were eager to gather to their new Zion in Utah. The Perpetual Emigration Fund, previously mentioned, had been established to aid the emigration of the poor, but the money raised was not sufficient to meet the demands. Writes W. H. Kimball from London on november 8, 1855: "The fire of emigration blazes throughout the pastorate to such an extent that the folks are willing to part with all their effects and toddle off with a few things in a pocket handkerchief." [458]

In answer to the many calls for help in migrating, Brigham Young set forth his plan to F. D. Richards, president of the European mission: "I have been thinking how we should operate another year. We cannot afford to purchase wagons and teams as in times past.

---

[458] L. R. Hafen, The story of the migration to Utah by handcarts, 1856-1860; master's thesis, MS. university of Utah. This thesis is the basis for the handcart story given here.

I am consequently thrown back upon my old plan – to make hand-carts, and let the emigration foot it, and draw upon them the necessary supplies, having a cow or two for every ten. They can come just as quick, if not quicker, and much cheaper – can start earlier and escape the prevailing sickness which annually lays so many of our brethren in the dust." [459]

In the Thirteenth General Epistle, issued by the Mormon church authorities in october, 1855, the official call is made: "Let all the Saints who can, gather up for Zion and come while the way is open before them; let the poor also come, whether they receive aid or not from the [P.E.] Fund; let them come on foot, with handcarts or wheelbarrows; let them gird up their loins and walk through, and nothing shall hinder or stay them."

Says an editorial of march 1, 1856, in the *Millennial Star,* Mormon organ at Liverpool: "Ancient Israel travelled to the promised land on foot with their wives and little ones. The Lord calls upon Modern Israel to do the same."

The proselytes from Europe, after crossing the Atlantic in sailing vessels, were transported by railroad to Iowa City, Iowa. Here was to begin the handcart journey.

The carts provided were similar in size and shape to those used by street sweepers today. They were made of Iowa hickory and oak and weighed about fifteen pounds. The axles were of wood, but the wheels had thin iron tires. Some of the carts were open, others were covered.[460] Clothing, cooking utensils and supplies were piled on the handcarts in amounts to fit the number of persons assigned to each cart.

---

[459] Letter of september 30, 1855.

[460] One of these carts may be seen in the Utah state capitol.

The first handcart company left Iowa City, june 9, 1856. Two days later, the second company followed. However, through most of the trip they traveled together. The parties totaled four hundred and ninety-seven persons, and their outfit consisted of one hundred handcarts and five ox-drawn wagons carrying the twenty-five tents and the groceries.

Across Iowa the journey led through partially settled country. The handcarts were not to receive their full loads until the Missouri river was reached, so they made good time to Nebraska. But the ordeal was exacting. Summer heat, dust and sand, made tired legs and swollen feet as they trudged along, pulling their two-wheeled wagons.

A short stop at Florence and the handcart emigrants were again on their way. A semi-military order of march was maintained. They rose, breakfasted, set out on the day's travel, camped, and retired, at calls from the bugle. The handcart song, comprising six stanzas, was frequently sung to keep up the spirits of the emigrants. The chorus ran thus:

> "Some must push and some must pull
> As we go marching up the hill,
> As merrily on the way we go
> Until we reach the valley, oh."

So westward along the Platte river trail plodded the footsore train. There were thunderstorms and windstorms, Indian scares and buffalo stampedes to vary the monotonous journey along that shining, winding, never-ending Platte. There were breakdowns and troubles, amusing incidents and jolly social parties, and on occasion a happy marriage celebration or the sad rites over a fresh grave on the prairie. At the evening camp, tired bodies and hopeful spirits gathered about the fires, or clustered in groups for social recreation. A considerate helpfulness born of common trials, and a general cheerfulness begotten of religious fervor, permeated the camp and the march.

Fort Laramie was a haven toward which they looked. Here they would find not only white habitation, but needed supplies and facilities for repairing their carts. These dust-browned emigrants pulling their creaking loads up to the fort must have seemed strange indeed to the soldiers, used to wagon caravans and pack trains upon the overland road. The hundred carts with the five hundred pushing, pulling, sweating travelers bespoke an enthusiasm that rivaled the gold-seekers' urge.

Supplies from Salt Lake valley were sent out to meet the handcart companies. The first company reached Salt Lake City, september 26. Church dignitaries, a brass band, a military detachment and hundreds of citizens welcomed the newcomers. Young and his associates were gratified at the success of their experiment.

A third company of handcart emigrants reached Utah safely on october 2, but the fourth and fifth companies were marked for tragedy. Some of the persons who were to compose these companies were late in sailing from Europe. Upon arriving at Iowa City in late june and early july a fatal delay occurred while carts were being made. The fourth company did not set out from Iowa City until july 15 and the fifth remained at that place until july 26. The fourth company numbered about 500; there was a handcart to every four or five persons and an ox-drawn wagon to each one hundred persons. The fifth company consisted of 576 persons equipped in the same proportion. Florence, Nebraska, was reached by the two companies on august

11 and 22, respectively, and a week's further delay was necessary for repair of the carts. The summer being far advanced, it was by some thought unsafe to attempt the further journey during the current season. But a large majority were for pushing on, buoyed by a faith that the Lord would protect them.

Upon setting out, a hundred pound sack of flour was placed on each cart in addition to the luggage. But sand had ground down the wooden axles, and this added weight caused many breakdowns. One evening the oxen of the fourth company were stampeded by buffalo and thirty of the cattle were permanently lost.

This company did not reach Fort Laramie until the first of september. Here numbers of the emigrants traded their watches and other valuables for provisions. A survey showed their supplies to be inadequate for the remainder of the journey. So the allowance of flour for each person was reduced from one pound to three-fourths of a pound per day. Later it was cut to ten ounces.

As they pushed on to the Sweetwater the nights grew colder. Scarcity of food, fatigue and the cold weakened endurance. Finally the snow came. The lead company made camp in some willows. The next morning the snow was over a foot deep, the cattle had strayed widely during the storm, the flour was all gone, and five persons had died during the night. It was decided that the company should remain in camp while messengers continue on, meet the expected supply train from Salt Lake and urge it to the rescue. Three days thereafter the supply train with food and clothing reached the camp.

In the meantime the fifth company, which had left the Missouri river about two weeks behind the fourth company, was undergoing similar experiences. It reached Fort Laramie october 8 and there procured one hundred buffalo robes to supplement clothing and bedding. On the further journey supplies ran short, and several times rations were cut.

There were many older people in this company, including three veterans of the battle of Waterloo who were between seventy-five and eighty years of age.

On october 20 they met the snow. "It continued falling three days," writes Josiah Rogerson. "Deaths began to multiply until a burying squad was appointed to prepare the graves each night for those who died during the day." "On the 20th of october," writes Mrs. Jackson, "we travelled, or almost wallowed for about ten miles through snow. At night, weary and worn out, we camped near the Platte river, where we soon left for the Sweetwater. We were visited with three days more snow. The animals and immigrants were almost completely exhausted. We remained in camp several days to gain strength. About the 25th of october I think it was, we reached camp about sundown. My husband had for several days previous been much worse. He was still sinking and his condition now became more serious. He tried to eat but failed. He had not the strength to swallow. I put him to bed as quickly as I could. He seemed to rest easy and fall asleep. About nine o'clock I retired. Bedding had become very scarce so I did not disrobe. I slept until, as it appeared to me, about midnight. I was extremely cold. The weather was bitter. I listened to hear if my husband breathed, he lay so still. I could not hear him. I became alarmed. I put one hand on his body, when to my horror I discovered that my worst fears were confirmed. My husband was dead. I called for help to the other inmates of the tent. They could render me no aid; and there was no alternative but to remain alone by the side of the corpse till morning. Oh, how the dreary hours drew their tedious length along. When daylight came, some of the male part of the company prepared the body for burial. And oh, such a burial and funeral service. They did not remove his clothing – he had but little. They wrapped him in a blanket and placed him in a pile with 13 others who had died, and then covered him up with snow. The ground was frozen so hard that they could not dig a grave."

On the last day of october the supply train arrived.

The news that the fourth and fifth handcart companies were on the plains had not reached Salt Lake City until early in october. The big semi-annual conference of the Mormon church was then in session. Brigham Young immediately suspended all other business and calling for volunteers organized trains to go to the rescue. He states in a letter of october 20: "We had no idea there were any more companies upon the Plains, presuming that they would consider their late arrival in America and not start them across the Plains until another year."

With the aid of the supply trains the two bereft companies reached Salt Lake City – the first, on november 9; the other, not until november 30. Deaths in the fourth company numbered 67, in the fifth between 135 and 150. The historic Donner tragedy of 1846, with its loss of nearly forty lives, pales before this winter toll from snow and hunger – over two hundred dead.

Although the misfortunes of the late handcart companies arrested enthusiasm for the plan, they by no means put an end to this method of migration. The Mormon authorities endorsed the continued use of the handcart, but ruled against companies starting overland later than july.

An eastbound handcart company set out from Salt Lake City in april, 1857. It was composed of seventy missionaries bound for the eastern states and Europe. Not a single horse, mule, ox, or cow accompanied this party. The food, tents, bedding, and clothing were transported in handcarts by man power. They made the trip from Salt Lake to Florence, Nebraska, in forty-eight days – about half the time usually taken by ox teams.

The Mormon emigration of 1857 was rather small, but two handcart companies were organized and successfully crossed the plains. There was little emigration to Utah in 1858 and none by handcart. The difficulties between the Mormons and the United States government account for this. One handcart company trekked to Utah in 1859 and during the following year two companies made the journey. These were the last; thereafter this method was abandoned. By 1861 the Mormons had a surplus of live stock in Utah and they found that the journey from Salt Lake to the Missouri river and back could be made in one season. Emigrants thereafter were carried westward along with freight by these round trip teams.

The handcart scheme, one of the most unique and interesting of western ventures, had sent 3,000 people in ten companies across the plains to Utah pushing 662 carts. And every company had welcomed the cool clear waters of the Laramie after the hot muddy waters of the Platte, and many had found succor in the friendly walls of the fort.

But not all westbound emigrants were making the journey by handcart. Even among the Mormons the covered wagon continued as the chief agency of travel.

From 1856 to 1860, the wagons carried over 5,000 emigrants to Utah.[461]

The companies of homeseekers bound for California and Oregon continued to stream past the fort on the Laramie. Each spring companies formed on the Missouri frontier and with their worldly effects under wagon covers trekked the Oregon trail.

A party traveling eastward from Fort Laramie in the spring of 1856, met the first California-bound emigrants at the crossing of the South Platte, and thereafter "passed trains almost hourly." [462] James Ure, clerk of the eastbound company, records:

"SATURDAY [may] 31 [a little east of Fort Kearny]. Started about 5:30 A.M. Met a number of government teams on their way to Fort Laramie, with supplies for the soldiers and corn for their horses. Yesterday and today we met upwards of two hundred wagons with from five to six yoke of cattle to a wagon. Each wagon carrying from 50 to 60 cwt.

"During the whole week the road has been literally covered with wagons, cattle, horses and mules with men and their families on their way to California. From the time we crossed the South Platte, we have met teams almost hourly and it seemed as if Missouri would be totally drained of cattle." [463] And another member of this party, after commenting on the large emigrant and freight caravans encountered along the road on the south side of the Platte, remarks: "From appearances the emigration on the north side of the Platte far exceeds that on the south." [464]

Charles Ford, who reached Fort Laramie from the

461 G. O. Larson, Perpetual emigrating fund company; M.A. thesis, university of Utah (MS.).

462 L.D.S. *Journal history,* may 29, 1856.

463 *Ibid.,* august 6, 1856.

464 George A. Smith's letter in the *Deseret News,* VI, 136.

west on may 28, 1856, reports: "We were in want of provisions and had to apply to the colonel for rations, a sufficiency of which he gave to all who had not means to purchase to serve them to the next fort. After leaving Laramie we met the California emigration, over 350 wagons and about 25,000 head of cattle." [465]

More impressive than the emigrant travel past Fort Laramie in 1857 and 1858 was the great freight transportation that dominated the plains travel of those years. The sending of the army to Utah in 1857, its maintenance there, and the campaign against the Cheyennes – topics to be treated in the following chapter – all involved extensive provision for the carriage of supplies.

The magnitude of this freighting business is indicated by figures for the year 1858. The great firm of Russell, Majors & Waddell received the contract for freighting the supplies to the army in Utah. On march 25, 1858, they ran the following advertisement in the *Nebraska Advertiser:*

ARMY OF THE WEST!

16,000 yoke good working cattle, from four to seven years of age wanted at Nebraska City, N.T., for hauling freight from that point to Utah, for which SEVENTY-FIVE dollars per yoke will be paid. . .

"FIFTEEN HUNDRED TEAMSTERS also wanted, to commence april 15, 1858. They will be paid twenty-five dollars per month, there and back, unless other wise agreed, for eight months or thereabouts.

"None but men of good health need apply.

"The use of intoxicating liquors as a beverage, card playing and profane language are prohibited. Each man will be presented with a bible and hymn book. Early application had better be made.

RUSSELL, MAJORS & WADDELL."

Realizing that it would be almost impossible to move all the freight from one depot, the facilities being too restricted for the handling and grazing of the necessary

---

[465] *Journal history*, august 6, 1856.

stock, the contractors arranged that only half of the freight be delivered at Fort Leavenworth, and the remainder be sent to a point to be selected farther up the river.[466]

The new town of Nebraska City was chosen as the other outfitting point. The *Nebraska News,* jubilant over the business this government contract would bring, calculated that it would require 2,000 wagons, each carrying 5,000 pounds, 16,000 cattle, two acres of ox yokes, and 2,000 drivers. The newspaper then drew a picture of the scene:

"Suffice it to say that a thousand whips are cracking, sixteen thousand tails are gaily snapping the flies of june away, two thousand drivers shrieking, eight thousand wagon wheels squeaking, all eager to join the anti-Mormon fray, when at the closing recitative, a herd of buffalos and six hundred Indians break in upon the train and a general stampede ensues, then, and not till then, do we show our true musical strength." [467]

The freighting firm had insisted, as one of the conditions for its location at Nebraska City, that the town suppress the liquor traffic. As an additional moral encouragement the company gave each of its employees a Bible and had them agree not to drink or swear while in the company's employ.

Mr. Majors appears to have been the principal leader in this move. A report in the *Kansas Chief* of july 21, 1859, indicated his activity and spirit: "On saturday evening Mr. Majors visited the encampment on the prairie and preached a sermon to the teamsters. It is said that he 'talked to them like a Dutch uncle.' "

---

[466] Alexander Majors, *Seventy years on the frontier,* 76.

[467] Quoted in *Publications of Nebraska state historical society,* XX, 295. See also the special edition of the *Nebraska Daily News-Press* (Nebraska City), november 14, 1929.

One of the interesting characters who worked with the company was Buffalo Bill [William F. Cody], then a youngster. In his autobiography he relates:

"That spring my former boss, Lew Simpson, was busily organizing a 'lightning bull team' for his employers, Russell, Majors & Waddell. Albert Sidney Johnston's soldiers, then moving West, needed supplies, and needed them in a hurry. Thus far the mule was the reindeer of draft animals, and mule trains were forming to hurry the needful supplies to the soldiers.

"But Simpson had great faith in the bull. A picked bull train, he allowed, could beat a mule train all hollow on a long haul. All he wanted was a chance to prove it.

"His employers gave him the chance. For several weeks he had been picking his animals for the outfit. . .

"A mule train was to start a week after Simpson's lightning bulls began their westward course. Whichever outfit got to Fort Laramie first would be the winner. No more excitement could have been occasioned had the contestants been a reindeer and a jack-rabbit. To my infinite delight Simpson let me join his party. . .

"We made the first hundred and fifty miles easily. . . The ordinary bull team could do about fifteen miles a day. Under Simpson's command his specially selected bulls were doing twenty-five, and doing it right along. . .

"Presently Stewart's train came shambling up, and a joyful lot the 'mule skinners' were at what they believed their victory.

"But it was a short-lived victory. At the end of the next three hundred miles we found them, trying to cross the Platte, and making heavy work of it. The grass fodder had told on the mules. Supplies from other sources were now exhausted. There were no farms, no traders, no grain to be had. The race had become a race of endurance, and the strongest stomachs were destined to be the winners.

"Stewart made a bad job of the crossing. The river was high, and his mules quickly mired down in the quicksand. The more they pawed the deeper they went.

"Simpson picked a place for crossing below the ford Stewart had chosen. He put enough bulls on a wagon to insure its easy progress, and the bulls wallowed through the sand on their round bellies, using their legs as paddles.

"Stewart pulled ahead again after he had crossed the river, but soon his mules grew too feeble to make anything like their normal speed. We passed them for good and all a few days farther on, and were far ahead when we reached the North Platte.

"Thus ended a race that I shall never forget." [468]

The contract prices arranged on january 16, 1858, by the Quarter-master-general for the freighting of the army supplies provided a schedule that varied with the time of the year when deliveries were to be made. The rate for each hundredweight per hundred miles varied from $1.35 in summer to $4.50 in winter. The rate to Fort Laramie (figuring the distance at 700 miles), would thus be 9.45 cents per pound in summer and 31.5 cents in winter. This rate was to apply only to the first 10,000,000 pounds; the next 5,000,000 would cost 25 per cent more; and any freight above 15,000,000 pounds should pay 35 per cent more than the original rate.[469]

Alexander Majors writes that in fulfilling his government freighting contract in 1858, his company employed 3,500 wagons, 40,000 oxen, 1,000 mules, and

[468] W. F. Cody, *An autobiography of Buffalo Bill*, 25-28.

[469] *Ex. docs.*, no. 99, p. 4, cong. 35, sess. 1.

over 4,000 men. Trail wagons had not yet come into use and one driver was required for each wagon.[470]

The fact that Russell, Majors & Waddell did not monopolize the freighting business of the plains is indicated by a table which appeared in the *Freedom's Champion* of october 30, 1858. It lists the twenty-four trains that left Atchison, Kansas, in 1858 for Fort Laramie, Salt Lake City and other western points. The combined figures made a total of 775 wagons, 1,114 men, 7,963 oxen, 142 horses, 1,286 mules and 3,730,905 pounds of merchandise.[471]

The freighting activity of Russell, Majors & Waddell at Leavenworth greatly impressed Horace Greeley on the editor's western tour in may, 1859. "Such acres of wagons!" he exclaimed, "such pyramids of extra axletrees! such herds of oxen! such regiments of drivers and other employees! No one who does not see can realize how vast a business this is, nor how immense are its outlays as well as its income. I presume this great firm has at this hour two millions of dollars invested in stock, mainly oxen, mules and wagons. (They last year employed six thousand teamsters, and worked forty-five thousand oxen)." [472]

In 1859 this great freighting firm added a third outfitting point, White Cloud, Kansas, to its depots. The *Kansas Chief,* of that city, which had printed scathing criticism of the firm in march, 1858, now spoke only praise.

The *American Railway Times* of january 26, 1861, reports that during the preceding year 18,000 tons of

[470] Majors, *op. cit.,* 143, 145.

[471] The table is reprinted in W. E. Connelley, *A standard history of Kansas and Kansans* (1918), I, 168.

[472] Horace Greeley, *An overland journey, from New York to San Francisco, in the summer of 1859,* 47-48.

freight were carried from the Missouri river to New Mexico, Utah, and the Pike's Peak country. One firm of freighters owned 15,500 oxen and sent out that year 51 trains of 26 wagons each; another 32 trains of 26 wagons each. Nearly 12,000 men, 8,000 mules, 68,000 oxen and 6,900 wagons were employed in freighting on the Plains.

Fort Laramie, as the great farwestern outpost, was a depot of supplies, repair station, and base of operations, not only for the army and its provision trains, but a way station of importance for all the freighting and emigrant travel on the Oregon trail.

News of a gold discovery on the South Platte near the mouth of Cherry creek reached Fort Laramie in the summer of 1858. Immediately, a number of traders, hangers-on and emigrants set out from the fort for the reputed gold fields. Among these were George A. Jackson and John H. Gregory, who were to make the most important early gold finds in Colorado and give their names respectively to Jackson Diggings and the Gregory Lode. The Janis brothers (early trappers), Big Phil, the Cannibal, and twenty Sioux were among those that accompanied Jackson to the South Platte.[473]

John Richard, Indian trader, and others from Fort Laramie, as well as members of the original prospecting parties, carried the golden news back to the Missouri valley towns. Soon the frontier was aflame with excitement. A number of parties were quickly organized and hurried across the plains to pick up the choice locations in the new El Dorado. Other thousands restrained themselves with thoughts of the approaching winter and planned their journeys for the following spring.

The fortune seekers who reached the mouth of

[473] L. R. Hafen (ed.), "George A. Jackson's diary, 1858-1859," in *Colorado Magazine*, XII, 202.

Cherry creek in the fall of 1858 did not find the sands of the stream yellow with gold, but they did find "color" and sufficient prospects to hold most of them through the winter. Experienced town promoters among them saw in real estate speculation an easier and surer fortune than was to be won from mining. They platted Denver and Auraria at the mouth of Cherry creek and made claim to other choice town sites in the region.

For these Argonauts, camped some two hundred miles south of Fort Laramie, this fort was the nearest post office and the point of contact with the outside world. They established a mail express to the fort during the winter of 1858-59. Jim Saunders, trapper, accompanied by his squaw, made the december trip in a little wagon drawn by four Indian ponies,[474] and George A. Jackson and Big Phil reached the fort on january 31 with another mail on horseback.[475] About a hundred miners were reported to have come in to Fort Laramie to spend the winter.[476]

The goldseekers that clustered about the mouth of Cherry creek, present Denver, in the fall of 1858 made plans for political organization. They held an election in november and chose H. J. Graham to represent them in congress. Although the political entity they so spontaneously launched was not yet christened, as Graham proceeded to Washington the press reported that he was the representative of the territory of Laramie.[477] The name of the proposed territory was soon changed to Jefferson, but its liberal boundaries included the Fort Laramie region. In a convention that met in pio-

---

[474] *Reminiscences of General William Larimer and of his son William H. H. Larimer, two of the founders of Denver City,* 136.

[475] Jackson's diary, *op. cit.,* 209.

[476] *Chicago Press-Tribune,* december 24, 1858.

[477] Pease and Cole, *Complete guide to the gold districts of Kansas and Nebraska,* 14, quoting the *Chicago Press-Tribune.*

neer Denver on april 15, 1859, and planned the creation of a state, Fort Laramie was designated one of the election precincts. But we have no record of an actual election being held at the post.[478] When congress finally created the territory of Colorado in 1861, the area was reduced to the present boundaries and Fort Laramie was beyond the territorial limits of the new territory.

The great Pike's Peak gold rush of 1859, which lured some hundred thousand would-be miners from their homes in the states, does not especially concern us here.[479] For although the principal route to the mines was along the Platte river, the goldseekers' road turned from the Oregon trail at the upper California crossing of the South Platte (near Julesburg) and continued up that stream to the vicinity of the mines. Early in the spring of 1859 the Leavenworth and Pike's Peak Express established direct stagecoach service between Leavenworth and Denver and Fort Laramie's connection with development in the Colorado region became increasingly remote.

But with the mail service on the North Platte, to Fort Laramie, Salt Lake City and beyond, our fort continued to be concerned. When last mentioned in our story, the carriage of this mail had been awarded to W. M. F. Magraw in 1854. The Indian uprising following the Grattan massacre had brought heavy losses on the contractor. He submitted his case and condition to the government and his annual compensation was increased from $14,440 to $36,000. The following year he submitted similar claims. The higher compensation was continued another year but the contract was then annulled.[480] In the meantime the mail service to Fort

---

[478] *Rocky Mountain News*, april 23, june 11, august 6, 20, october 20, 1859.

[479] See L. R. Hafen, *Colorado, the story of a western commonwealth*, chapter 7.

[480] L. R. Hafen, *The overland mail*, 60-61.

Laramie was very irregular and the officials of the post frequently had to depend on special military expresses to carry mail and dispatches.

The new mail contract, of october, 1856, was awarded to Hiram Kimball of Utah, agent of Mormon leaders who had plans for building up a great carrying company to operate by way of Fort Laramie. Brigham Young had proposed such an undertaking even before the mail contract was awarded, but with this aid their plans were now perfected, and the B. Y. Express Carrying company was formed. The Mormons planned not only to establish stations but to found settlements at intervals along the line, these to furnish supplies and protection for the emigrants as well as for the mail. The severity of the weather during the winter of 1856-57 delayed the launching of the enterprise, but in the spring companies were organized with outfitting teams and farming tools to form the settlements.[481] By midsummer, however, the mail contract was annulled and an army was on its way to Salt Lake City. With the suspension of regular communication with Utah, Fort Laramie also was deprived of the monthly mail.

In the spring of 1858 Fort Laramie was given a much improved mail service. John M. Hockaday and associates had obtained a contract for carrying the mail in four-mule wagons or carriages from Independence, Missouri, to Salt Lake City. The service was to be weekly and was to operate on a twenty-two day schedule.[482] Bringing from the Missouri river to the fort news but twelve days old, this service was a boon to the soldiers, for their isolation and the infrequency of communication had been looked upon as principal handicaps of life at the post.

481 *Ibid.*, 62.
482 *House ex. docs.,* cong. 35, sess. 2, no. 109, XI, 863.

A change of policy in the post office department, following the death of Postmaster-general Brown in march, 1859, resulted in a general curtailment of western mail lines. The service to Fort Laramie was reduced to a semi-monthly schedule. Financially embarrassed by the reduction, the mail contractors disposed of their contract and equipment to Jones, Russell and company, the organization that had just launched the Leavenworth & Pike's Peak Express on the Republican river route. The two lines were combined during the summer and were routed on the Platte river road.[483]

A rivalry among western mail lines, and especially between the Southern, or Butterfield, route by way of El Paso and Tucson and the Central route, by South Pass and Salt Lake City, was to result in a new and important development in western communication. The first improved overland mail service to the Pacific coast had been established on the Southern route in september, 1858, providing for semi-weekly stagecoach service on a twenty-five day schedule and costing the government $600,000 per year.[484] Partisans of the Central route had endeavored to secure the contract and service for the route they favored, but had failed of their goal. The postmaster-general, with southern sympathies, had decided that the southerly route was surest and best, especially as a year-round undertaking. With a view to demonstrating the practicability of the Central route for year-round travel from Missouri to San Francisco, and with the hope of obtaining an enlarged mail contract, the mail carriers on the Fort Laramie route now boldly undertook the launching of a project – the famous Pony Express.

William H. Russell, who had traveled the Platte

483 Hafen, *The overland mail,* 150-51.
484 *Ibid.,* 90.

river route to California in 1846, and who in 1859 was heavily engaged in western freighting and stagecoaching, may be considered the father of the Pony Express. While in the national capital during the winter of 1859-60 he had discussed with Senator Gwin of California the desirability of launching a fast express over the Central route. The senator had favored the project and had agreed to obtain from congress a subsidy for the undertaking.[485] The Central route was acknowledged as the shortest to the Golden Gate. What was needed was a practical demonstration of its feasibility for year-round travel. A swift express might not only accomplish this, but by its spectacular achievement of clipping two-thirds of the time from the schedule would center the attention of the nation upon the route and upon the organizers and conductors of the express. Government support was sure to follow.

Having decided on their enterprise, Russell and his partners pushed their preparations with vigor. His partner, Alexander Majors, who supervised the organizing, explains in his memoirs:

"Five hundred of the fleetest horses to be procured were immediately purchased, and the services of over two hundred competent men were secured. Eighty of these men were selected for express riders. . . Relays were established at stations. . . At each station a sufficient number of horses were kept, and at every third station the thin, wiry, and hardy pony-riders held themselves in readiness to press forward with the mails. . .

"The distance between relay riders' stations varied from sixty-five to one hundred miles, and often more. The weight to be carried by each was fixed at ten pounds or under, and the charge for transportation was $5 in

485 Alexander Majors, *Seventy years on the frontier*, 182.

gold for each half of an ounce. . . The horses were mostly half-breed California mustangs. . . Only two minutes were allowed at stations for changing mails and horses." [486]

Within two months after the plan was decided upon, everything was in readiness for the initial express. Weekly trips on a ten day schedule were provided.[487] "Pony Express – nine days from San Francisco to New York," ran the advertisement in the *San Francisco Bulletin* [march 17, 1860], "For Telegraphic Dispatches, 9 days; for Letters, 13 days." And St. Louis writers marveled at this "new enterprise in this fast age." [488]

On april 3, 1860, all was in readiness for simultaneous starts from the two ends of the line. In San Francisco a clean-limbed pony stood waiting for his precious letter packets. Two little flags adorned his head-stall and from the pommel of his saddle hung a bag, lettered Overland Pony Express.[489] This animal had but a short run to the boat which would carry the express to Sacramento. Here began the real Pony Express. Harry Roff, on a spirited half-breed broncho, started eastward from the California capital, covering the first twenty miles, including one change of mounts, in fifty-nine minutes.

At the eastern terminus, St. Joseph, Missouri, a large crowd gathered to witness the start. The Hannibal and St. Joseph train bringing the New York mail was late, and it was not until darkness was settling down that the roar of a cannon from the express office announced the arrival of the train with the letters, and with it the

---

[486] *Ibid.,* 173-175.

[487] Accounts of the pony express are given in Arthur Chapman, *The pony express* (1932); G. D. Bradley, *The story of the pony express* (1913); and W. L. Visscher, *A thrilling and truthful history of the pony express,* (1908).

[488] Hafen, *Overland mail,* 169-170.

[489] *San Francisco Bulletin,* april 3, 1860.

inauguration of the Pony Express. Lots had been cast among the riders and the first stretch was drawn by Billy Richardson, a young sailor.[490] He leaped into the saddle on the bright bay mare and dashed away to the ferry. From the west bank of the Big Muddy he careered into the darkness.

Along the emigrant trail, thudding the sand hills, splashing the creeks, lunging through dangerous gullies, dodging the Indians, the relay of riders flew westward. Up the Platte, past Court House Rock and Chimney Rock to Fort Laramie station. Here from a pocket of the *mochila* [saddlebag] local letters were taken for the soldiers, and new letters were picked up for points farther west. Six hundred miles covered in three days! It must have taken about ten riders and twenty horses to do that stretch of the two thousand miles toward the Golden Gate.

Arrangements had been so well planned that the first express was carried through on schedule time. Receptions of the ponies along the route and at the ends of the line were enthusiastic. News of the approach of the westbound express having been telegraphed ahead from Genoa, Nevada, J Street, Sacramento, was lined its entire length for hours before the fleet messenger arrived.[491]

The reception in San Francisco is graphically described in the *Bulletin* of april 14.

"It took seventy-five ponies to make the trip from Missouri to California in 10½ days, but the last one — the little fellow who came down in the Sacramento boat this morning had the vicarious glory of them all. Upon him an enthusiastic crowd were disposed to shower all

---

490 Hauck, The pony express celebration, in *Missouri historical review*, XVII, 437.

491 Letter from Sacramento, in the *San Francisco Bulletin*, april 16, 1860.

their compliments. He was the veritable Hippagriff who shoved a continent behind his hoofs so easily; who snuffed up sandy plains, sent lakes and mountains, prairies and forests, whizzing behind him, like one great river rushing eastward. . .

"The boat waited for the Pony Express at Sacramento until 5 o'clock, yesterday afternoon. The instant it arrived it came on board, and the *Antelope* put on all steam to accomplish an early trip. Meanwhile at the theatres it had been announced that on the landing of the boat there would be ceremonies of reception, music, jollification and some speeches. . . The California band traveled up and down the streets waking all the echoes, fetching out the boys, and making the night melodious. Bonfires were kindled here and there on the plaza and on the wharves. . . The organized turn-out reached the foot of Broadway at midnight. With waltzes and Yankee Doodle, the airs of all the nations and several improvised black-oak dances, the spirits were maintained until near one o'clock when the *Antelope* came steaming down, wheeled, threw out her hawsers, was made fast and the glorified pony walked ashore.

"The crowd cheered till their throats were sore; the band played as if they would crack their cheeks . . . the boys stirred up their bonfires and the speech makers studied their points. The procession reformed, opened right and left, and the pony, a bright bay . . . paced gaily up to his stand. The line closed again, the band went ahead, the firemen followed with their machines, the center of attraction, the Hippagriff, came next, and citizens fell in behind. There was one lady on the ground. As the pony trotted into line, she tore the ribbons from her bonnet and tied them around his neck.

All moved up to the Pony Express office. While the twenty-five letters that were brought were being distributed, the speech-makers were proceeding to uncork the bottles of their eloquence. Their friends said 'hear hear,' but the boys would leave it to the pony. He considered a moment, eyed the ribbon around his neck, looked a bit sleepy, thought of his oats, and uttered a loud neigh. So the speeches were corked down again, the speech-makers tied comforters around their throats, the dashaways cheered hoarsely, the rag-tag-and-bobtail took something warm, the morning papers went to press, the crowd to bed and the pony to his stable. . . Long live the pony!"

As winter approached, the experiment was watched with great interest. Not only was the Pony Express being tested, but the Central route itself was on trial, the question being determined whether the first daily overland mail and the railroad could use this most direct route to the Pacific coast. Although the crossing of the Rockies and the Sierras during the winter entailed an extension of the time schedule, the mail went through. Only one trip was missed, and the average time between the telegraph termini for twenty-two midwinter trips was 13.8 days.[492]

The demonstration succeeded. On march 2, 1861, congress passed an act providing for a daily mail and a semi-weekly Pony Express on the Central route, the compensation for the joint undertakings to be $1,000,000 per annum.[493] When this measure went into effect on july 1, 1861, the Pony Express rate was reduced to one dollar per half ounce letter. And on that basis it con-

---

[492] Data gathered from the California papers are tabulated in Hafen, *Overland mail*, 186.

[493] *U.S. statutes at large*, XII, 206.

tinued until the Express was displaced by the first overland telegraph, completed october 24, 1861.[494]

In the days before the coming of the railroad, the
Pony Express was the acme of speed in overland travel.
About this spectacular institution has gathered a halo
of romance that grows in glamour with the passing
years. Over the same trail, in the dust of the speeding
pony, crept the humble handcart – homeseekers trudg-
ing the weary road to a new land of promise.

From her vantage point beside the overland trail,
Fort Laramie saw these strange carriers come and go –
the patrician and the plebian of early western travel,
yet each a vital agency in the conquest of the West.

[494] *San Francisco Bulletin,* october 25, 1861.

The Cheyenne and the Utah Expeditions

After the departure of the last troops of the Harney expedition in the spring of 1856, there remained four companies stationed at Fort Laramie. The monthly post returns sent to the war department record the number of men as varying from 261 to 267 for the months from july to december, 1856. Through the succeeding winter the number gradually declined until it reached 244 in may, 1857.[495]

In the meantime the war department had decided to abandon Fort Laramie. Apprised of this intention, Major Hoffman, in a letter of april 20, 1857, had suggested that a small guard be retained to protect the public property in case the post should be needed again. Assistant-quartermaster J. P. Higgins, in his annual buildings report of june 30, 1857, said, "As the post, according to orders recently received, is to be abandoned very soon, no additional buildings are required." [496] But already an order had been issued, may 29, 1857, as follows: "Ft. Laramie, Nebraska terr., heretofore directed to be abandoned, will be kept up as a military post until further orders."

Instead of abandonment, the fort was to become more important than ever before. It was to be a supply depot for the Sumner Indian campaign that was already under way and was to hold a key position in the operations about to be undertaken against Utah.

---

[495] Monthly post returns from Fort Laramie, in old files of Adjutant-general's office, Washington, D.C.

[496] Fort Laramie records at Fort Meyer, Virginia.

Before we recount the story of these expeditions, it may be well to take a closer view of our fort at this period. The old adobe structure bought by the government in 1849, and which was in bad repair when purchased, had been gradually replaced by other buildings and one part after another had been abandoned and torn down.

The report of the inspector of public buildings, june 30, 1856, gives an inventory and description of structures at Fort Laramie:

"BARRACKS AND QUARTERS

"1   One two-story building containing four sets of captain's quarters, two rooms and a kitchen to each set of quarters. The kitchen in second story not fit for the purpose. The piazzas yet remain unfinished. The roof is much injured by wind and leaks – a new roof is necessary.

"2   One two-story building built for two companies – now used by G and D, Sixth infantry, is yet unfinished, never having been plastered and only partly lathed. The roof is bad – should be renewed. In consequence the occupants suffer from cold in winter.

"3   An adobe building with mud roof – two rooms and a kitchen – occupied by the chaplain. In such a ruinous condition it cannot be repaired.

"4   The quarters of company B Sixth infantry, part of an old stable, is in such a dilapidated condition, that it has been found necessary to abandon it as quarters. It cannot be repaired. Its mate built same time and of same character has already fallen down.

"5   The building used as a hospital which was part of the old fort purchased from the American Fur company became untenable, and has been torn down. There is now no hospital at the post. The sick are in tents.

"ADDITIONS

"During the past year seven adobe buildings have been erected.

"6   One building, mud roof – four ground rooms, 16 feet square, for officers quarters. Two of these rooms have board kitchen adjoining, very temporary – without floors, and canvas roofing.

"7   Three buildings – mud roofs, two rooms each, 15 feet square used as temporary officers quarters.

"8   Two buildings – two rooms each 36 x 21 feet. One occupied by company c, Sixth infantry. The other is used by g and d companies as mess rooms and kitchen. Mud roofs and without floors.

"9   Two very temporary stables with earth roofs, for the two mounted companies at the post. One is now used for the public animals of the quartermaster's department. The other as a commissary storeroom.

"10   An addition to the bake house.

"11   Two temporary corn houses slated and covered with paulins, 120x26 feet, are under construction.

"The adobe buildings above enumerated, have been so located as to make them available and useful for various purposes, when permanent buildings are erected.

"It is proposed to put floors in the two large buildings when convenient.

"Store Houses

"The property of the quartermasters' department is stored in an old slab building, mud roofed, and nearly gone to decay. This property is constantly liable to damage both from rain and the falling of the building. Three store tents are also in use.

"The commissary supplies are stored – in part – in an old dilapidated slab building, mud roofed, put up some years since as a stable – and partly in one of the temporary stables put up last year. Both these buildings afford very inadequate protection to the stores they contain.

"An old stable used as a commissary storehouse and for animals of the quartermaster's department fell down recently and has been removed.

"Additional buildings required are: quarters for one field officer, two sets of captain's quarters, nine sets of subaltern's quarters, three sets of company quarters, hospital, quartermaster and commissary store houses.

"Plans and estimates for these buildings were forwarded last year.
    J. C. Kelton, *Assistant-quartermaster 6th Infantry*" [497]

Colonel Hoffman, commander of the fort, writing from the post on august 19, 1856, gives additional information: "From the experiments I have made here I am satisfied that the adobe is the best, and much the

---

[497] Report found among Fort Laramie papers stored at Fort Myer, Virginia, in june, 1936.

cheapest material that can be used for building in this country.

"Last summer I commenced building in august with only three rough masons and not a man who had ever made an adobe, and by november seven adobe buildings were up and occupied. Any handy man can be taught to make and to lay adobes in a wall in a very little while.

"I have a steam saw mill running – 35 miles from the post – which will furnish an abundance of lumber for nearly all purposes. It warps very much and is therefore unfit for doors and therefore these and window sashes and window blinds will have to be sent out from St. Louis.

"With the engineer we now have to take charge of the sawmill; a master builder to superintend carpenters and masons, and 14 carpenters and 10 brick and stone masons, and 3 plasterers – enlisted men – I am sure all the quarters and store houses required at this post to accommodate four companies can be erected and made inhabitable during next year, at a very little greater expense than the extra pay of the soldiers employed on the work. During the coming winter all the lumber required can be got out. There is one mason and one carpenter in the command and other handy men who assist them. It is imperative that the enlisted mechanics required be sent out this fall.

"Having been obliged to tear down part of the old adobe fort, which was used as a hospital, I am now putting up an adobe building to be used as a hospital this winter – which will hereafter form a back building – comprising kitchen, store room and ward or mess room for the permanent hospital." [498]

---

[498] Records in old files, war department.

As noted in a previous chapter, the Sioux difficulties were quieted by Harney's campaign and his peace treaty signed in march, 1856. The Cheyennes, who were not concerned in the Sioux difficulties, were soon involved in troubles of their own with the whites.

In april, 1856, a small party of Cheyennes came to the upper Platte bridge [near present Casper, Wyoming] to trade. The commander of the troops stationed there demanded of the Indians the return of four horses, stolen or estray, that were in the Indian band but which belonged to whites. Three of the horses were brought in, but about the fourth there were conflicting statements and misunderstanding. Thereupon the commandant took three of the Indians prisoners. While attempting to put them in irons, two tried to escape. One of these succeeded in freeing himself, the other was shot down. The rest of the band fled into the Black Hills. During the succeeding night they met and killed Ganier, an old trapper. The third Indian prisoner was brought to Fort Laramie and was confined there in irons, Indian agent Twiss trying in vain to secure his release.[499]

The Cheyennes in the Fort Laramie region, hearing of the upper Platte bridge affair, retreated to the Arkansas river and joined their tribesmen there.

In the following august a Cheyenne war party, said to have been sent against their enemies the Pawnees,

---

[499] Agent Twiss's report in commissioner of Indian Affairs annual report of 1856, 87. *House ex. docs.,* cong. 34, sess. 3, no. 1, vol. I, part 1, p. 638. The Cheyenne prisoner was held at Fort Laramie until april 16, 1857, when he died of the effects of his confinement. See Colonel Hoffman's report of april 17, 1857, in the old files of the Adjutant-general's office, Washington, D.C. The *New York Tribune* of may 21, 1857, also reports the prisoner's death and says that the Indians' demand for the prisoner's body was refused by the fort commandant. Thereupon the Cheyennes were reported to be ready to meet the whites in battle.

was in the vicinity of Fort Kearny. Two young Indians approached a mail wagon to beg tobacco. The driver mistook their intentions and fired at them; whereupon one of the Indians shot an arrow and wounded the driver. The wounded man reported the affair at Fort Kearny. Next morning troops from the fort attacked the Cheyenne band and killed six of the warriors. The fleeing Indians crossed the Platte and attacked an emigrant train, killing two men and a child and taking a woman captive, whom they afterwards killed. With the hostile spirit aroused other war parties left the main Cheyenne camp to raid the emigrant road. One party attacked a small white camp, killed one woman and took a child captive. Another party attacked and killed Hon. A. W. Babbitt, secretary of Utah territory, and his two companions who were encamped near o'Fallon's Bluffs on the Platte, and on the following night attacked another party and killed two men, one woman and a child and took a woman captive.[500]

The *Council Bluffs Bugle,* quoted in *The Mormon* (New York) of november 15, 1856, gives some details about the death of secretary Babbitt. It appears that after he had fired his double-barrelled shot gun and his two revolvers, one of the Indians crept behind the wagon and tomahawked him. The Indians reported that he "fought like a grizzly bear." This paper states that about 18 whites had been killed by the Cheyennes in the recent raids. The frontier attitude was expressed by this newspaper thus: "His [Babbitt's] loss is irreparable, and the government should send at once a

---

[500] *House ex. docs., op. cit.,* 650-51. Letter of Major-brevet-lieutenant-colonel W. Hoffman, commander of Fort Laramie, september 26, 1856, in the old files of the Adjutant-general's office, Washington, D.C. See also A. W. Hoopes, "Thomas S. Twiss, Indian agent on the upper Platte, 1855-1861," in *Mississippi valley historical review,* XX, 361, for a list of the Indian outrages.

sufficient force to punish, yes to exterminate this tribe who for the last three months have been murdering and plundering her emigrants."

Wrote Major Hoffman at Fort Laramie on september 27, 1856: "Anticipating that a campaign will be made against the Cheyenne Indians, I have caused a map of their country to be prepared. . . They are well armed and well mounted and have the reputation of being enterprising and warlike." [501]

Colonel Hoffman and agent Twiss, who had carried on a sharp controversy at Fort Laramie in regard to Sioux affairs, continued their disagreement in reference to the Cheyennes. Hoffman did not want annuities given to the Indians nor permission given them to camp within 75 or 100 miles of the fort. [502]

Agent Twiss held several councils with the Cheyennes in the fall of 1856. In the third of these, on october 16, 1856, he met 42 chiefs and headmen and arranged a general cessation of hostilities. [503]

But the military had in mind another method of procedure and wholly ignored the Indian agent's arrangements.

As early as june 7, 1856, Captain H. W. Wharton had written: "The Cheyennes have been pursuing this same outrageous course for some years past, but this time, in open and daring violation of the treaty just made by them it calls most loudly for punishment." [504] Major-general P. F. Smith wrote from Fort Leavenworth on september 10, 1856: "This tribe must be severely punished . . . but no trifling or partial punishment will suffice, and as no one can be spared from this neighbor-

---

[501] Letter in old files Adjutant-general's office, A.G.O., 10/A.B.

[502] *Ibid.* Hoffman's letters of august 8 and september 27, 1856.

[503] Hoopes, *op. cit.*, 362.

[504] *Ibid.*, 361.

hood I will postpone extensive operations until the spring." [505]

The punitive expedition against the Cheyennes was organized in the spring of 1857, with Colonel Edwin Vose Sumner in command. He was familiarly called "the old Bull o' the Woods." One of the soldiers speaks of the colonel as "the ideal veteran commander," "idolized by his men." "Although then (in 1857) well advanced in years, with hair and beard white as snow, he was still quite vigorous, every inch a soldier, straight as an arrow, and could ride like a Cheyenne." [506]

The plan of campaign provided for a movement in two divisions, one up the Arkansas and the other up the Platte. Accordingly, on may 18, Major John Sedgwick set out from Fort Leavenworth with four companies of cavalry, with Fall Leaf and some other Delawares as scouts and hunters. They made their way up the Arkansas to the vicinity of present Pueblo, Colorado, and then turned north to the South Platte river, without encountering the Cheyennes.[507] Colonel Sumner left Fort Leavenworth may 20 with two companies of cavalry, took up two companies of the Second Dragoons at Fort Kearny and continued his march up the Platte to Fort Laramie.[508]

While the two columns made their respective ways up the Arkansas and the Platte, the Cheyennes slipped into the 200-mile strip between these rivers. From the vicinity of Fort Riley and from points in the rear of the Sumner troops came stories of Indian outrages. Most

---

[505] Quoted in J. P. Dunn, *Massacres of the mountains,* 239.

[506] R. M. Peck, "Recollections of early times in Kansas territory," in *Transactions of the Kansas state historical society,* VIII, 485.

[507] A good account of this expedition, especially the Sedgwick division, is given by R. M. Peck in the article cited above, 486-500.

[508] Report of Colonel Sumner in *House ex. docs.,* cong. 35, sess. 1, no. 2, p. 98.

of these stories, that appeared in the frontier newspapers, were pure fabrications. One of these had it that Sumner had encountered the Cheyennes at Ash Hollow just as they were attacking an emigrant train. Sumner had lost 150 men but had defeated the enemy. The Indians had been urged on by the Mormons.[509] Other stories with as little foundation, but generally less sensational, went the rounds of the frontier press.

Leaving behind the two Dragoon companies, in conformity with orders received, and adding three companies of the 6th infantry from Fort Laramie, Colonel Sumner set out from the fort on june 27 to form a juncture with Sedgwick's command, as per previous arrangement, and then to seek out the Cheyennes.[510] The two commands joined forces on the South Platte, near the mouth of Crow creek, on july 5.

Hearing that the Cheyennes were assembled in force in the Republican river country and were planning resistance, Colonel Sumner decided to leave his wagon train, tents and all encumbrances behind, and strike for the hostile villages. He sent the wagons back to Fort Laramie with orders to meet him in twenty days at the lower crossing of the South Platte. Putting the most urgently needed supplies on pack mules, and driving his beef on the hoof, he struck across country southward in search of the enemy.

On july 29, while following the Cheyenne trail down the Solomon river in western Kansas, Colonel Sumner came suddenly upon about three hundred hostiles drawn

---

[509] The *Kansas Chief,* july 23, 1857. For other stories see the *Kansas Herald,* june 20, 1857; the *Elwood Advertiser,* july 2, 1857; *Herald of Freedom,* july 4, 1857. The *Kansas Chief,* of september 10, 1857, talks of a battle in which Colonel Sumner killed four or five hundred Indians, including men, women and children.

[510] Sumner's report, *op. cit.,* 98.

up in battle array. He immediately ordered a charge by the cavalry.

"The Indians were all mounted and well armed," reports the colonel. "Many of them had rifles and revolvers, and they stood, with remarkable boldness until we charged and were nearly upon them, when they broke in all directions, and we pursued them seven miles. Their horses were fresh and very fleet, and it was impossible to overtake many of them. There were but nine men killed in the pursuit, but there must have been a great number wounded. I had two men killed, and Lieutenant J. E. B. Stuart, and eight men wounded; but it is believed they will all recover. . . I have the pleasure to report, what will give the lieutenant-general commanding the army the highest satisfaction, that in these operations not a woman nor a child has been hurt." [511] This last, an apparent fling at General Harney's engagement of 1855.

An explanation of the Indian conduct in this engagement is given by Robert C. Miller, Indian agent of the upper Arkansas agency. It appears that the Cheyennes had taken their position beside a little lake "in which they had but to dip their hands, when the victory over the troops would be an easy one – so their medicine man told them – and that they had but to hold up their hands and the balls would roll from the muzzles of the soldiers' guns harmless to their feet. Acting under this delusion, when Colonel Sumner came upon them with his command, he found them drawn up in regular line of battle, well mounted, and moving forward to the music of their war song with as firm a tread as well disciplined troops, expecting no doubt to receive the harmless fire of the soldiers and achieve an easy victory.

[511] *Ibid.*, 96. An official account of the engagement appeared in the *Herald of Freedom*, october 10, 1857.

But the charm was broken when the command was given by Colonel Sumner to charge with sabres, for they broke and fled in the wildest confusion, being completely routed." [512]

On the second day after the fight Colonel Sumner came upon the principal Cheyenne village, with 171 lodges standing and evidence that about as many more had been hastily removed. He destroyed the lodges and a large amount of supplies, including 15,000 to 20,000 pounds of buffalo meat which the Indians had left in their headlong retreat.[513]

Sumner followed the Indians to the Arkansas but found that they had scattered beyond his reach. Having learned by the Santa Fe mail that the Indian agent had gone up to Bent's Fort with the annuities for the Cheyennes, the colonel decided to turn west with the pick of his cavalry for that point. He hoped for another engagement with the Cheyennes, but failing in that, he would at least prevent distribution of presents and supplies to the hostiles.

At Bent's Fort on august 19, he took over the annuities which agent Miller had stored in Bent's new Fort, threw the powder, lead and flints into the river and directed the giving of most of the supplies to friendly Indians. The next day he began his march back to the Missouri, taking agent Miller with him.[514] Thus ended the Sumner campaign against the Cheyennes. It had chastised a few Indians, embittered many more and overawed none. Both Sumner and Miller expected that further punishment would be necessary. But a larger military movement, the Utah Expedition, was already

[512] Report of agent Miller, in *Report of the commissioner of Indian Affairs* (1857), p. 147.

[513] *Ibid.,* 147, and Sumner's report, *op. cit.,* 98.

[514] Miller's report, 146; Sumner's report, 98.

under way and was to absorb most of the troops of the Cheyenne expedition.

The causes that brought about the Utah Expedition are largely beyond the scope of our story. Suffice it to say that the reports sent by Judge W. W. Drummond of the federal court in Utah, former mail contractor W. M. F. Magraw, and Indian agent Thomas S. Twiss were the chief documents upon which was based the decision to send an army to Utah. According to the information from these sources, the Mormons were in rebellion against the United States government. These reports, colored though they were by personal bias, led the Buchanan administration to authorize a military expedition to accompany newly-appointed territorial officers to Utah.[515] As matters developed, the expedition turned out to be largely a fiasco, but at its inception it was enthusiastically acclaimed and supported by the press of the country.

General Winfield Scott, commanding-general of the army, issued an order on may 28, 1857, for the assembling and organization of twenty-five hundred troops at Fort Leavenworth to march to Utah.[516] Brigadier-general W. S. Harney was at first placed in command, receiving his instructions on june 29.[517]

The first detachment of troops, comprising eight companies of the Tenth infantry, and the entire Fifth infantry, left Fort Leavenworth july 18, under command of Colonel E. B. Alexander. These were soon followed

---

[515] For a study of the causes that brought about the Utah Expedition see L. H. Creer, *Utah and the nation*, chapter VII, and the references therein cited. See also E. W. Tullidge, *History of Salt Lake City*, and W. A. Linn, *The story of the Mormons*. President Buchanan, in his first annual message to congress, december, 1857, explained his purpose in sending the expedition. See J. D. Richardson, *Messages and papers of the presidents*, V, 454-55.

[516] *House ex. docs.*, cong. 35, sess. 1, no. 71, pp. 4-5.

[517] *Ibid.*, 7-9.

by other detachments, the remaining companies of the Tenth infantry being led by Colonel C. F. Smith.[518]

Great activity was shown in procuring the necessary supplies, forwarding them to Fort Leavenworth, and starting them across the plains. The assistant-quarter-master-general at Fort Leavenworth, on july 5, reported on hand for the Utah Expedition, 413 six-mule wagons and harness, 18 six-mule ambulances, 1870 mules, and other equipment.[519] In advance went "two thousand head of beef cattle, together with a huge and unwieldy convoy." [520]

The Cheyennes saw a chance now to retaliate for Sumner's campaign against them. They stampeded a drove of some 800 cattle, about 20 miles west of Fort Kearny, killing one driver and wounding another.[521] Later they attacked one of the supply trains a little west of the South Platte crossing and killed three of the men.[522] But difficulties encountered by troops and supply trains east of Fort Laramie were insignificant as compared with what they were to experience west of that post.

Colonel Alexander and his command reached Fort Laramie on september 1. Jesse A. Gove, captain of I company, Tenth infantry, writes from the fort on september 2: "We arrived here yesterday about 11 A.M. Encamped near the post. It is a very pretty site and the houses are quite elegant. Col. Hoffman, in command, called yesterday on all the ladies and gentlemen in garrison. Invited to dine today at 1 P.M. with Col. Hoff-

---

[518] Creer, *op. cit.*, 130.

[519] *Publications of the Nebraska historical society*, XX, 290, quoting the *Missouri Republican* of july 20, 1857.

[520] H. H. Bancroft, *History of Utah*, 498.

[521] *Kansas Free State*, august 22, 1857. Also, *Publications of the Nebraska state historical society*, XX, 291.

[522] *Leavenworth Journal*, october 27, 1857.

man. Shall go. Mrs. H. is a high headed piece of furniture, fully corroborating what I have heard of her before. The Colonel is a very agreeable man." [523]

At this point important unofficial news reached the advance troops. Captain Gove, in the above-quoted letter, reports: "Col. Johnston of the cavalry is ordered to take command of the expedition. Good! the old woman [Colonel Alexander] feels it sensibly. He grows more worthless every day he lives." There was foundation for the report, for the war department had some weeks before decided to keep General Harney in Kansas and had recalled Colonel Johnston from Texas to assume new duties. But it was not until august 29 that he was assigned to the command of the Utah Expedition.[524] Colonel Johnston repaired immediately to Fort Leavenworth and shortly afterward set out for the farther west, reaching Fort Laramie on october 4.

Six companies of the Second Dragoons, under the command of Colonel P. St. George Cooke, commander of the Mormon Battalion in the Mexican War, left Fort Leavenworth on september 16. Accompanying Cooke and escorted by his cavalry, went the newly appointed Utah executive, Governor Alfred Cumming, and other recently chosen officials for the territory. They reached Fort Laramie about october 20.[525]

Before the military expedition left Fort Leavenworth orders had been issued placing forts Kearny and Laramie under the command of the leader of the Utah Expedition. Upon reaching the latter post on october 4,

---

[523] O. G. Hammond (ed.), *The Utah expedition, 1857-1858. Letters of Captain Jesse A. Gove*, etc., 50.

[524] R. P. Bieber (ed.), *Frontier life in the army, 1854-1861*, p. 47, citing original orders in the war department archives.

[525] Creer, *op. cit.*, 138.

Colonel Johnston assumed direction. He retained Lieutenant-colonel Hoffman in command of the post.[526]

Let us turn now to examine developments in another quarter. The first Mormons to learn of the contemplated military expedition to their region were Feramorz Little and Ephraim Hanks, who arrived at Independence, Missouri, in late february, 1857, with Utah mail. A. O. Smoot, mayor of Salt Lake City, while in the east as an agent of the Brigham Young Express and Carrying company, learned of developments. Being refused the mail at Independence, he decided to break up the stations along the route and take the outfits back to Utah. Upon arriving at Fort Laramie he met Orin P. Rockwell and Judson Stoddard. The three decided to hurry with the news to the Mormon capital. Taking four good horses and a light wagon, they covered the 513 miles, reaching Salt Lake City on the evening of july 23.[527] Brigham Young was not in the city, having gone with a large number of the citizens to Big Cottonwood canyon to celebrate Pioneer day, the tenth anniversary of the arrival of the Saints in the Salt Lake valley.

The news of the approach of an army caused great consternation among the Mormons. Having previously suffered much persecution, they believed that a recurrence of such conditions was to be experienced. They recalled the fact that Joseph Smith, founder of their sect, had been murdered by a mob while he was presumably under the protection of the civil authorities. They had been peaceful and industrious in their newly-

[526] Special order no. 32, of october 5, 1857, in Fort Laramie papers, war department old files.

[527] Creer, *op. cit.*, 131.

made mountain home. Now, they thought, jealous and malicious enemies had won the ear of the government and were coming out to destroy them. The popular uproar against them, as reflected in the press of the country, gave credence to their fears.

Looking upon the expedition as a military invasion that was without justification, the Mormon leaders decided to defy the government and defend their homes. They planned for a vigorous defense, making preparations with religious fervor. "We have transgressed no law," proclaimed Brigham Young, head of the Mormon church, "neither do we intend to do so; but as far as any nation coming to destroy this people, God being my helper, it shall not be." [528] The far-flung colonies of Saints in San Bernardino, California, and Carson valley, present Nevada, were recalled for the defense of Zion. Firearms were manufactured and repaired, scythes converted into bayonets, troops enlisted and drilled.

Captain Stewart Van Vliet of the commissary department hurried to Utah ahead of the United States troops to make arrangements for the purchase of forage and supplies. Upon arrival at Salt Lake City on september 8, he was astonished at the attitude he encountered. "The governor," writes the captain, "informed me that there was an abundance of everything I required for the troops, such as lumber, forage, etc., but that none would be sold to us. . . In the course of my conversation with him and the influential men of the territory, I told them plainly and frankly what I conceived would be the result of their present course; I told them that they might prevent the small military force now approaching Utah from getting through the narrow defiles

---

[528] *Deseret News*, september 23, 1857.

and rugged passes of the mountains this year, but that next season the United States government would send troops sufficient to overcome all opposition. The answer to this was invariably the same. 'We are aware that such will be the case; but when these troops arrive they will find Utah a desert; every house will be burned to the ground; every tree cut down, and every field laid waste. We have three years' provisions on hand which we will 'cache' and then take to the mountains, and bid defiance to all the powers of the government'. . ." [529]

On the day following the departure of Captain Van Vliet, Brigham Young, who had been governor of Utah since the creation of the territory in 1850, declared martial law in Utah and forbade any military forces to enter the territory.[530]

Lieutenant-general Daniel H. Wells, commander of the Mormon forces, established headquarters at the mouth of Echo canyon. This narrow twenty-mile defile with its high perpendicular walls was especially adapted to effective defense, and through it lay the only direct route from Fort Bridger to Salt Lake City.

General Wells sent a small detachment to reconnoiter the position and condition of the United States troops and then dispatched Major Lot Smith to destroy supply trains. This wily leader succeeded in burning 74 wagons laden with supplies and driving off nearly 1,000 head of cattle. Among the supplies destroyed by Smith were 12,700 pounds of bacon, 167,000 pounds of flour, 1,400 pounds of sugar, 13,333 pounds of soap and 134 bushels of dried peaches.[531]

---

[529] Report of Captain Van Vliet, september 16, 1857, in *House ex. docs.*, cong. 35, sess. 1, no. 2, vol. XI, part 2, p. 24.

[530] A photostatic copy of this proclamation of september 15, is reproduced in O. G. Hammond, *op. cit.*, opposite p. 60.

[531] Report of commissary department, in *House ex. docs.*, cong. 35, sess. 1, no. 71, p. 63.

Let us return now to the United States troops and note the progress being made by the expedition. Colonel Alexander, in command of the advance forces, left Fort Laramie on september 5 [532] and made his way up the Platte and the Sweetwater and over South Pass. As he advanced, the grass became scarcer, the animals weaker. He crossed Green river on september 27 and during the succeeding night made a forced march of twenty-two miles to Ham's Fork to protect the advance supply train that had reached that point.[533] Here he established Camp Winfield.

Having received a copy of Young's martial law proclamation and having been apprised by Captain Van Vliet of the attitude and purpose of the Mormons, he decided to await directions from the commanding officer. In early october the Mormons began to destroy supply trains in his rear. Finally, urged on by his officers, Alexander decided to assume responsibility and continue the march.[534] Instead of taking the direct route by way of Fort Bridger and Echo canyon, he decided to take the round-about one by Soda Springs, present Idaho. Wrote Captain Gove on october 8: "The order is out for a movement tomorrow. The battery, first followed by its train; next the 10th inf. followed by its train; then the immense trains of supplies concentrated here of Russell's & Wharton, ox trains; then follows Reno's siege train; then the 5th inf. The whole command when straightened out will reach 7 or 8 miles." [535]

As the train moved slowly up Ham's Fork it was harassed by the Mormon raiding parties, who burned

---

[532] Hammond, *op. cit.*, 51.

[533] *Ibid.*, 66.

[534] Colonel Alexander's letter of october 8, in *House ex. docs.*, 71, *op. cit.*, 39-40.

[535] Hammond, *op. cit.*, 72.

the grass and drove off numbers of the animals. The infantry and ox-trains, with no cavalry, were almost helpless. The vacillating colonel, uncertain for days what course to pursue, finally stopped the train and ordered it to turn about. On october 21, Captain Gove wrote: "Our march has been directly back over the same road we went up the Fork. When we passed over the road before most of the officers then thought that Col. A. had at last taken a step towards doing something for himself and the service. But, alas, the weakness of old women! It has been a severe trial for us all that we are humiliated into the position that we have an officer in the army, yes, at the head, by accident, of this gallant little army, and still more in a personal point of view, a colonel of the 10th inf. who is no more qualified for his position than a child ten years old, who changes his mind as often as the wind blows; who does not know what to do or how to do; whose intellect is blunted; who issues orders to do one thing and the next breath do the contrary; whose whole care is a grass plot for his tent and a feeding spot for his own animals; whose conduct is that of an insane man; who has marched up and down this valley to his eternal disgrace and injury to an immense amount of public property, such as loss of mules, wagons, cattle, etc." [536]

When Colonel Johnston reached the advance troops on november 3, confidence in the leadership of the army was restored and the morale of the men immeasurably improved. He gave orders to proceed on the direct route to Salt Lake City, heading first for Fort Bridger.

Then on november 6 it commenced to snow. The next day the temperature fell below zero and the thin animals began to die like flies. Captain Gove recorded on

[536] *Ibid.,* 82.

the 9th: "Made about 7 miles, animals lying along the road every rod, almost, and daily and hourly dying as they are driven along the road. Snow about 7 inches deep. Fort Bridger is our hope. If we once get there we shall be safe with our stores. Hundreds of animals die every twenty-four hours . . . had Gen. Harney been at Green river when he should have been we would have saved all this, and been in Salt Lake City. When he was absent and Alexander, the 'old woman,' found himself in one of the prettiest positions an officer could desire, assumed command, did nothing, made an ass of himself, was crazy, fooled away the entire month of beautiful october marching up Harris Fork and down again, when had he done his duty, or done as he was advised by those who would and who could sustain him, we should have been in or before the walls of the Saint's city. Either would have been successful. Now our struggle is with the season and the elements that belong to it." [537]

The cold and the accompanying difficulties continued. The cattle died so rapidly that only one train at a time could be moved. Two weeks were consumed in making the thirty-five miles to Fort Bridger. Before reaching this point the expedition had lost nearly 600 mules, about half of the battery horses, two-thirds of the cavalry mounts, nine-tenths of the casualties having occurred within the last month.[538] And by this time all hope of reaching Salt Lake City the current season had been blasted. Fort Bridger and Fort Supply, farther up the river, had been destroyed by the Mormons before the troops reached them.[539] General Johnston was there-

[537] *Ibid.*, 92.

[538] Bieber, *op. cit.*, 48.

[539] A good account of these destructions are given in the journal of J. W.

fore compelled to build winter quarters for his men, which he did by establishing Camp Scott about two miles above the site of the burned Fort Bridger.

Hardships did not end when the marching ceased. Inadequate shelter and a shortage of flour, bacon, salt and other essentials made the winter an ordeal. And while soldiers went hungry at Camp Scott, quantities of supplies intended for them were in storage at Fort Laramie. L. P. Higgins, acting assistant quartermaster, reported on december 26, 1857, that the following supplies destined for the Utah Expedition were at Fort Laramie: 293,854 pounds of flour, 46,265 pounds of bacon, 20,130 pounds of coffee, 38,947 pounds of sugar, 25,296 pounds of beans, 20 half barrels of molasses, 13,974 pounds of rice, etc. Ammunition and numerous field and mountain howitzers were also at the fort. But, wrote the commander of the post, "We have not a team of mules at the post that I think would stand the journey from this place to Fort Bridger and haul one of these guns. We have some six or seven teams that we haul wood with, but they are very poor. No mules can be purchased at this place at any price." [540]

The troops and supply trains at Camp Scott were in such a plight that reenforcements and quantities of supplies were imperatively needed before any forward advance could be made in the spring. On november 24 Colonel Johnston dispatched Captain R. B. Marcy through the mountains to New Mexico for horses and mules.[541] He instructed the commanding officer at Fort

---

Crosby, who was a member of the party that burned the posts. His journal is in the Mormon church archives, Salt Lake City.

[540] Reports from Fort Laramie, dated december 24 and 26, 1857, in *Sen. docs.*, cong. 35, sess. 2, no. 1, pp. 49-50.

[541] For a graphic account of the mid-winter march across the Rockies, see R. B. Marcy, *Thirty years of army life on the border*, 224-63.

Laramie to escort the supply train at that post to the
headquarters of the army of Utah "as soon in the spring
as practicable." [542]

In delivering his first annual message to congress in
december, 1857, President Buchanan said: "This is the
first rebellion which has existed in our territories, and
humanity itself requires that we should put it down in
such a manner that it shall be the last." [543] He recommended the raising of four additional regiments.
Congress responded by authorizing the raising of 3,000
troops. It was estimated that 4,500 wagons, 50,000 oxen,
4,000 mules and the employment of 2,000 teamsters
would be required for this reenforcing expedition, at
a total expense of about $5,000,000.[544]

Upon learning that draft animals were not available
at Fort Laramie to move the supplies stored at that post,
Colonel Johnston requested that a mule train be sent
from Fort Leavenworth to assist in this important work.
In response, a train of 200 wagons, to be escorted by
two companies of infantry and two of cavalry, was ordered. Colonel Hoffman, who had been called east to
attend a court martial, was placed in command of the
expedition. He reached Fort Kearny on april 1 and
arrived at Fort Laramie on the 21st. Here he loaded
his train with supplies, added three companies of infantry to his command and set out for Camp Scott on
april 24.[545]

Five days after leaving the fort he encountered a
severe storm. Snow fell to a depth of two feet and the
train was stalled. When about ready to resume travel

[542] Bieber, *op. cit.*, 49, citing original orders.
[543] Richardson, *Messages and papers of the presidents*, v, 456.
[544] L. H. Creer, *Utah and the nation*, 145.
[545] *Sen. ex. docs.*, cong. 35, sess. 2, no. 1, part 2, pp. 177-78.

another storm came. Two weeks were lost.[546] On april 27 Colonel Johnston wrote to Hoffman directing him to send ahead any surplus beef or draft cattle he had and about three weeks later directed the sending of a lightly-loaded train with flour, beans, rice and salt.[547] Men and mules from Camp Scott were sent out to help this express train along and speed its progress. In the meantime rations for the army had been cut and matters were becoming critical.

But the anxiously awaited supplies came in time. Part of the beef cattle arrived may 27 and the other supplies came in early june.[548] Captain Marcy brought in his stock from New Mexico on june 9.[549] Colonel Johnston, his army again provisioned and equipped, began his march for Salt Lake City on june 13.[550]

But in the meantime important events had occurred to change entirely the face of matters. Colonel Thomas L. Kane, on his own responsibility, had assumed the role of mediator. He traveled from New York, by way of Panama, to Los Angeles and thence to Salt Lake City, arriving there on february 25, 1858. After conferring with the Mormon leaders, he set out for Camp Scott, where he arrived on march 12. He convinced Governor Cumming of the wisdom of going on to the Utah capital, assuring him safe conduct if the troops were left behind. On april 5 the governor and Colonel Kane set out for Salt Lake City. Upon arrival, the governor was recognized in his official capacity and was shown every courtesy by the citizens.[551]

546 *Ibid.*, 179.

547 Bieber, *op. cit.*, 52.

548 Hammond, *op. cit.*, 277, 314.

549 Marcy, *op. cit.*, 263.

550 *Sen. ex. docs.*, cong. 35, sess. 2, no. 1, part 2, p. 117.

551 Creer, *op. cit.*, 147-150. See also *The private papers and diary of Thomas Leiper Kane*, ed. O. O. Winther.

But the Mormons were still adamant against entry of the troops. Governor Cumming wrote to secretary of state Cass on may 2, as follows: "The people, including the inhabitants of this city, are removing every settlement in the northern part of the territory. The roads are everywhere filled with wagons loaded with provisions and household furniture, the women and children, often without shoes and hats, driving their flocks, they know not where. They seem not only resigned, but cheerful. . . The masses everywhere announce to me that the torch will be applied to every house, indiscriminately throughout the country, so soon as the troops attempt to cross the mountains. I shall follow these people and attempt to rally them." [552]

While Colonel Kane was making his mid-winter trip to Utah, Dr. John M. Bernhisel, Utah's delegate to congress, had journeyed to Washington. He interviewed President Buchanan and proposed the withdrawal of the troops and the appointment of a commission to settle the difficulties. The president was reported as having rejected the proposal.[553] However, in april following, he appointed senator-elect L. W. Powell of Kentucky and Major Ben McCulloch of Texas as peace commissioners to Utah and entrusted them with a signed proclamation of pardon, dated april 6, 1858.

The peace commissioners reached Salt Lake City on june 7 and soon presented their terms to the Mormon leaders. The authority of the United States must be maintained, the constitution and laws enforced. The army, they promised, would be used not to deprive the people of their rights but only to insure the execution of the laws.

---

552 Cumming's report in *Sen. ex. docs.*, cong. 35, sess. 1, no. 31, pp. 96-7.
553 *New York Herald*, february 5, 1858.

Brigham Young responded with the assertion that his people were law-abiding and ever had been. But they had been persecuted and they feared an armed mob. If the pardon was for the destruction of army supplies, he would accept it. "We are willing," he said, "those troops should come into our country, but not to stay in our city. They may pass through it, if needs be, but must not quarter less than forty miles from us. If you bring your troops here to disturb this people, you have got a bigger job than you or President Buchanan have any idea of. Before the troops reach here, this city will be in ashes. . . Our wives and children will go to the canyons, and take shelter in the mountains; while their husbands and sons will fight you; and as God lives, we will hunt you by night and by day, until your armies are wasted away. No mob can live in the homes we have built in these mountains. That's the program gentlemen, whether you like it or not. If you want war, you can have it; but if you wish peace, peace it is; we shall be glad of it." [554]

Terms were agreed upon. The troops were to enter unresisted, but were to pass on through the city and make their encampment at Cedar valley, 36 miles beyond the city.

In the meantime the people "on the move south," still distrusting the promises of the president's representatives and the proclamation of General Johnston, remained away from their homes. When the soldiers entered Salt Lake City on june 26 they found the streets deserted and everything ready for the firing of the houses. But with the establishment of Camp Floyd, at Cedar valley, confidence was restored and the people returned to their homes.

---

[554] Creer, *op. cit.*, 156-157, quoting the journal of Wilford Woodruff.

The peace settlement came just as the government's campaign was getting well under way. Brigadier-general Harney had been placed in command of the reenforcing expedition and, following the departure of Colonel Hoffman's detachment from Fort Leavenworth in march, 1858, had dispatched five columns of troops from that frontier fort at intervals during may and early june, 1858.[555]

On june 30 his command included 38 companies, comprising 3,699 men; of these, 112 men, under Major J. Lynde, constituted the garrison at Fort Laramie. Several of the marching companies were east of this post and others were west of the fort when the june 30 report was made. On the same date Colonel Johnston's army, already in Utah, totaled 2,645 men.[556] General Harney had reached Lone Tree, a point on the South Platte near the present Colorado-Nebraska boundary line, when the express reached him on july 8, with orders for halting and re-directing the troops.

Changes of plans were effected at once and on july 28 the first of the returning troops had reached Fort Leavenworth.[557] By november 30, 1858, the troops had been disposed as follows: four companies of the troops in Utah had been returned to New Mexico, two companies were returned to the department of the West, and four were sent to Oregon. The places of these ten companies were taken by ten from General Harney's command, leaving the number in Utah at the same figure. Of Harney's other troops, twelve companies were assigned to the district of the Platte, ten were returned to

555 *Publications of the Nebraska state historical society*, XX, 300.

556 Report of Adjutant-general S. Cooper, in *House ex. docs.*, cong. 35, sess. 2, no. 2, vol. XI, part 2, pp. 780-83.

557 *Missouri Republican*, august 2, 1858, in *Publications of the Nebraska state historical society*, XX, 302.

the department of the West, and six were sent to Washington territory.[558]

An indication of the cost for one year of the Utah Expedition is given in the report of the Quartermaster-general for the fiscal year ending june 30, 1858:

"The expenditures on account of the Expedition to Utah, as far as ascertained, exceed five millions of dollars. Besides the vast supplies provided for the service, the operating columns were furnished with nine travelling forges, 22 ambulances, 29 light wagons, 988 baggage wagons, 6,447 mules, 254 horses, in addition to the horses furnished for the mounted corps. And for the transportation of supplies for the army, and for the depots at Fort Kearney and Fort Laramie, on the route, 3,908 wagons, 33 mules, and 46,896 oxen, were required; being 4,956 wagons and carriages, and 53,430 draught animals." [559]

With the end of the "Utah war," in which no fighting had occurred, there was less activity in the Fort Laramie region and matters resumed their former aspect. On august 2, 1858, Lieutenant-colonel John Munroe of the Fourth artillery assumed command of the fort, relieving Major Isaac Lynde of the Seventh infantry. The orders he issued the following day give an idea of routine life at the post. Drill and dress parade were to be held daily except saturday and sunday. Full uniform was to be worn on guard mounting and dress parade. The calls were to be as follows: reveille, 5 o'clock A.M.; fatigue, 5:15; recall from fatigue, 6:45; breakfast, 7:00; surgeon's call, 7:30; guard mounting, 8:00; fatigue call, 8:30; church call (sundays), 11:00; first sergeant's call, 12:00; recall from fatigue, 12:45; din-

558 Report of Adj.-gen. Cooper, *op. cit.*, 780-83.
559 *Ibid.*, 797.

ner, 1:00; fatigue, 2:00; recall for all men who were
to attend drill, 4:30; drill, 5:00; recall from drill, 6:00;
dress parade one-half hour before sunset; tattoo, 9:00;
taps, 9:15.[560]

Another phase of life at the fort is indicated by the
record of a garrison court martial held september 23,
1858. Ten men were brought before the court, the case
of Private Casper B. Renick being typical. He was
charged with absence without leave and with drunken-
ness, to which he plead guilty. His sentence was "to
forfeit six dollars of his pay for one month and to be
confined to hard labor in charge of the guard, for one
week." [561]

Through the winter of 1858-59, Lieutenant-colonel
Munroe was in command of Fort Laramie with a garrison of between 220 and 230 men. During the spring
and summer numerous changes occurred with companies coming and going at frequent intervals. Arrivals
in april and may increased the force to 315; then de-
partures in june, mostly for Fort Randall, reduced the
garrison to 90. In july it was again raised to 266 and in
the fall was increased to about 380 and was maintained
at nearly that figure through the winter of 1859-60.
Changes in command were noted as follows: Lieutenant-colonel Munroe was relieved in june, 1859, by Captain Francis A. Clark, who was supplanted in august by
Captain Christopher Lovell, and he was relieved in
september by Major Hannibal Day, who maintained
command until may, 1860.[562]

During this period housing accommodations at the

[560] Old records division, Adjutant-general's office, Washington, D.C. Fort
Laramie order book, no. 47, orders no. 63.

[561] *Ibid.*, orders no. 103.

[562] Fort Laramie monthly post returns, in war department old files, Washington, D.C.

fort were somewhat improved. New construction during the year ending july 1, 1859, included two sets of captains quarters, one storehouse (78 by 24 feet in size), four new stables (120x27 feet), and an addition to the hospital (16x24 feet).[563]

Colonel E. B. Alexander assumed command of Fort Laramie on july 16, 1860,[564] and retained the position most of the time during the remainder of the year and was in command at the outbreak of the Civil war. There were changes of troops during the period but the garrison was maintained with a force of from 250 to 300 men.

The Englishman, Richard F. Burton, who visited the fort august 14, 1860, on his western tour, has left this description of the post: "The straggling cantonment requires no description: it has the usual big flag, barracks, store-houses, officers' quarters, guard-houses, sutlers' stores, and groceries. . .

"Fort Laramie, called Fort John in the days of the American Fur company, was used by them as a storehouse for the bear and buffalo skins, which they collected in thousands. The old adobe *enceinte,* sketched and described by Fremont and Stansbury, soon disappeared after the place was sold to the United States government. Its former rival was Fort Platte, belonging in 1842 – when the pale face first opened this road – to Messrs. Sybille, Adams, and co., and situated immediately on the point of land at the junction of Laramie Fort [k] with the Platte."[565]

Though the Utah war was over, Fort Laramie, Fort

---

[563] Fort Laramie buildings report, july 1, 1859.

[564] General orders no. 98, Fort Laramie, july 16, 1860. Captain Samuel H. Starr and Captain John Dunovaur had been in command in may and june, respectively.

[565] R. F. Burton, *The city of the saints, and across the Rocky mountains to California,* 90.

Bridger and Camp Floyd had to be supplied. For this undertaking over 900 freight wagons were employed in 1859. Over the trail past Fort Laramie, trekked some 3,500 emigrants during this season, bound for California or Utah. Some 130,000 loose cattle, 6,000 sheep, and large numbers of horses were driven over the same road.[566]

Some of the surplus stock and equipment employed in the Utah Expedition were sold in Utah in 1859. Nineteen hundred mules that had cost on an average $157 each were sold at $75 and government wagons with iron axles were disposed of at $20 each.[567]

In february, 1860, Colonel Johnston left Camp Floyd for Washington. His place was taken by Colonel Smith, who was in turn replaced by Colonel Cooke. Most of the troops were ordered from Utah to Arizona and New Mexico in may, 1860. Then with the outbreak of the Civil war the next year, the remaining troops were withdrawn and Camp Floyd was abandoned. Large stores of provisions and equipment were disposed of at great sacrifice. It was said that goods worth $4,000,000 were sold for $100,000.[568]

---

[566] *Missouri Republican,* august 24, 1859.
[567] L.D.S. *Journal history,* august 18, 1859.
[568] O. F. Whitney, *Popular history of Utah,* 176-77.

The Civil War and the Uprising of the Plains Indians

With the outbreak of the Civil war in the spring of 1861, the attention of the nation was centered upon that tragic conflict. Troops needed for the defense of the Union were withdrawn from various posts in the West. But Fort Laramie, doubtless because of its key position on the line of communication with the Rocky mountains and Pacific coast regions, was not at first heavily drawn upon. Approximately 250 men were retained at this post until november, 1861, when the force was reduced to 132.[569]

Following the secession of seven states and the formation of a southern confederacy, the congress of the United States enacted a law on march 2, 1861, moving the Butterfield overland mail from the route via El Paso and Tucson to the Central route by way of Fort Laramie. The stagecoach service was to be increased to a daily schedule, the Pony Express was to run semi-weekly until the overland telegraph was completed, and the compensation for the combined service was to be $1,000,000 per year.[570] In conformity with the law the daily mail was inaugurated on july 1, 1861. The coach that left St. Joseph, Missouri, on that date reached San Francisco on the evening of the 18th.

Fear was entertained as to the treatment the Indians would give the daily mail, especially in view of the

---

[569] Fort Laramie post returns of 1861. War department old files.
[570] *United States statutes at large,* XII, 206.

withdrawal of so many troops from service on the Plains. But through the activity of Senator Latham of California, the war department issued orders on july 25, 1861, accepting one regiment of infantry and five companies of cavalry from California to protect the overland mail route.[571] With this precaution taken, no Indian difficulties of consequence developed on the route during 1861.

Earlier in the year had occurred an incident that is reflected in the following order issued at Fort Laramie on may 9, 1861, by Captain L. H. Marshall: "Second-lieutenant O. P. Gooding, 10th infantry, with a detachment of one non-commissioned officer and 30 men will proceed immediately in pursuit of a number of Cheyenne Indians who stole one or more horses from Mr. Ward's herd last night. Lieut. Gooding will recapture the horses and bring back to the post the thieves. If they make any resistance he will attack the band and take no prisoners. Jack Steed, the mountaineer, will accompany the party." [572] Apparently the matter was settled without resort to arms.

The daily overland mail and the Pony Express kept the inhabitants of Fort Laramie in rather close touch with happenings in the outside world. And as news of battles reached the soldiers they fretted at their inactivity in this far-away outpost. Interesting stagecoach passengers, officials and businessmen visited the fort. Mark Twain, accompanying his brother who was the newly-appointed secretary of Nevada territory, passed the fort in the summer of 1861. Unfortunately, Twain, who has given such a fascinating picture of the trip in *Roughing It,* failed to give his impressions of Fort

571 *San Francisco Bulletin,* august 3, 13, 1861.
572 Fort Laramie records, book 56, Adjutant-general's office, Washington.

Laramie. It appears that he passed the fort in the night, which would account for his failure and our loss.

Emigrants continued to pass the post. The Mormons, having given up their handcart scheme, now started their trains from Utah in the spring, picked up their loads of passengers and freight on the Missouri river, and returned with them to Zion in the fall. On september 12, 1861, the *Deseret News* of Salt Lake City, in reporting the return of the trains of Captains Milo Andrus and John Murdock, said that they had set out on the eastward journey on april 23, and had "made the trip to Florence [Nebraska] and back, including all delays and hindrances, in one hundred and forty-three days."

During the summer of 1861 the transcontinental telegraph was being extended across the Plains toward Fort Laramie. Back in 1859 the California legislature had offered $6,000 a year to the first overland telegraph,[573] and congress, by an act of june 16, 1860, had pledged $40,000 a year for ten years for carrying government messages.[574] Under these inducements the work was begun in 1860, but the line was run only to Fort Kearny from the east and to Fort Churchill, Nevada, from the west, during 1860.[575]

There was some question as to the route to be taken over the Rocky mountains. Edward Creighton, superintendent of the Western Union and Missouri Telegraph company, came to Denver in july, 1860. He informed the inhabitants of Colorado that if they would subscribe $20,000 of stock in the enterprise the company would run the line through Denver; otherwise the emigrant and mail route via Fort Laramie and

---

573 *San Francisco Bulletin,* november 7, 1861.

574 *United States statutes at large.*

575 L. R. Hafen, *The overland mail,* 185-86.

South Pass would be followed.[576] The required support was not forthcoming from Denver, so the line was routed up the North Platte. The building of the telegraph was pushed forward through the late summer and fall of 1861. Across the treeless plains the bringing in and distribution of poles was one of the principal problems. Number nine and number ten annealed wire was used.[577]

The line from the east reached Fort Laramie in september and was completed to Salt Lake City, where it connected with the line from the west coast, on october 24, 1861. The day before, when construction work was completed, but before through connection had been made, the *San Francisco Bulletin* had this to say:

"Great epochs approach with moccasined feet – great events glide in with muffled oars. One of these great events, a grand epoch for California, is just at hand – the opening of telegraphic communication from New York to San Francisco. It comes without half the fuss that the Bactrian camels made – it makes no such stir, breeds no such celebration as the Atlantic cable laying begot, but to us it is more important by far than that famous project would have been even if it had not proved a failure. One of the wonders of the age is just about being revealed a perfected fact, and it scarcely makes as much sensation as a $1,000 fire would do."

Indian difficulties began to threaten the Fort Laramie region in the spring of 1862. Early in april stage stations between Fort Bridger and the North Platte were burned, the stock was driven off, stages were attacked and a number of men were killed or wounded.[578] News

---

[576] *Rocky Mountain News,* august 1, 1860; *Western Mountaineer* (Golden, Colorado), august 2, 1860.

[577] *San Francisco Bulletin,* november 7, 1861. An excellent summary of the building of the telegraph is given here.

[578] *Alta California* (San Francisco), april 4, may 26, june 23, 1862.

of the raids were telegraphed east and west, but the reduced forces at Forts Laramie and Bridger were able to do little more than defend their respective posts. The Colorado Volunteers had departed six weeks before to fight back the Texan invasion of New Mexico. On april 28 President Lincoln telegraphed to ex-Governor Young of Utah for a force of cavalry to protect the mail and telegraph lines. A company was immediately raised and, under the captaincy of Lot Smith – who will be remembered as the raider on government trains in 1857 – hurried to the Independence Rock region.[579]

Colonel William O. Collins and his battalion of Ohio Volunteer cavalry were ordered west. They made a hurried march up the Oregon trail and arrived at Fort Laramie on may 30, 1862.[580] After recuperating a few days at the fort they continued farther west, establishing headquarters at South Pass and maintaining detachments at other points to protect the stage stations. With the troops along the line, serious depredations ceased.

Young Caspar Collins, who had accompanied his father the colonel, described the situation thus in a letter to his mother from Sweetwater bridge, june 16, 1862: "The Indians keep stealing horses and other stock from the mail stations, and now and then they shoot a man, but troops cannot get near them. Wherever there are a few men stationed, they are as quiet as lambs." In a letter two weeks later he observed: "I never saw so many men so anxious in my life to have a fight with the Indians. But ponies are faster than American horses, and I think they will be disappointed."[581]

Colonel Patrick E. Connor and his regiment of Cali-

---

579 *Deseret News*, XI, no. 348.

580 Letters of Colonel Collins, may 31, 1862, printed in A. W. Spring, *Caspar Collins, The life and exploits of an Indian fighter of the sixties*, 115.

581 *Ibid.*, 117, 121.

fornia Volunteers was ordered east. He set out from California in july and in the fall established himself at Camp Douglas, on the outskirts of Salt Lake City.[582]

The Indian disturbances prompted the transfer of the mail line in july, 1862, from the old route to one by way of the Cherokee trail and Bridger Pass. This latter route, considerably shorter than the old emigrant road, followed up the South Platte to the Cache la Poudre, turned northwest to traverse the Laramie plains, and followed approximately the present Lincoln highway from Laramie city to Fort Bridger.[583] Company A of the Eleventh Ohio Volunteer cavalry escorted the mail company property on the move south from the Sweetwater to the new route.[584]

With this change of route, Fort Laramie was left more than a hundred miles to the north of the mail line and it became necessary to establish another fort to guard the coaches. Such a post, located at the north base of Elk mountain, where the Cherokee trail rounded the Medicine Bow range, was built in the late summer and fall of 1862 and was named Fort Halleck, in honor of the then-popular Union general. With the telegraph on the South Pass route and the stagecoaches running by Bridger Pass, two lines of communication had to be kept open by the troops.

The large emigration also needed protection. Caspar Collins, from the South Pass region, wrote on august 13: "The Mormon emigration has just commenced passing. Three hundred wagons passed today." And in his letter of the 31st he reported: "A large Mormon

---

582 O. F. Whitney, *Popular history of Utah,* 189.

583 For a fuller description of this new route, the Overland trail, see L. R. Hafen, *The overland mail,* 230-32.

584 Spring, *op. cit.,* 42-43, letter of J. J. Hollingsworth, a member of company A.

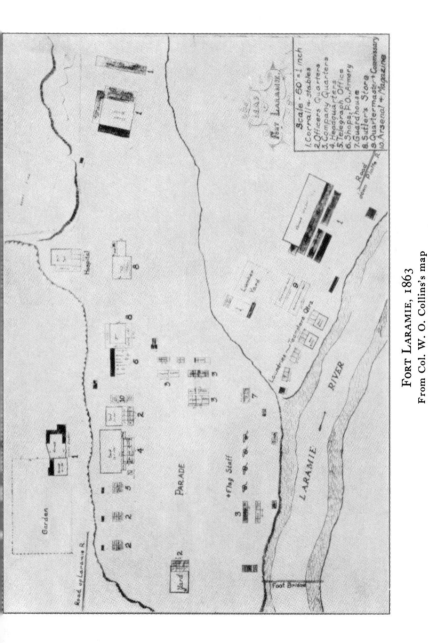

FORT LARAMIE, 1863
From Col. W. O. Collins's map

train passed here yesterday, of 80 wagons, most of them with 5, 6 and 7 yoke of cattle. All of them were from Denmark and Sweden, and very few could talk English." [585]

One important engagement was fought with Indians during the winter of 1862-63, but it was rather far removed from Fort Laramie. On the Bear river, in southern Idaho, Colonel Connor attacked a camp of Bannocks and Shoshones on january 29, 1863, and inflicted a severe blow that broke the power of these Indians. [586]

But at Fort Laramie the winter passed rather quietly. Bands of peaceful Cheyennes made frequent visits to the fort. Caspar Collins reports the arrival on september 20 of ninety warriors with thirty lodges and three hundred women and children. Old Smoke, a Sioux chief, and his contingent were there also. The chief, at the solicitation of General Craig, commander of the fort, had some of the Indians dive in the Platte to attempt recovery of some guns the General's men had recently lost in the stream while duck hunting.

Young Collins gives other sidelights on life at the fort in his various letters: "I saw a little pagan shoot one of the general's pigeons this morning as it was eating, a little piece back of the fort. . . General Craig has an old antelope which is very tame and runs about the garrison and butts people and eats bread and is very fat, which the young Indians watch with a great deal of attention, and the little wretches look as if they would like to try their hands on larger game than blackbirds. . .

"There are cats enough at this place to delight you

for ten years. I saw several Indians barbecuing a very fine fat one this morning. They were nearly through skinning her and were going to boil her in a capacious kettle or caldron, like the witches in Macbeth. . .

"Cattle can be kept here all winter without feeding them at all. No rain, except a little in may and june, falling in the year, and the grass dries like hay. Mr. Majors, the contractor for the carriage of the corn used by this department, has some 1500 head to winter here. They have not fed the government herd a particle thus far [december 15], and yet the beef is so fat that it is unpleasant." [587]

Of social life at the fort, Collins remarks: "They make the soldiers wear white gloves at this post, and they cut around very fashionably. A good many of the regulars are married and have their wives and families with them." They had a circulating library, organized a band, had amateur theatricals, and had an occasional ball. [588]

On february 23, 1863, word came to Fort Laramie that the Utes were stealing horses from the mail stations on the Overland trail. Troops were immediately dispatched to Fort Halleck. In making the trip they encountered a severe storm; two of the soldiers froze to death and others were badly frostbitten. [589] The Indians had run away, but they returned to make other forays during the spring and summer.

A party of soldiers from Fort Halleck went in pursuit of a Ute band early in july. Coming upon them, they demanded the return of the animals, but the Indians refused, protesting that the horses had been stolen from the Sioux and not from the whites. A sharp en-

---

[587] Spring, *op. cit.,* 132, 135, 136, 149.

[588] *Ibid.,* 40-41, 140, 146, 153.

[589] *Ibid.,* 46-48.

gagement followed, in which one soldier was killed and four were wounded. The Utes escaped with the stolen horses. Six companies of the First Colorado cavalry, under Major Ed. W. Wynkoop, were sent into the field, but they were unable to find the Indians, who had disappeared into the mountains.[590] In the fall of 1863, a peace settlement was effected with the Utes at Conejos, Colorado, and further war with these Indians was averted.[591]

A council was held with the Shoshones at Fort Bridger by Governor Doty of Utah and a treaty of peace was signed on july 2, 1863. Chief Washakie and the head men of the eastern bands agreed not to molest the telegraph or mail lines and consented to the construction of a railroad through their country.[592] Treaties with other bands of Shoshones were made during the summer.

Dr. John Evans, governor and superintendent of Indian affairs of Colorado territory, and Indian agents Loree and Colley attempted to make a peace treaty with the Sioux, Arapahos and Cheyennes. In july, 1863, they sent the trader Elbridge Gerry, grandson of the Elbridge Gerry who signed the Declaration of Independence, to gather the Indians for a council. But even Gerry, who was married to an Indian woman and was very friendly with the various tribes, was unable to induce them to meet the white commission. His promise of a distribution of goods was unavailing. They asked him what was to be requested of them, and when told

---

[590] The annual report of Governor John Evans, superintendent of Indian Affairs in Colorado, in the *Report of the commissioner of Indian Affairs for the year 1863*, 123. See also the *Denver Commonwealth*, july 2, 16, 1863.

[591] C. J. Kappler, *Indian affairs, laws and treaties*, II, 856-59.

[592] *Ibid.*, 848-50. See also, Grace R. Hebard, *Washakie, an account of Indian resistance of the covered wagon and Union Pacific railroad invasions of their territory.*

that the governor wanted them to settle down on a reservation and live like white men, they replied: "You can just go back to the governor and tell him we are not reduced quite that low yet." [593]

News of the very serious conflict between the whites and Indians in Minnesota during the year 1862 had reached the western plains. Also, emissaries from the southern confederacy were reported to be in contact with the Indians of the Oklahoma country. To what extent such developments affected the Indians of the high plains it is difficult to determine, but the result was doubtless anything but quieting.

In november, 1863, Robert North, a white man who had lived among the Indians since boyhood and was married to an Arapaho, came with important news to Governor Evans. He said that the various plains tribes had "pledged one another to go to war with the whites as soon as they can procure ammunition in the spring." [594]

These developments gave a foreboding of what was to occur the following year. During 1862 and 1863 the plains Indians had acquired many horses and guns, and to observant persons it appeared that a general uprising was being planned. Governor Evans repeatedly communicated such information to the authorities at Washington. [595]

In response to requests in 1863, additional troops were placed along the lines of travel and communication in the fall of that year. Company B of the First

[593] "Interview with ex-Governor Evans," in 1884. (MS. in the Bancroft library, university of California.) An account of the effort to hold a council with these tribes is given in Governor Evans's annual report, *op. cit.*, 124-25, and Gerry's report, *ibid.*, 129-130.

[594] North's statement, in Governor Evans's annual report, found in the *Report of the commissioner of Indian Affairs for the year 1864*, 224-25.

[595] See Governor Evans's correspondence published in the *Rocky Mountain News*, august 25, 1864, and his annual reports of 1863 and 1864 as superintendent of Indian Affairs for Colorado territory.

Colorado cavalry established a camp near Laporte on the Cache la Poudre branch of the South Platte.[596]

Colonel Collins, who had gone east from Fort Laramie in the summer of 1863 to procure more men, recruited four companies. These set out across the plains on september 2 and arrived at Fort Laramie on october 10.[597] Eight companies of the Seventh Iowa cavalry were dispatched up the Platte River trail in september and october and were distributed along the emigrant road.[598]

Relations between the whites and the Indians of the plains were approaching a crisis. White encroachments had been increasing rapidly in recent years, and it was becoming evident to the Indians that they were being crowded from their own hunting grounds. Back in the days of the fur trappers and traders occasional conflicts with the white men had occurred, but in general, peace had prevailed because the trade was of mutual advantage. But the traders had been followed by the endless chains of white-topped wagons bearing homeseekers into the west and supplies to the ever-increasing military forts. Then the goldseekers had come and squatted on their lands, burrowing holes in the mountains, cutting down and burning the trees and building towns and cities on the edge of the buffalo plains. The "Indian's cattle" were his food, shelter and clothing, and as he saw the buffalo slaughtered he read his own fate in the whitened bones on the prairie. Now the white men were fighting among themselves. Perhaps the Great Spirit

---

[596] A. W. Spring, "The founding of Fort Collins, u.s. military post," in *Colorado Magazine*, x, 48.

[597] A. W. Spring, *Caspar Collins,* 50-51. See also L. F. Crawford, *Rekindling campfires, the exploits of Ben Arnold* (Connor). Arnold was one of the soldiers.

[598] E. F. Ware, *The Indian war of 1864.* Ware belonged to this Iowa regiment.

had brought on the Civil war that his red children might make a successful stand against the white invaders.

Through the first months of 1864 no Indian hostilities occurred. In fact there is some question as to whether or not the Indians intended to launch a war against the whites. Dr. George Bird Grinnell, scholar and friend of the Indians, contends that the Cheyennes and other tribes of the plains favored peace and were forced into hostility by attacks from the white soldiers.[599] Governor Evans of Colorado, certain pioneer settlers and military men were convinced that the Indians planned war.[600] In any event troubles began in the spring.

Early in april Irwin and Jackman, government contractors, reported that about 170 head of their stock on the headwaters of the Big Sandy, east of Denver, had been stolen. Colonel Chivington sent Lieutenant George Eayre with troops from Camp Weld, near Denver, to recover the cattle.[601] About the same time stock were reported stolen from ranches on the South Platte north of Denver and Lieutenant Dunn of the First Colorado cavalry was sent in pursuit. Both of these detachments came into conflict with the Indians and lives were lost, but the question as to who began the attack in each case is still unsettled.[602]

With both whites and Indians considering themselves unjustly attacked, hostility grew and conflicts increased. Lieutenant Eayre set out immediately on a second expe-

---

[599] See G. B. Grinnell's chapter, "Harrying the Indians, 1864," in his *The fighting Cheyennes*, 131-142.

[600] See Governor Evans's annual report in *Report of the commissioner of Indian Affairs for the year 1864*, 216-58.

[601] *Ibid.*, 226.

[602] Governor Evans says Lieutenant Dunn was attacked by the Indians, *ibid.*, 218; Grinnell says, *op. cit.*, 136, "According to the statements of Indians who were of the party the troops charged on them without any warning."

dition, going east to the Smoky Hill and then south to the Arkansas. Near Fort Larned, Kansas, he had a fight with the Cheyennes, in which he is reported to have killed 25 or 30 Indians.[603] The following day the Cheyennes raided the stage road east of Fort Larned. Soon after, Kiowas came north to the Arkansas river and ran off Eayre's horses. Chief Left Hand and his Arapahos came in to offer assistance in recapturing the horses and the soldiers fired on the Arapahos. These Indians now became hostile and carried on a raid up the Arkansas river and to the west of Fort Larned.[604]

Early in may Major Jacob Downing attacked a village of Cheyennes at Cedar canyon, north of the South Platte. He reported the killing of 26 Indians, the wounding of 30 and the capture of 100 horses. His own loss was one killed and one wounded.[605]

In early june horses were stampeded from freighters on the "cut-off" road northeast of Denver and on the 11th an assault was made on a ranch on Running creek, some thirty miles east of Denver. Mr. Hungate, his wife, and two children were murdered and scalped. Their mutilated bodies were brought to Denver and placed on exhibition. Feeling ran high and rumors spread that all the settlements were to be attacked. Denver was in panic. The governor ordered business houses closed at 6:30 and all able-bodied men to meet for drill at seven o'clock. He appealed to the heads of the military departments of Kansas and New Mexico for assistance.[606] The immediate danger to Denver did not materialize and the excitement subsided somewhat.

[603] Governor Evans's report of june 15, 1864, in *Report of the commissioner of Indian Affairs for the year 1864*, 239.

[604] Grinnell, *op. cit.*, 139-41.

[605] Grinnell, *op. cit.*, 137-38. *Rocky Mountain News*, may 4, 1864.

[606] *Denver Commonwealth*, june 15, 22, 1864.

Governor Evans telegraphed for authority to raise volunteer militia companies and place them in the federal service. He also asked for and received permission to attempt a separation of the peaceful Indians from the hostiles. On june 27 he issued a proclamation calling on the friendly bands to gather in to designated military posts, where they would be protected. The Kiowas and Comanches were to go to Fort Larned; the southern Arapahos and Cheyennes, to Fort Lyon; the northern Arapahos and Cheyennes, to Camp Collins; and the Sioux to Fort Laramie.[607] There was little immediate response.

In middle july Indian raids were made on the stage road along the South Platte. Five men were killed and over a hundred horses were run off.[608]

Until this time the Sioux, except for a small band who usually accompanied the Cheyennes, had not been involved in the difficulties. But their relations with the whites were rather strained. Brigadier-general Robert B. Mitchell, commander of the department of Nebraska, had held a council with some of them at Cottonwood on the South Platte river, april 16, 1864. He said he wanted them to stay out of the Platte valley and away from the emigrant road. The Indians would not agree to this and countered with a demand that the whites close the Smoky Hill road, which ran through good buffalo country. Both sides blustered and bluffed, but neither would concede. Mitchell adjourned the conference and arranged for another meeting the following month.[609]

---

607 Evans's annual report, *op. cit.,* 218.

608 *Rocky Mountain News,* july 18, 22, 23, 1864.

609 Ware, *op. cit.,* 144-161. Ware was present at the council and gives an excellent account of the proceedings.

In late may the general came up the Platte again. He sent old-time traders south to interview the Cheyennes, but his emissaries were chased back with the word that these Indians were on the warpath. A large number of Brulé Sioux however, under Chief Spotted Tail came in, as did some Oglalas and Miniconjous. Beeves were killed and large quantities of bacon, coffee and hard bread were issued. But the conference was practically a repetition of the one held in april. The Indians wanted the Smoky Hill route closed and would not agree to stay out of the Platte valley. Mitchell told ᵗʰem they must restrain their young men or there would be war. He also wanted them to make peace with the Pawnees. Failing to get an agreement signed, he arranged for a third council.[610]

In conformity with arrangements, General Mitchell met the Sioux for a third time near the Cottonwood Springs post on july 19. He was accompanied by about eighty Pawnees and by company D of the Seventh Iowa cavalry. By this date so many Indian conflicts had occurred that he had no hope of a peace settlement between the whites and Indians. But to save his face he attempted to make a peace between the Sioux and the Pawnees. In this too he failed, having considerable difficulty in keeping them from actually fighting with each other at the meeting. After the breakup of the council the Sioux splashed through the Platte, yelling back their taunts to the Pawnees and the whites.[611]

General Mitchell continued on up the Platte river road with 160 white men and 80 Pawnee soldiers. He reached Fort Laramie on july 27, 1864, and placed Major Wood of the Seventh Iowa cavalry in command

[610] *Ibid.*, 198-204.
[611] *Ibid.*, 219-228.

of the post.[612] There had been minor Indian raids in this region of the upper North Platte, but no wholesale uprising. The tribes, as such, had not declared war, but parties of young men had occasionally conducted raids of their own. The troops were employed in scouting and in guarding emigrant and freight trains.

One day a number of detachments that had been out for three days in various directions for hostile Indians, returned to Fort Laramie and reported that no Indians were within twenty-five miles of the post. The scouting parties were disbanded on the parade ground about noon. And as the ground here was level and sandy, and the horses were tired, the officers ordered the saddles removed and the horses turned loose so that they might rest themselves by rolling in the sand. Just as the horses were enjoying this brief freedom a band of some thirty Indians dashed through the parade ground yelling, shooting and waving buffalo robes. They stampeded every animal on the parade ground and made away with them in a cloud of dust. "Boots and saddles" was sounded, horses remaining in the stables were saddled, rations provided and within an hour troops were on the trail. They followed it for two days and nights but the only horses they recovered were a few worn-out and discarded stragglers.[613]

Lieutenant Ware, who was stationed at the fort in august, 1864, writes: "My duties as post adjutant were very light. I had to superintend guard-mount at nine o'clock in the morning, and act in dress parade every evening at six. The old regular army traditions of the post had been kept up, and everything was done exactly as it had been done before the war. Every little matter

---

612 *Ibid.*, 270. The Pawnees were released and sent back down the road before Fort Laramie was reached.

613 *Ibid.*, 286-90.

OFFICERS AT FORT LARAMIE, 1864

Bottom row (1) Capt. Levi Monroe Rinehart, Co. G, 11 Ohio Volunteer cavalry,
killed by Indians at La Bonta station, february 13, 1865
(2) 2nd Lt. Caspar W. Collins, killed by Indians july 26, 1865

of detail had been handed down, and was perpetuated with nicety and zest." [614]

General Mitchell attempted to bring in the Indians and hold a council at the fort in late august. Only a few unimportant ones could be induced to come in. Rations were issued to these, but the council was a failure. Unsuccessful in this peace effort, the general decided to strengthen the defenses along the road. He ordered a fort built near Julesburg on the South Platte (Camp Rankin, later Fort Sedgwick), one near Scotts Bluffs (Fort Mitchell), and fortified structures established at Mud Springs (midway between the North Platte and South Platte) and at the old mail station of Ficklin (67 miles below Fort Laramie). Each of these was to have a telegraph operator. The road was to be patrolled.

In the meantime, and while conditions were comparatively peaceful on the North Platte, the worst outbreak of the summer occurred on the South Platte and on the road farther east. On august 8 an attack was made upon some trains at Plum creek, thirty-five miles west of Fort Kearny. Fourteen men were reported killed and some women and children taken prisoners. Three men were killed west of the fort. On the 10th the valley of the Little Blue was raided, trains were captured and some prisoners taken.[615] Panic seized the Nebraska frontier.

Upon learning of the raids on the Platte river road, Governor Evans issued a proclamation: "Patriotic citizens of Colorado: I again appeal to you to organize for defense of your homes and families against the merci-

[614] *Ibid.*, 273.
[615] *Rocky Mountain News*, august 9, 10, 11, 1864. *Official records, union and confederate armies*, LXXXIV, 612.

less savages. . . Any man who kills a hostile Indian is a patriot. . ." And the *Rocky Mountain News* added: "A few months of active extermination against the red devils will bring quiet and nothing else will." [616] The governor "authorized all citizens of Colorado, either individually or in such parties as they may organize, to go in pursuit of all hostile Indians . . . and to hold to their own private use and benefit, all property of said Indians that they may capture." In response to his appeal to the war department he was authorized to raise a regiment of "one hundred days men" to fight the Indians.[617]

The hostiles were assembled in a great camp on the Solomon river and from this center sent out their raiding parties. Some troops approached this camp and were driven back, the officer reporting, according to George Bent, that he "chased them ten miles, after which the Indians had turned around and chased him thirty." [618]

The raiding along the Platte road continued through august. The daily mail was stopped and all travel and freight transportation was paralyzed. Raids along the Arkansas river brought travel there also to a stand still.

On the night of august 19 two friendly Cheyennes came to Elbridge Gerry's ranch at the junction of Crow creek and the South Platte and warned Gerry to take his stock away from the river, for two nights thereafter the Indians were going to make a general attack on practically the whole Colorado frontier. Gerry mounted his horse and sped the 65 miles to Denver with the news. Messengers were dispatched to all the threatened locali-

---

[616] *Rocky Mountain News,* august 10, 1864.

[617] *Ibid.,* august 13, 1864.

[618] Quoted in Grinnell, *op. cit.,* 150.

ties and preparations made for defense. When the Indians appeared at the appointed time and found that their secret had been divulged they made only minor attacks. In one of these, unfortunately, Gerry's drove of horses was driven off.[619]

The Indians controlled some 400 miles of the Platte river road for about six weeks. The overland mail company drew off what stock and stages had not been captured. Mail from Denver for the East was sent west by stage to San Francisco and thence to New York by way of Panama. Food and supplies grew scarce in Colorado and prices began to soar, flour selling for $25 per hundred pounds and other things in proportion. Not until the latter part of september was the Platte road opened and travel and mail service resumed.[620]

In the meantime attempts had been made to end the war. William Bent had written to the Cheyenne chiefs urging them to make peace. This was answered on august 29 by a letter written by his own half-breed son, George, and signed "Black Kettle and other chiefs." They promised to stop fighting provided the peace included the Kiowas, Comanches, Arapahos, Apaches and Sioux. They reported having some prisoners which they were willing to exchange.[621]

Responding to the letter, Major Edward W. Wynkoop, in command of Fort Lyon, went to the Indian camp. He obtained the prisoners – four white children – and brought Black Kettle, White Antelope and other Indian chiefs to Denver for a peace council. Governor Evans, General Chivington and others met the

---

[619] Governor Evans's annual report, *op. cit.*, 219, 232.

[620] *Ibid.*, 254. Also *Rocky Mountain News*, august 24, september 3, september 24, 1864; *Alta California*, october 3, 1864.

[621] Letter quoted in Grinnell, *op. cit.*, 152.

Indian leaders, but nothing was accomplished. The
military authorities thought it folly to make peace before the Indians had been punished. Major-general S.
R. Curtis telegraphed from Fort Leavenworth on september 28, 1864: "I shall require the bad Indians delivered up; restoration of equal numbers of stock – also
hostages, to secure. I want no peace till the Indians
suffer more." [622]

The chiefs returned to their camp and presently several hundred of their tribesmen came in to Fort Lyon,
apparently with the understanding that they would be
protected, in conformity with Governor Evans's proclamation of the preceding june calling upon peaceful
Cheyennes and Arapahos to assemble at Fort Lyon.
These Indians were fed a short time at the fort and
were then directed to hunt for their food. They set up
camp on their reservation at Sand creek, about forty
miles north of Fort Lyon, where they were soon to be
involved in one of the most famous, or infamous, tragedies of western history.

On the early morning of november 29, 1864, General
Chivington, in command of about 750 soldiers, suddenly
charged the camp, while some detached troops cut off
the horse herd. The village, made up of some hundred
lodges and containing 500 to 600 men, women and children, was taken entirely by surprise, as the Indians had
considered themselves safe from attack. Great terror
and confusion reigned as the soldiers opened fire. Black
Kettle had run up the American flag when he saw the
troops coming and he and White Antelope protested
friendship, but this had no effect. Black Kettle finally
ran and escaped, but White Antelope stood with arms
folded and was killed while singing his death song.

---

[622] Evans's annual report, *op. cit.*, 221.

The slaughter was terrible, the fleeing men, women and children being shot down as they ran. It is impossible to determine the exact number of Indian losses. Chivington at first reported that 500 were killed, but the figure given by George Bent – over 150 – is probably nearer the truth. The white losses were 10 killed and 38 wounded.[623]

The fugitive survivors from Sand creek made their way to another Cheyenne camp on the Smoky Hill river. Enraged at their unjust treatment they held a council and sent pipe bearers to the Northern Arapahos and to the Sioux on Solomon river, telling of what they had suffered and inviting them to join in a war on the whites. These responded, inhaled bitterness from the Cheyenne pipe and heartily joined in a campaign for revenge.

An attack on Julesburg, prominent junction point and supply depot, was decided upon. About one thousand warriors of the combined tribes were in the party that moved toward the South Platte on january 7. They attempted to lead the soldiers from Camp Rankin (a post established in the preceding august, one mile west of Julesburg) to an ambush in the sandhills and did succeed in killing fourteen of the troops. The Indians then sacked Julesburg and carried away loads of flour, sugar and other supplies.[624]

---

[623] The most extensive data about the Sand creek affair is contained in the *Massacre of Cheyenne Indians,* the report of "The joint committee on the conduct of the war." This committee of congress held hearings, took testimony and published its findings. By it Chivington and the troops were strongly condemned. Grinnell presents a good account and quotes the description of the massacre given by George Bent, who was with the Indians and was wounded in the conflict. Perhaps the best account presented from the standpoint of the soldiers is found in Irving Howbert's *Memories of a lifetime in the Pike's Peak region,* 95-163. Howbert was a participant as a member of the Third Colorado cavalry.

[624] Grinnell, *op. cit.,* 175-79.

A small party of ex-soldiers traveling eastward along the Platte was intercepted and killed. Upon opening the white men's valises the Indians found in them scalps which they recognized as taken from certain Indians killed at Sand creek. Thereupon they hacked the bodies to pieces.[625]

Upon learning of this Julesburg raid of jan. 7, General Mitchell collected over 600 cavalry at Camp Cottonwood and with four twelve-pound mountain howitzers and about one hundred wagons lightly loaded with supplies set out on january 15 to punish the Indians. He went south to the Republican river and endured a hard winter march of over three hundred miles, but failing to find the hostile village returned to the Platte on the 26th.[626] Instructions were wired to telegraph stations and by night a 300-mile fire was sweeping the plains, burning the feed of Indian ponies.[627]

The following day the Indians launched wholesale attacks on the South Platte. They completely wrecked seventy-five miles of the road, burning stations and ranches, driving off herds of cattle, capturing wagon trains and destroying the telegraph line. Julesburg was sacked again and was burned on february 2. After reveling for several days in quantities of supplies the Indians moved northward with what they could carry, heading for the Powder river country.[628]

These raids on the South Platte and the breaking of

---

[625] *The Rocky Mountain News,* january 16, 1865, says there were two soldiers in the party; Grinnell, *op. cit.,* 184, gives the number as nine.

[626] Ware, *op. cit.,* 454-486. Ware was acting Assistant-adjutant-general during this expedition.

[627] *Ibid.,* 488-90.

[628] *Ibid.,* 490-506; *Rocky Mountain News,* january 28, 1865. Barnes in his *From the Atlantic to the Pacific, overland,* 25, says that 6,000 bushels of corn were destroyed at Julesburg. Birge in his *The awakening of the desert,* 126, places the loss in the attack on Julesburg at $115,100.

the line of communication caused great excitement in Denver. On february 6 Colonel Moonlight, who had replaced Colonel Chivington in command of the district of Colorado, announced that martial law would be proclaimed on the 8th and that business houses would be closed until 360 men were furnished to protect the road to Julesburg. Men came forward, the road was opened and the telegraph line was repaired.[629]

In the meantime the Indians had moved north toward the North Platte. The advance party reached Mud Springs on february 4 and ran off the stock. Word was telegraphed to Fort Laramie, 105 miles away. Colonel Collins ordered Lieutenant Ellsworth who was at Camp Mitchell, forty-five miles above the threatened station, to proceed at once to the rescue. He complied promptly, and after an all night march arrived at Mud Springs at daybreak. Colonel Collins left Fort Laramie with 120 men on the evening of february 4, reached Camp Mitchell the next day, and after a short rest hurried with twenty-five picked men to Mud Springs, reaching the station at 2 A.M. on the 6th. The rest of his command, some of whom had been badly frozen, arrived six hours later.[630]

A general assault was made on the Mud Springs station by the Indians on the 6th, but the troops were able to successfully defend it. The next day the Indians moved off to the northeast. Colonel Collins, being outnumbered, followed them cautiously. On the North Platte some sharp engagements occurred, after which the big Indian encampment moved on toward Powder river, and the troops wisely decided not to follow.[631]

---

[629] *Rocky Mountain News,* february 6, 13, 20, 1865.

[630] Spring, *Caspar Collins,* 61-62.

[631] *Ibid.,* 62-66; Grinnell, *op. cit.,* 187-194.

In the general region of the Powder and Tongue rivers the Indian tribes spent the rest of the winter, living rich on the spoils of their raids. But the whites were preparing for vigorous and extensive campaigns and to carry the war into the heart of the Indian country.

War and Peace, 1865-1869

With the closing of the Civil war the United States government was in a position to divert large numbers of troops into the struggle with the western Indians. General Grenville M. Dodge was in command of the department of Missouri, General Connor was given charge of the district of the Plains, and Colonel Moonlight was made commander of Fort Laramie.[632] Additional troops were distributed along the Oregon and Overland trails, and the lines of travel and communication were generally kept open. Early in 1865 plans were laid to strike the Indians from various angles and especially to carry the war north of Fort Laramie into the Indian country. But these were slow in being put into execution and it was mid-summer before the various columns were on the march.

In the meantime, during the early months of 1865, the combined hostile tribes, holding their feasts and war dances in the choice valleys of the Powder and Tongue rivers, talked of what they would do when grass grew again. After shifting camp several times during march and april to procure forage and game, they moved in may up the Tongue river to the base of the

---

[632] G. M. Dodge, *The battle of Atlanta and other campaigns, addresses, etc.,* 63. The department of Kansas having been merged with the department of the Missouri, General Dodge assumed command february 8, 1865. *The War of the rebellion: a compilation of the official records,* etc., series I, vol. XLVIII, part I, (serial 101) p. 780. The districts of Utah, Colorado and Nebraska were merged into the district of the Plains and were placed under the command of Brigadier-general P. E. Connor by an order dated march 28, 1865. *Ibid.,* 1285.

Big Horn mountains. Here they held a war council and decided that as soon as their horses were strong enough they would raid the North Platte and South Platte roads.[633] Their general attacks began late in may and grew in extent and intensity during june and july.

Colonel Moonlight, having heard that the Cheyennes were assembled in the Wind river valley, decided to conduct a campaign against them. With about 500 cavalry from the Eleventh Ohio, Eleventh Kansas and Seventh Iowa regiments, he set out from Fort Laramie on may 3. Although guided by the old scout Jim Bridger, he did not find the Indians, and after traveling 450 miles he returned to the fort on the Laramie without having struck a blow.[634] Soon after his return a much-discussed event occurred. Two Face and Black Foot, two Oglala Sioux, arrived at the fort with the captives, Mrs. Eubank and her baby, who had been taken in the raid on the Little Blue of eastern Kansas in june of the preceding year. Some accounts say the two Indians were captured; others assert that they came in willingly to surrender the captives, expecting a reward. Against the protest of sutler Bullock and the wishes of Mrs. Eubank, Colonel Moonlight ordered the Indians hanged by chains.[635] Their bodies were left

[633] Grinnell, *The fighting Cheyennes*, 210.

[634] *War of rebellion records*, series 101, p. 255-56, gives Colonel Moonlight's report. See also W. E. Connelley, *The life of Preston B. Plumb*, 197. Diary of J. J. Pattison in *Nebraska history magazine*, XV, 84-85. S. H. Fairfield, "The Eleventh Kansas regiment at Platte bridge," in *Transactions of the Kansas state historical society*, VIII, 354.

[635] Colonel Moonlight's official report of the hanging is found in *War of the rebellion*, serial 101, p. 276. Grinnell, *op. cit.*, 181, says: "The two Sioux, Two Face and Blackfoot, were friends of the whites. They had bought the woman and her child at their own expense from the Indians who had captured them and had brought them to the fort and given them up to prove their friendliness. The drunken officer in command of the post ordered the two Indians hanged in chains, and this was done." Pattison's diary, *op. cit.*,

dangling for months on a scaffold on the bluff northeast of the post.

The Indians in the meantime, began their raids on the North Platte emigrant road and telegraph line. On may 20 they attacked Deer Creek station, killed one soldier and ran off twenty-six horses. About a week later they burned St. Mary's station, the soldiers escaping to South Pass. Attacks on Sweetwater station were repulsed. On june 3 Indians appeared at Platte bridge, and in that vicinity they had a fight with Colonel Plumb, in which two soldiers were killed.[636]

At the same time, other parties of Indians were attacking the Overland trail. They killed two emigrants near Bridger Pass on june 2 and raided the country for fifty miles along the mail line. On the 8th they attacked a station near Fort Halleck, drove off the horses, burned the station and killed five of the seven men located there. On june 11, General Connor ordered Colonel Plumb to proceed to Fort Halleck with five of his companies and reopen the mail line. He arrived on the 24th, distributed his troops along the route, and carried or escorted the mail until regular service was resumed.[637]

A village of Brulé Sioux, who had taken no part in the war, were encamped at Fort Laramie in the spring of 1865. Unable to hunt lest they be mistaken for hostiles, the band remained at the post and was fed from the supplies there. To reduce the heavy expense entailed by this arrangement, General Dodge ordered them sent farther east, where the cost of food would be less. Colonel Moonlight directed Captain Fouts, with

85, reports that the hanging occurred on may 26. B. F. Rockafellow, on july 25, 1865, saw the bodies still hanging from the gallows on the bluff. His diary, MS.

[636] Connelley, *op. cit.,* 198. A. W. Spring, *Caspar Collins,* 75-77.

[637] *Rocky Mountain News,* june 8, 12, 1865. See also Connelley, *op. cit.,* 199.

139 of the Seventh Iowa cavalry, to escort the Brulés to Fort Kearny. These Sioux did not relish the idea of being taken down into the country of their enemies, the Pawnees, but despite their objections they were started upon the march on june 11. As they proceeded, their discontent and fears increased and they soon decided to attack their guards, flee to the north and join the hostiles. At the camp on Horse creek they carried out the plan. Captain Fouts and four soldiers were killed and the Indians made good their escape.[638]

Colonel Moonlight, advised by telegraph of what had happened, led a force north from Fort Laramie in search of the fugitives. Upon reaching Dead Man's Fork, 120 miles northeast of the fort, and not having found the Indians, he turned his horses loose to graze. Thereupon the Indians charged his camp and made off with the animals. Moonlight, outshone by this daylight raid, burned his saddles and equipment and made his way back to the Laramie afoot. He was censured for his loss and was soon thereafter mustered out of the service.[639]

The Brulés joined the combined hostiles in time to participate in the major attack of the summer on the North Platte road. Sioux, Cheyennes and Arapahos, aggregating about 3,000 warriors, moved down toward Platte bridge, near present Casper, Wyoming. While most of the band remained hidden in the sand hills north of the Platte, a small force approached the fort

---

[638] Grinnell, *op. cit.*, 215-16. Dodge, *op. cit.*, 86-87.

[639] General Dodge says that he ordered him mustered out. *War of the rebellion*, serial 101, p. 332. Fairfield, *op. cit.*, 355, asserts that the soldiers were bitter against Colonel Connor for having Moonlight mustered out, and says, "It was a cruel order and a great injustice to a brave soldier. Colonel Moonlight was the peer of any officer that ever drew sword west of the Missouri River."

in an effort to lead the soldiers into an ambush. But the soldiers would not follow. Early the next day about half of the Indians secreted themselves in the brush and timber below the bridge, while the other half hid above the bridge.

Platte bridge station, on the south bank of the North Platte, was one of the important posts on the route. Protected by a pine log stockade, fourteen feet high, and defended by about 120 men under command of Major Anderson of the Eleventh Kansas cavalry, it appeared safe from successful assault.

At 2 A.M. on July 26 word came to Platte bridge that a wagon train of five wagons escorted by ten soldiers was traveling toward the post from Sweetwater station. Nothing was done to warn the train or send relief under cover of darkness. But at 7 o'clock Lieutenant Caspar Collins, who had arrived at Platte bridge from Fort Laramie the night before, was ordered to lead twenty-five men to relieve and bring in the wagon train. The young lieutenant, realizing the great danger he faced and believing he would not return alive, gave his cap to a friend as a memento and thundered over the bridge to the north side of the river with his gallant twenty-five. The Indians soon closed in on them. The soldiers fought their way forward for a time, but in the face of the overwhelming odds, finally turned about and attempted to reach the bridge. Collins and four of his men were killed in the engagement.

The Indians now crossed the river and cut the telegraph line about a mile east of the post. In the afternoon thirty men were sent to repair the break. These were attacked and suffered a loss of two men.

Despite warnings, Sergeant Custard with the wagon

train, continued to move down the river toward Platte
bridge. When about three miles from the post he sent
out an advance party of five men. Three of these finally
reached the post alive. As the Indians began to surround the train, the sergeant corraled his wagons and
succeeded in holding off the Indians for about an hour.
But he was overpowered and all the men were killed.
The white men who lost their lives at the Platte bridge
fights numbered twenty-six.[640]

Following these engagements a party of Indians
raided the road toward Fort Laramie, killing a number
of soldiers and destroying some ranches and stations.
Then most of the Indians moved north, returning to
the Powder river country.[641]

But some remained behind to re-visit the stage line
on the Overland trail. On august 4 they killed twelve
whites near Rock creek. E. N. Lewis, hospital steward
at Fort Halleck, told of one of the captured men being
scalped and tied to the wheel of a wagon, that bacon
was then piled around him and he was burned in its
flame.[642]

By this time the general offensive against the Indians was well under way. Doubtless it was this drive
that had caused the withdrawal of most of the Indians
from the North Platte road after the Platte bridge fight.
General Dodge had planned to push three columns
into the Powder river country in the spring. But he
encountered difficulties and suffered delays. Supplies
were not purchased until may and after reaching Leavenworth moved slowly up the road. Troops were de-

---

640 Spring, *op. cit.*, 94. Mrs. Spring gives one of the best accounts of these
engagements. See also Grinnell and Fairfield, cited above.

641 Grinnell, *op. cit.*, 217.

642 *Rocky Mountain News*, august 10, 16, 1865.

layed at Fort Laramie from four to six weeks waiting for supplies to arrive.[643]

Soldiers were obtained with difficulty and held uncertainly. Many of the men who had enlisted for the duration of the Civil war were demanding their release. Appealing to their congressmen, they applied political pressure that resulted in orders for muster out. General Dodge lists 4,740 men ordered to his assistance who, after having been equipped and marched varying distances out onto the plains, were mustered out without having given him any assistance. Instead of the 4,500 men intended for the operations, only 2,500 were obtained.[644]

The campaign against the Indians north of Fort Laramie, commonly known as the Powder River Expedition, was directed by General Connor and was to operate as three converging divisions. One column, under Colonel Nelson Cole, was to move up the Loup Fork of the Platte, along the east base of the Black Hills of South Dakota, across to the forks of the Little and Big Powder rivers, and thence to a point on Tongue river about fifty miles above Yellowstone river. A second column, under Lieutenant-colonel Samuel Walker, was to march north from Fort Laramie, along the west base of the Black Hills, and meet Cole's command at the junction point on Tongue river. The third column, under General Connor's personal direction, with supplies for the three divisions after their convergence, was to move up the North Platte to its northerly bend, north to the Powder river and, after establishing Fort Connor on this stream, to move along the east base of

---

[643] *War of the rebellion,* serial 101, p. 336.
[644] *Ibid.,* 346.

the Big Horn mountains to the point of junction on Tongue river.[645]

Colonel Cole set out from Omaha on july 1 with 1,400 men and a train of 140 six-mule wagons. He followed in general the course outlined, but his maps were inadequate, his guides poorly informed and the country rough. His progress was therefore slow, and his difficulties multiplied. Instead of taking the offensive in the Indian country, he was hard pressed to defend his own train. The minor skirmishes he had with the Indians resulted in nothing decisive. Fatigue and lack of food wore down his men and animals. During a storm in early september he lost 414 animals "at the picket ropes or along the road between camps. This loss necessitated the destruction of wagons, cavalry equipment, harness, and all tools and implements not absolutely essential to the command." [646]

Colonel Walker's division left Fort Laramie july 5. Being equipped with pack animals instead of wagons it was more mobile and did not experience the difficulties Cole's column suffered. These two columns effected a junction, but through misunderstandings or misinterpretations of the topography, they did not meet the third division where expected.

General Connor set out from Fort Laramie on july 30 with about 800 men, including 75 Pawnees under Captain Frank North and 70 Winnebagoes and Omahas under Captain E. W. Nash. A train of 185 wagons, with 195 teamsters and wagonmasters, accompanied the troops. The command reached Powder river august 11, and three days thereafter began the building of a stockade, called Camp Connor. Leaving part of his force

---

[645] *Ibid.,* 336.
[646] *Ibid.,* 376. Cole's report.

and supplies here, the General pushed on down Powder river. He had several engagements with the Indians, the most important of which was a battle in late august with the Arapahos under Black Bear. A number of Indians were killed; the village and a large herd of horses were captured. The winter supplies of this band and 250 of their lodges were burned.[647]

General Connor moved down the Tongue river to the place of expected meeting with Cole and Walker, but found no signs of them. On september 4 news came of an Indian attack west of Tongue river on Colonel Sawyer's train – a party that had been opening an emigrant road to the Montana mines by way of the Niobrara. General Connor sent troops to the rescue.[648]

Becoming uneasy as to the whereabouts of Colonels Cole and Walker, General Connor began to send out scouting parties to find them. One of these came back with a report of having discovered 500 dead horses, apparently of Cole's command. On september 19, Major North and his Pawnees located the two commands and found the men almost starving. North led them to Camp Connor.[649] General Connor retraced his steps and joined them at that point on september 24. Here he found orders recalling him and relieving him of the command. The troops returned to Fort Laramie and the Powder River Expedition was at an end. It had failed of its purpose. The Indians were unpunished; in fact, certain detachments of the troops were

[647] H. E. Palmer, "History of the Powder river Indian expedition of 1865," in *Transactions and reports of the Nebraska state historical society,* II, 204, 207, 219. Captain Palmer of Connor's command, gives us our fullest account of the movements of the general's column. Connor's report was not published with the others.

[648] *Ibid.,* 220.

[649] Grinnell, *op. cit.,* 203-4.

fortunate to have escaped starvation and annihilation.

General Connor and his division leaders have been given blame for the outcome. But back of them are other persons and factors that also affected the situation. We have mentioned the difficulties experienced in getting the men and supplies needed. Congress and the cabinet were demanding economy and retrenchment in the military arm of the government. Then, there were active advocates of peaceful rather than military measures in dealing with the Indians and these were gaining a temporary ascendency.[650] They had stopped the military expedition under General J. B. Sanborn that was going up the Arkansas to fight the southern Indians and had replaced it by a peace gesture that resulted in the treaties of the Little Arkansas on october 14-18, 1865.[651] Similar developments on the upper Missouri were to culminate in the Fort Sully treaties of october 10-28, 1865, with various bands of the Sioux.[652]

The officials at Washington had decided to try peaceful measures with the Indians of the Fort Laramie region also, regardless of the outcome of the Powder River Expedition. Major-general John Pope, on september 2, had informed General Dodge that Connor was being transferred to Utah and that Brevet-major-general Wheaton would assume command of Nebraska and the portion of Dakota west of Nebraska, with headquarters at Fort Laramie.[653]

General Dodge, although opposed to the peace party plan, was ordered to undertake negotiations with the

[650] J. R. Perkins, *Trails, rails and war. The life of General G. M. Dodge*, 181-83.

[651] C. J. Kappler, *Indian affairs, laws and treaties*, II, 887-95.

[652] *Ibid.*, 883-87, 896-908.

[653] *War of the rebellion*, serial 101, p. 355.

northern Indians.[654] From Denver on october 2, he informed General Wheaton that he was sending Big Ribs and other friendly Sioux to Fort Laramie and that these were to act as emissaries to the Sioux and Cheyennes, inviting them to Camp Connor or Fort Laramie for a peace settlement.[655]

These emissaries returned to Fort Laramie from the hostile Sioux on january 16, 1866, bringing with them a deputation led by Swift Bear. Colonel Henry E. Maynadier, who had replaced General Wheaton in command of Fort Laramie, held a preliminary council with these Indians.[656] He then sent out runners to the other tribes with invitations for a general peace council at the fort in june.

On march 9 Colonel Maynadier reported to the commissioner of Indian Affairs an occurrence which he considered of great significance and one auguring success for the peace measures. Pegaleshka, or Spotted Tail (sometimes rendered Shan-tag-a-lisk), head chief of the Brulé Sioux, had come to the fort the preceding day, bringing the body of his daughter and requesting that she be buried among the whites.[657] The story of this girl is one of the romances and tragedies of Fort Laramie history.

Her name was Ah-ho-ap-pa, the Sioux word for wheat flour, the whitest thing these Indians knew. Her father, the brave and renowned Spotted Tail, had won his chieftainship by daring deeds, having counted twenty-six coups on enemies. But the chief, fierce

---

[654] Letter of General Dodge in *Personal recollections and observations of General Nelson A. Miles*, 141-42.

[655] *War of the rebellion*, serial 101, p. 364.

[656] *Report of the commissioner of Indian Affairs for the year 1866*, 204-6. Report of Colonel Maynadier, january 25, 1866.

[657] *Ibid.*, 207. Colonel Maynadier's report of march 9, 1866.

against enemies, was tender to his child. As she grew to girlhood he noted with pride her haughtiness and queenly bearing. She came with her father to Fort Laramie and was fascinated at the manoeuvers of the soldiers in uniform.

In the summer of 1864, Lieutenant Ware, adjutant at Fort Laramie, was distributing goods to the Indians. The women and children, he says, had formed a circle around the barrels and boxes of flour, crackers, bacon and coffee that had been placed on the parade ground. One girl, tall and well dressed, stood apart. Through the interpreter he told her that she must get in the circle or she would lose her share.

"I am the daughter of Shan-tag-a-lisk," she replied, without moving.

"I don't care whose daughter she is," retorted the lieutenant. "Tell her if she doesn't get into the ring she won't get anything to eat." Back from her through the interpreter came her answer: "I have plenty to eat; I am the daughter of Shan-tag-a-lisk."

At the subsequent distribution of rations she always came and stood outside of the ring alone.

"During the daytime," writes Ware, "she came to the sutler's store and sat on a bench outside, near the door, watching as if she were living on the sights she saw. She was particularly fond of witnessing guard-mount in the morning, and dress-parade in the evening. Whoever officiated principally on these occasions put on a few extra touches for her special benefit, at the suggestion of Major Wood, the post commander. The officer-of-the-guard always appeared in an eighteen-dollar red silk sash, ostrich plume, shoulder-straps, and about two hundred dollars' worth of astonishing raiment, such as, in the field, we boys used to look upon with loathing and contempt. We all knew her by sight, but she never spoke to any of us. Among ourselves we called her 'the princess.' She was looking, always looking, as if she were feeding upon what she saw." [658]

Charles Elston, early trader, who had known the girl from babyhood, told the officers at Fort Laramie in 1864: "She won't marry an Indian; she always said that. Her father has been offered two hundred ponies for her, but won't sell her. She says she won't marry anybody but a 'capitan,' and that idea sort of pleases her father for more reasons than one. Among the Indians every officer, big or little, with shoulder-straps on, is a 'capitan.' . . She tried to learn to read and speak English once of a captured boy, but the boy escaped before she got it. She carries around with her a little bit of a red book, with a gold cross printed on it, that General Harney gave her mother many years ago. She's got it wrapped up in a parfleche [piece of dressed rawhide]. You ought to hear her talk when she is mad. She is a holy terror. She tells the Indians they are all fools for not living in houses and making peace with the whites." [659]

When the Sioux went on the warpath in the fall of 1864, Spotted Tail and his daughter were with them. During the following year they were in the Powder river country.

The aspirations of Ah-ho-ap'pa seemed impossible of fulfillment. The hard life weakened her. During the cold winter of 1865-66 she took sick and grew steadily worse. Then in february came messengers calling the Indians to Fort Laramie to make peace. But the news came too late for her. She told her father that she

[658] E. F. Ware, *The Indian war of 1864*, 571.
[659] *Ibid.*, 573.

wanted to go and had him promise to take her for burial in the white cemetery at Fort Laramie.

After her death, her body was tightly wrapped in smoked deer skin, was placed on the backs of her two white ponies (tied side by side), and the 260-mile journey over the frozen hills began. Her father notified Fort Laramie of his approach and asked permission to comply with his daughter's wish. Colonel Maynadier responded gallantly. An ambulance, guarded by a company of cavalry in full uniform was dispatched, followed by two twelve-pound howitzers, with postilions in red chevrons. The body was placed in the ambulance and was followed by the girl's two white horses. Colonel Maynadier with officers and men went out and met the cavalcade and escorted Shan-tag-a-lisk to headquarters.

A coffin was made, a scaffold prepared, and to the poles of the scaffold were nailed the heads and tails of the two white ponies. Just before sunset the body was taken to the cemetery, mounted on an artillery caisson. The relatives and the officers of the post followed, and after them the soldiers in uniform. The post chaplain, Reverend Wright, conducted the burial service, using the little red book – an episcopal prayer-book – which General Harney had given and Ah-ho-ap'pa had carried. Funeral offerings were put on the coffin by red and white alike, the colonel placing there a pair of white kid cavalry gloves. The coffin was raised and placed on the scaffold, covered with a buffalo robe and tied firmly in place by thongs. An honor watch remained and fired a gun at half-hour intervals throughout the night.

Next morning Spotted Tail attended a conference held at post headquarters. The commanding officer told of the white commissioners that were to come to the post later in the spring to make peace. Pointing to the silk flag hanging on the wall he said: "My Indian brother, look at those stripes. Some of them are red, and some of them are white. They remain peacefully side by side – the red and the white – for there is room for each." [660]

During march, 1866, a number of chiefs were communicated with and a cessation of hostilities until the convening of the peace council, was arranged.

At Fort Laramie on june 1, 1866, the peace commission assembled. It consisted of E. B. Taylor, superintendent of the northern superintendency, Colonel H. E. Maynadier, Colonel R. N. McLaren of Minnesota, and Thomas Wistar of Philadelphia. Charles E. Bowles of the Indian department was secretary. The Brulé and Oglala Sioux were represented by their principal chiefs, with about 2,000 of their tribesmen in attendance. After a preliminary discussion it was decided to postpone further action until more of the sub-bands came in. Wrote the head of the commission: "A band numbering perhaps three hundred warriors, headed by Red Cloud, a prominent·chief of the Ogalallahs, refused to come in. They are known as the Bad Faces, and are composed of the most refractory and desperate characters of the tribe." [661]

About the middle of june, calculating that seven-eighths of the Brulés and Oglalas were present, the commissioners proceeded to negotiate a treaty.

In the meantime, and without waiting to learn the outcome of negotiations, the war department had started an expedition with instructions to open the Powder

[660] *Ibid.*, 581.

[661] *Report of the commissioner of Indian Affairs for the year 1866*, 211. Report of Superintendent E. B. Taylor.

river road to Montana and establish forts upon it.
Colonel Henry B. Carrington, with about 2,000 troops –
less than half of whom were to continue with him to
the Powder river – set out from Fort Kearny on may
19. The expedition's own thirty-piece band enlivened
the march past Dobey Town (on the outskirts of the
fort). The train of 226 mule teams was loaded with
equipment and supplies, including a saw mill, mowing
machines, shingle and brick machines, blacksmith and
harness-making equipment, axes, saws and tools of all
kinds. There were rocking chairs, churns, quantities
of canned fruit, turkeys, chickens, pigs and cows – to
equip and stock the new posts when established.[662]

Colonel Carrington and his troops reached Fort
Laramie on june 13, while the peace council was still
in session. Their appearance had a decidedly disquiet-
ing effect. As one chief expressed it, "Great Father
sends us presents and wants new road, but white chief
goes with soldiers to steal road before Indian say yes
or no." [663] Red Cloud and Man-Afraid-of-his-horses
made no secret of their opposition and withdrew with
their fighting men from all association with the treaty-
makers.

While at Fort Laramie Mrs. Carrington, wife of the
colonel, and other ladies of the command went shop-
ping at the sutler's store. The lady's picture is enlight-
ening:

"The long counter of Messrs. Bullock and Ward was
a scene of seeming confusion not surpassed in any popular, overcrowded store of Omaha itself. Indians, dressed

---

[662] H. B. Carrington, *Absaraka, land of massacre*, etc., 36-45. Most of this
book was written by Mrs. H. B. Carrington. See also G. R. Hebard and A. E.
Brininstool, *The Bozeman trail*, I, 268.

[663] Carrington, *op. cit.*, 79-80.

FORT LARAMIE, 1868
From U.S. Geological Survey collection

and half dressed and undressed; squaws, dressed to the same degree of completeness as their noble lords; papooses, absolutely nude, slightly not nude, or wrapped in calico, buckskin, or furs, mingled with soldiers of the garrison, teamsters, emigrants, speculators, half-breeds, and interpreters. HERE, cups of rice, sugar, coffee, or flour were being emptied into the looped-up skirts or blankets of a squaw; and THERE, some tall warrior was grimacing delightfully as he grasped and sucked his long sticks of peppermint candy. Bright shawls, red squaw cloth, brilliant calicoes, and flashing ribbons passed over the same counter with knives and tobacco, brass nails and glass beads, and that endless catalogue of articles which belong to the legitimate border traffic. The room was redolent of cheese and herring, and 'heap of smoke;' while the debris of mounched crackers lying loose under foot furnished both nutriment and employment for little bits of Indians too big to ride on mamma's back, and too little to reach the good things on counter or shelves." [664]

Mr. Julius C. Birge, who visited the fort at this time, also paid his respects to the sutler and his store. "We modestly approached the pompous Mr. Ward, who we were told was the sutler. He wore fine clothes, and a soft, easy hat. A huge diamond glittered in his shirt front. He moved quietly round as if he were master of the situation, and with that peculiar air so often affected by men who are financially prosperous and self-satisfied. He seemed to be a good fellow and was in every respect courteous. . .

"As a business proposition, it was manifestly to the advantage of the sutler and agents that some treaty be made, for the reason that every Indian treaty in-

[664] *Ibid.,* 76-77.

volves the giving of many presents and other valuable considerations. Whatever the Indians may finally receive become articles of exchange in trade. In this the astute sutler profits largely, as the Indian has little knowledge of the intrinsic value of manufactured goods and the sutler enjoyed exclusive rights of traffic with them at the posts." [665]

Despite the withdrawal of Red Cloud and his followers, a thousand or more Sioux remained at the peace council. These finally signed the proffered treaty. A number of the chiefs and head men of the Cheyennes who were present signed a similar treaty and it was left at the fort for the signatures of other Cheyennes when they should arrive. [666]

Now came the event, long awaited by the Indians. Mr. Birge writes:

"The treaty of 1866, at which we were present, such as it was, having been concluded by the chiefs of the thousand Indians who remained, the coveted presents were distributed. In a few hours more the friendly camps were ablaze with mounted Indians decked in yellow, red, and other brilliantly colored cheap fabrics flying in the winds. To their simple tastes these tawdry stuffs were more attractive than diamonds. Gilded jewelry was received by them in exchange for articles of real value. We were informed that they received firearms and ammunition, which they greatly prized, but this statement is not made from my personal knowledge." [667]

The treaty provided for the opening of the Powder

---

[665] J. C. Birge, *The awakening of the desert*, 178-79.

[666] *Report of the commissioner of Indian Affairs for the year 1866*, 208, 211. A few Arapahos came in toward the end of june and said they were for peace.

[667] Birge, *op. cit.*, 181.

river, or Bozeman, road to the Montana mines. Discoveries of gold in that region in 1862 had led to a rush to Virginia City and the other camps in 1863 and 1864. The first routes to these mines were round-about — one leading north from Fort Hall on the Oregon trail, a second going east from the Oregon country, and a third leading up the Missouri river. In 1864 Jim Bridger and John M. Bozeman had led parties north from the upper North Platte, the former by a route west of the Big Horn mountains, the latter by a route east of that chain.[668] The Bozeman trail had proved to be a practicable and desirable route, and the whites were determined to secure and use it.

From the Indians' standpoint there was serious objection to the road. It traversed the best hunting grounds of the Sioux. The white man had previously established the Oregon, Overland and Santa Fe trails. Now he was invading the last large game reserve of the northern plains. So it is easy to understand why the Indians who signed the Fort Laramie treaty of 1866 did so with reluctance and why others of their leaders spurned the white man's offer and refused to sign away their heritage.

Colonel Carrington and his troops set out from Fort Laramie on june 17, 1866, and reached Fort Connor on the 28th. Leaving some of the men to garrison this post (soon to be moved a short distance and re-named Fort Reno), he marched on sixty-seven miles to the northwest, selected a site at the foot of the Big Horn mountains and began the building of Fort Phil Kearny.[669]

He had been warned that the erection of new forts

---

[668] Hebard and Brininstool, *op. cit.*, I, 201-35, 268.
[669] Carrington, *Absaraka*, 80-110.

would be tantamount to a declaration of war. And the accuracy of the forecast was soon demonstrated. Within forty-eight hours after beginning the construction, they lost part of their horses through an Indian attack. Later the same day, july 17, Louis Gazzous, a French trader, and five of his men were killed. Five wagon trains were attacked during the next twelve days.[670] The fort was under an almost constant siege. No party was safe outside the post and the watch could never be relinquished.

Early in august Colonel Carrington sent two companies of troops about ninety miles farther northwest along the Bozeman trail to begin the construction of Fort C. F. Smith.[671] In the meantime the soldiers left at Fort Phil Kearny were busily employed in cutting and bringing in timbers for the stockade and the quarters at their post. These wood trains and cutters had to be carefully guarded and numerous minor skirmishes with Red Cloud's warriors occurred. Early in december a wood-train escort of forty men under Captain W. J. Fetterman gave chase to some Indians and were led into an ambush. Only the timely arrival of Carrington with additional troops saved the imperiled soldiers. The episode taught the colonel caution, but the impetuous captain appears to have learned nothing from the experience.

On december 21, a distress signal came from the wood train, and troops were ordered to the relief. They were to have been led by Captain Powell, but Captain Fetterman pled his seniority and was given command. He was directed to protect the train but was specifically ordered not to pursue the Indians beyond the Lodge Trail ridge. But after the train was safe, a little group

---

[670] *Ibid.,* 119-124.
[671] *Ibid.,* 125.

of audacious warriors lured him on and into a trap. Then from every side hundreds of Indians closed in on Fetterman and his eighty men, killing them to a man.[672]

The fort with its reduced force was now in jeopardy. News of the Fetterman tragedy and an appeal for reinforcements and supplies must be carried to Fort Laramie, 235 miles away. The weather had turned suddenly cold and a blizzard was raging, but in the face of the terrible odds John (Portugee) Phillips, trader and scout, volunteered to attempt the journey.

Wrapped in a great buffalo coat, with hardtack for himself and a little grain for his horse, he disappeared in the darkness. With skill and hardihood Portugee and his fine horse – a Kentucky thoroughbred belonging to Colonel Carrington – made their way over the plains to Fort Laramie. The faithful horse dropped on the parade ground, never to rise, while Phillips staggered into the post after having made one of the great rides of American history. It was just before midnight on Christmas night, and a gay ball in Bedlam (officers' quarters) was in full swing, but as the tragic news spread through the fort festivities terminated and plans were laid for relief.[673]

General H. W. Wessels soon set out from Fort Laramie with four companies of infantry and two of cavalry. Through sub-zero weather they pushed northward, reaching Fort Phil Kearny in mid-January. They found the garrison safe, for during the inhospitable weather, the Indians had been content to nurse their

672 *Ibid.,* 200-210. Grinnell, *op. cit.,* 225-235, gives the Indians' account of the fight and says that fifty or sixty Indians were killed.

673 Hebard and Brininstool, *op. cit.,* I, 297-346, and II, 15-38, give full accounts of the Fetterman fight and of Phillips's heroic ride, with much original information.

own troubles.[674] General Wessels brought orders relieving Colonel Carrington of the command and directing him to proceed to Fort Caspar on the North Platte. He was being unjustly punished for the Fetterman tragedy.[675]

General Wessels attempted a winter campaign against the Indians, but it had no definite results, the severity of the weather militating against its success. Though the state of war continued, there was no important engagement until summer.

On august 2, 1867, the Wagon Box fight occurred. The escort of the Phil Kearny wood cutters was attacked while in an oval corral made of wagon boxes. Captain James Powell, his small force armed with new breech-loading rifles, gave the Indians an unexpected reception, repulsed their repeated assaults and held his position.[676]

With the general activity in the region and with Fort Laramie serving as a base for the Bozeman trail forts, a need was felt for repairs and more buildings at the fort on the Laramie. In january, 1867, some carpenters and blacksmiths were sent out from Omaha and on march 1 the following civilian employees were listed at the fort: 4 clerks, 3 storekeepers, 11 guides, 9 wagonmasters, 13 carpenters, 7 blacksmiths, 4 saddlers, 1 bricklayer, 1 engineer, and 10 watchmen. But the request from the fort for new buildings was denied: "The dep't commander has decided to make Ft. Laramie a five company post and the new buildings recommended will not be required." [677]

---

674 *Ibid.,* I, 319-320.

675 He demanded an investigation and was subsequently exonerated.

676 Hebard and Brininstool, *op. cit.,* II, 39-87.

677 Fort Laramie records at Fort Myer, Virginia. Letters of General Augur, march 1, and march 5, 1867.

A good picture of the fort at this time is given by the inspector's report of july 1, 1867:

No. and kind of buildings	Capacity	Condition
1 Adjutant's office	3 rooms, 10 desks	Good
6 Officers quarters	30 rooms	Good
1 Provost marshall's office	1 room, 2 desks	Serviceable
2 Officers stables	20 horses	Good
1 Arsenal magazine	2 rooms	Good
1 Building, company shops	8 benches	Very bad
1 Bakery	Can bake bread for 1,200 men per day	Unserviceable
3 Kitchens for barracks	3 companies	Unserviceable, 1 very bad
5 Barracks	3-1 company each; 2-2 companies each	4 good, 1 very bad
1 Farriers quarters		Unserviceable
2 Mess houses for barracks	400 men	1 good, 1 very bad
1 Guard house	40 men	Good
1 Band room	10 men	Serviceable
1 Ice house	100 tons	Good
1 Musicians quarters	2 rooms	Utterly worthless
3 Laundress quarters	8 laundresses	Utterly worthless
1 Saddle shop	10 benches	Unserviceable
1 Blacksmith's shop	6 fires	Good
3 Store houses, com. & Q.M.	Com. 250,000 rations	1 good, 2 unserviceable
1 Q.M. office & store house	Store room, 200 tons	Good
1 Com. off. store house	Store room, 250,000 rations	Good
1 Carpenter shop	14 benches	Good
1 Post office	2 rooms	Good
1 Hospital	24 patients	Good
3 Cavalry stables	200 horses	Serviceable

Respt'y. submitted,

BRVT.-MAJ. E. B. GRIMES [678]

---

[678] Fort Laramie records, Washington, D.C.

While events were happening in the Powder river
country and about Fort Laramie, the railroad, har-
binger of the red man's expulsion and frontier fort
abandonment, was nosing its way up the valley of the
Platte. The Union Pacific had reached Plum creek, two
hundred miles west of Omaha, when the Indians made
their first attack on the builders in august, 1866. They
swept down on a freight train and captured it. General
Dodge, who had now become chief engineer of the road,
but who found that he had not forsaken his military
role, came to the rescue with an armed force. This was
the beginning of twenty months of warfare.[679] Surveying parties and construction crews had thereafter to
be on guard and actual conflicts were common occur-
rences. Dodge was in a position to get military support
for his great project. For the government had not only
invested heavily in the bonds of the railroad company
but the war department looked upon the building of
the road as one of the most effective measures for sub-
duing the Indians of the West.

Writes General C. C. Augur, "The Union Pacific
railroad, beside its great national importance, is very
essential to the interests of the department in the way
of moving troops and supplies at a great saving of
money. I have, therefore, endeavored in every way
possible, to assist in its construction, deeming its completion to the Black Hills even, in its effect upon Indian
affairs as equivalent to a successful campaign. The
Thirtieth infantry, part of the Fourth, part of the
Thirty-sixth, four companies of cavalry, and four companies of Pawnee scouts have been occupied in its care
during the entire summer, escorting engineers and commissioners and protecting grading and working parties."

[679] J. R. Perkins, *op. cit.*, 202.

The engineers forsook the old emigrant road by way of Fort Laramie for a more direct route through the southern Wyoming country. And being left off the railroad line, the fate of the old fort was sealed. Through the pack horse and the wagon train years it had been the principal outpost of the principal western thoroughfare of the nation. Now a new era for the region was beginning with a new route and a new mode of travel. But Fort Laramie's sun was still above the horizon. Her existence was so entwined with that of the blanket Indians that she was to be abandoned only when the Red sun had set.

While the Indians were hectoring the builders of the Union Pacific, were raiding emigrant trains and coaches, stage and telegraph stations, were laying siege to the forts on the Bozeman trail, the government was changing its policy toward the Indians. Peace advocates were again in the ascendency.

Congress embodied the policy into law by the Act of july 20, 1867. This provided for a commission of seven members – four civilians (including the commissioner of Indian Affairs) and three generals of the army – who were to deal with the hostile tribes. In the event that the commission did not succeed in making peace with the Indians, then the secretary of war was to enlist 4,000 men to suppress the hostiles.[680]

The Indian commission, consisting of N. G. Taylor (commissioner of Indian Affairs), J. B. Henderson (chairman of the senate committee on Indian Affairs), J. B. Sanborn, S. F. Tappan, and generals W. H. Sherman, W. S. Harney, and A. H. Terry, met and organized at St. Louis august 6, 1867. They dispatched orders at once to the military forts and the Indian agen-

---

[680] *U.S. statutes at large,* xv, 17.

cies directing the sending out of runners and the gathering in of the northern Indians to meet the commission at Fort Laramie on september 13, and the assembling of the southern Indians at or near Fort Larned about the 13th of october. The commission then began the gathering of testimony in regard to Indian affairs, making a trip up the Missouri river for the purpose. From Omaha on september 11 they took rail for North Platte, where they found a large number of Indians, some friendly and others recently hostile. Without authorization of the commission, these Indians had been told that if they came in for peace they would be supplied with ammunition for the hunt. As a friendly gesture and to instill confidence, the promise was kept.

Learning that the northern Sioux, waging the war on Powder river, would be unable to meet at Fort Laramie at the time indicated, the commission postponed the meeting there until november 1, and then proceeded toward the appointed meeting place for the council with the Indians of the Southern Plains. Here they negotiated the Medicine Lodge treaties of october 21-28, 1867.

Returning to Fort Laramie for the postponed meeting, the commission found a few friendly Crows awaiting them, but the Sioux had refused to come in. Red Cloud, leader of the hostiles, sent word "that his war against the whites was to save the valley of the Powder river, the only hunting ground left to his nation, from our intrusion. He assured us that whenever the military garrisons at Fort Phil Kearny and Fort C. F. Smith were withdrawn, the war on his part would cease." [681] Later in the winter Red Cloud accepted their propo-

681 Report to the president by the Indian peace commission, january 7, 1868, in *Annual report of the commissioner of Indian Affairs for the year 1868*, 31.

The Peace Commission, 1867

Left to right: Gen. A. H. Terry, W. S. Harney, W. H. Sherman, a Sioux squaw, N. G. Taylor, S. F. Tappan, and C. C. Augur

sition to discontinue hostilities and to meet them in council the following spring.

The commissioners came again to Fort Laramie in april, 1868, and were now prepared to accede to the Indian demands for abandonment of the Bozeman trail. The peace was signed by the Brulé Sioux on april 29, and by part of the Oglalas on may 25.[682] But Red Cloud still distrusted the white man's word and would not sign until his demands were met literally. The president had ordered, on march 2, 1868, the abandonment of the three forts on the Bozeman trail, but not until transportation was supplied in august was the order carried out. As the Stars and Stripes were hauled down at Fort Phil Kearny and the troops marched out, the Indians took possession and soon the well-built quarters and the hated stockade were melting away in red flames.[683]

When the soldiers were all surely out of the Powder river country and the region was again the undisturbed land of the Indian and his native game, Red Cloud came in to Fort Laramie and signed the treaty of peace on november 6, 1868. The treaty was ratified by the senate on february 16, and proclaimed on february 24, 1869.[684]

It provided for a reservation comprising approximately that part of present South Dakota west of the Missouri river, and for agency buildings to be constructed on the Missouri river. Fort Laramie was thus outside the bounds of this new reservation and Brevet-brigadier-general A. J. Slemner, in command of the fort in the summer of 1868, informed special Indian

---

[682] C. J. Kappler, *Indian affairs, laws and treaties,* II, 998-1004.

[683] Hebard and Brininstool, *op. cit.,* II, 254.

[684] Kappler, *op. cit.,* 998, 1006.

agent J. P. Cooper that after the signing of the treaty no more Indians would be permitted to come to the fort on the Laramie.[685]

The railroad, that reached and made Cheyenne in the summer of 1867, was pushed on westward, the construction reaching its climax on may 10, 1869, when the golden spike was driven at Promontory Point on the Great Salt Lake. With the joining of the Union Pacific and the Central Pacific the nation was tied by a band of steel. Time and space were fore-shortened, old agencies were cast in the discard and in one sense the conquest of the continent was complete.

[685] *Annual report of the commissioner of Indian Affairs for the year 1868,* 251.

The Fight for the Black Hills

In conformity with the peace treaty signed by the Sioux at Fort Laramie in 1868, most of these Indians took up their residence upon the big Dakota reservation. But some of the bands were inclined to wander beyond the reserved tract. Fort Laramie had for so many years been the trade center for the Sioux that they were loath to give it up. Red Cloud expressly asked in 1870 that the agency and trading post for his people be located at Fort Laramie.[686] But the United States government wanted the Indians farther removed from the regular routes of white travel and would not consent to such a modification of the treaty.

To continue the work begun by the peace commission of 1867, congress provided by an Act of april 10, 1869, for the appointment of a board of Indian commissioners to assist the administrative departments in the conduct of Indian affairs.[687] Felix R. Brunot became chairman of this board,[688] and one of the members was Robert Campbell, whom we remember as the builder of the original fort on the Laramie in 1834. Through arrangements made by this board, Red Cloud and a number of his head men were taken to Washington in 1870 to see the Great Father. They were also escorted to New York and other large cities to be impressed

---

[686] *Annual report of the commissioner of Indian Affairs* (*1870*), p. 325.

[687] This Board held office until 1874. See *Annual report of the commissioner of Indian Affairs* (*1877*), p. 9.

[688] *Annual report of the commissioner of Indian Affairs* (*1869*), pp. 44-51.

with the numbers and resources of the white man.[689] In october of that year the commission met Red Cloud, American Horse and other Sioux at Fort Laramie and were promised that these Indians would select a site on the reservation for their agency.[690] But the following summer when Brunot again visited Red Cloud and his band at Fort Laramie, he found that they had not yet chosen an agency location and were still asking for a site on the North Platte.[691] A concession was made and a temporary agency established for them on this river, about thirty miles southeast of Fort Laramie.[692]

In its third annual report (1871), the Board of Indian Commissioners observed: "The remarkable spectacle seen this fall, on the plains of western Nebraska and Kansas and eastern Colorado, of the warlike tribes of the Sioux of Dakota, Montana, and Wyoming, hunting peacefully for buffalo without occasioning any serious alarm among the thousands of white settlers whose cabins skirt the borders on both sides of these plains, shows clearly that the efforts of the friends of peace in establishing confidence between the white people and the Indians, in this heretofore greatly disturbed section of the country, have been eminently successful." [693]

In 1872, writes General Augur, "not a white man was killed in the department of the Platte." [694] Reports

[689] *Annual report of the commissioner of Indian Affairs (1870)*, pp. 324-326.

[690] *Annual report of the commissioner of Indian Affairs (1871)*, p. 24. See also, Carrington, *op. cit.*, 298.

[691] *Annual report of the commissioner of Indian Affairs (1871)*, 22-29. Verbatim report of the conference.

[692] *Ibid.*, 4.

[693] *Ibid.*, 12.

[694] Carrington, *op. cit.*, 300. A series of orders issued at Fort Laramie by Colonel John E. Smith, commander of the post, 1872-74, are published in the *Annals of Wyoming*, IX, 755-759.

from other officials also were encouraging, but there was some misgiving in regard to the Sioux. Red Cloud still declined to leave the North Platte. Having expressed a desire again to visit Washington, he and twenty-seven of his men were taken on a month's excursion of eastern cities. They appeared to have been greatly impressed and indicated a willingness to take up farming.[695] They finally selected an agency site on White river [northwest corner of Nebraska], and to this location they and their agent moved in august, 1873.[696]

During the early 'seventies, while most of the Sioux were remaining on their reservation and keeping rather close to their agencies – where food and supplies were provided – a considerable number of the dissatisfied were in the Montana country. In 1872 these comprised about 450 lodges, mainly Uncpapas, but also disaffected factions of other tribes, and were under the leadership of Sitting Bull, Black Moon and other chiefs.[697]

These hostiles, with reinforcements from other bands, attacked the surveying expedition of the Northern Pacific railroad near Tongue river in early august, 1873. Colonel Stanley and Lieutenant-colonel Custer, in command of the military forces, sustained attacks for several days.[698] Numbers of the Indians whom they fought had come recently from the agencies and were clothed and equipped with goods drawn from the Indian Bureau.

"The Sioux at Red Cloud and Spotted Tail agencies," writes the commissioner of Indian Affairs, in

[695] *Annual report of the commissioner of Indian Affairs* (*1872*), 268. Report of agent J. W. Daniels.

[696] *Annual report of the commissioner of Indian Affairs* (*1873*), 243.

[697] *Annual report of the commissioner of Indian Affairs* (*1872*), 269.

[698] Carrington, *op. cit.,* 302-303.

his annual report of 1873, "have also assumed impudent manners and made hostile threats, which have prevented the proper administration of agency affairs." In view of these developments, he recommended that "provision be made at once for placing at each of the Sioux reservations a military force sufficient to enable the agents to enforce respect for their authority, and to conduct agency affairs in an orderly manner. Also, that all Sioux Indians be required to remain on the Sioux reservation, and that any found off, or refusing to come in and treat with the government, be forced in and brought to obedience by the military." [699]

Heretofore the troops, in compliance with the express provisions of the Fort Laramie treaty of 1868, had refrained from going on the Sioux reservation. But now the agents and their employees were feeling unsafe and were asking for protection. On the other hand, the Sioux had insisted that the whites stay off their reservation. Red Cloud had at first demanded that even the agency buildings be placed beyond the reservation boundaries, for he accurately foresaw that if one white man was permitted to enter, others would follow.

But despite Indian objection, military posts were established at the Red Cloud and Spotted Tail agencies in 1874.

Persistent rumors of gold in the Black Hills region of the Dakotas induced the government, in the spring of 1874, to send Colonel George A. Custer to make a reconnaissance of the region. Scientists, scouts, teamsters and practical miners accompanied the soldiers. From French creek, on august 2, Custer sent out this dispatch: "I have on my table forty or fifty small particles of gold in size averaging a small pin head, and most

[699] *Annual report of the commissioner of Indian Affairs (1873)*, 6.

of it obtained from one pan." [700] Other favorable reports followed and the news spread rapidly. Prospecting expeditions were being excitedly organized when General Sheridan, on august 27, issued this order to General Terry, in command of the department of Dakota: "Should companies now organizing at Sioux City and Yankton trespass upon the Sioux reservation, you are hereby directed to use the force at your command to burn their wagon trains, destroy the outfits and arrest the leaders, confining them at the nearest military post in the Indian country." [701]

This order disrupted most parties of prospectors. One slipped through the military ban, only to be stopped by the Brulés, with one man killed. However, another party, led by John Gordon, did get through. They reached the Dakota hills in early december and set about building a pine stockade on French creek. [702]

The commissioner of Indian Affairs, in his annual report at the end of 1874, pointed to the developments of the year as proof that the white policy was succeeding. "The feeding process," he writes, "which has been now continued for six years with the Sioux, has so far taken the fight out of them that it was impossible for a portion of the more warlike non-treaty bands to prevail upon their brethren, who have been sitting down at the agencies along the Missouri river, to risk the loss of their coffee, sugar, and beef in exchange for the hardships and perils of a campaign against soldiers. As a result, the Custer expedition penetrated to the very heart of their wild country and returned without meeting opposition, and the military camps at Red Cloud and Spotted Tail agencies are in safety, though

[700] Quoted in Doane Robinson, *History of South Dakota,* I, 260.
[701] *Ibid.,* 261.
[702] *Ibid.,* 262.

surrounded by a force of fighting men from ten to twenty times larger than their own number. To have tamed this great and warlike nation down to this degree of submission by the issue of rations is in itself a demonstration of what has been often urged – that it is cheaper to feed than to fight wild Indians." [703]

In february, 1875, John Gordon and a companion made their way from the stockade settlement on French creek back to Yankton on the Missouri. With them they carried the yellow fruit of their mining operations. The sight of the dust induced another wave of the gold fever. Parties were formed to push in to the Black Hills. The one led by Gordon was stopped by U.S. troops, the outfits were destroyed and the members were taken across the 200-mile stretch to Fort Laramie and lodged in jail. The remnant of the little party left in the stockade on French creek was also rounded up in april, 1875, and was marched off to the fort on the Laramie. [704]

Then, in an effort to gauge the authenticity of the reports and to determine the value of the region, the government sent a second expedition to the Black Hills. It was led by Professor W. P. Jenney of the School of Mines of New York City, and comprised a staff of trained assistants. They fitted out at Cheyenne and proceeded to Fort Laramie. Here they were given an escort of six companies of cavalry and two of infantry, under the command of Colonel R. I. Dodge. The expedition left the fort on may 25, 1875. Upon reaching the Black Hills in early june, Professor Jenney found prospectors already at work. The miners, he reported, "poured by hundreds into the hills, and accompany-

[703] *Annual report of the commissioner of Indian Affairs (1874),* 5.
[704] Robinson, *op. cit.,* 271.

ing me, gave me great assistance in prospecting the country." [705]

In august General Crook went to the Black Hills. He called all the miners to assemble at Custer City and asked them to voluntarily leave the Hills until the Indian title could be extinguished. He agreed to let six men remain to protect the claims already staked out. The main body of miners then left the district, going out to Fort Laramie and Cheyenne. But many remained behind, hiding out in the mountains. [706]

In the meantime, the government, hard pressed to hold back its own citizens, had approached the Sioux in an effort to purchase the Black Hills. A delegation of Indians was taken to Washington in may, 1875, and this was followed by the sending of a government commission to treat at the agencies. [707] This commission, headed by Senator W. B. Allison, was unable to obtain a cession of the desired land. Spotted Tail and some of his men, having visited the mining area in august, had formed a high estimate of the value of the area. So the reservation Indians, though willing to sell, demanded a price far in excess of what the government was willing to pay. And the non-reservation Indians, refusing to sell at any price, warned the whites to keep out.

After the failure to obtain a cession by treaty, the military made little pretense of excluding white men from the Black Hills and the miners rushed in by the hundreds.

Despite the seriousness of the situation, the commissioner of Indian Affairs in his report at the close of

[705] Report of geological survey of the Black Hills, in *Annual report of the commissioner of Indian Affairs* (*1875*), 181.

[706] Robinson, *op. cit.*, 272; R. E. Strahorn, *Hand-book of Wyoming*, 234.

[707] *Annual report of the commissioner of Indian Affairs* (*1875*), 7.

1875 stated that during the past year there had been "less conflict with Indians than for many previous years." He also repeated a statement made in his preceding annual report, that "such an event as a general Indian war can never again occur in the U.S." He did, however, recognize the possibility of conflict with the wild, non-reservation Sioux. "It will probably be found necessary," he writes, "to compel the northern non-treaty Sioux, under the leadership of Sitting Bull, who have never yet in any way recognized the United States government except by snatching rations occasionally at an agency, and such outlaws from the several agencies as have attached themselves to these same hostiles, to cease marauding and settle down, as the other Sioux have done, at some designated point. This may occasion conflict between this band of Indians and the soldiers." [708]

His attitude was adopted as a government policy and in december runners were sent out to the wild Sioux, ordering them to come in to the reservation by january 31, 1876. Failure to comply would result in the ordering of soldiers to fetch them.[709] The Indians ignored the demand and the military prepared for action.

General Sheridan consulted with generals Terry and Crook and ordered them to proceed against the hostiles. Crook was to move north from the Fort Laramie region, while Terry pushed west from the upper Missouri. Although cold weather prevented Terry from undertaking this expedition at once, Crook was able to launch his campaign. From Fort Fetterman on the

---

[708] *Ibid.,* 4-5.

[709] *Record of engagements with hostile Indians within the military division of the Missouri from 1868 to 1882, Lieutenant-general P. H. Sheridan commanding,* 57.

North Platte, eighty miles northwest of Fort Laramie, he set out on march 1, 1876, with about ten troops of cavalry and two companies of infantry. At dawn on the 17th the main force, under Colonel J. J. Reynolds, attacked a large village of Sioux and Northern Cheyennes near the mouth of Little Powder river, Montana. The Indians, surprised, at first scattered; but Crazy Horse soon rallied them and presently forced the soldiers to retreat. General Crook came up in time to save his cavalry, but the general engagement was a victory for the Sioux.[710] In the face of the Indian opposition and the extreme severity of the weather, General Crook withdrew his forces to Fort Fetterman.

Later in the spring he concentrated fifteen troops of cavalry and five companies of infantry at Fort Fetterman for another drive into the Indian country. In late may he moved to the north and on june 15 was joined by some 300 friendly Shoshones and Crows. Two days later, on the Rosebud, they met the enemy – and in much greater force than expected. The bands of non-treaty Sioux and Cheyennes had been greatly augmented by warriors from the agencies, so they attacked with confidence. And under the great generalship of Crazy Horse they presented a battle front unexcelled in the annals of Indian warfare. General Crook was hard pressed to save certain detachments of his men, and when the battle was over he "deemed it best to return to his supply camp, to await reinforcements and supplies, not considering it advisable to make another forward movement until additional troops reached him."[711]

---

[710] J. G. Bourke, *On the border with Crook*, 270-282, and *Record of engagements*, 58-59. See also P. I. Wellman, *Death on the Prairie; the thirty years' struggle for the western Plains*, 136-138.

[711] *Record of engagements*, etc., 60. Wellman, *op. cit.*, 139-146, gives a

Simultaneous with Crook's campaign, General Terry was moving west from Fort A. Lincoln, near Bismarck, with the entire Seventh cavalry, three gatling guns and six companies of infantry. He established a supply camp at the mouth of Powder river on june 7 and sent out scouting parties. Moving his main force up the Yellowstone river he formed a junction with Colonel John Gibbon, who had marched east from Fort Ellis, near Bozeman, Montana, with four troops of cavalry and six companies of infantry. The scouts having located Indians in the vicinity of the Little Big Horn river, Terry decided to move in that direction. He divided his command, directing Colonel Custer to go by way of the Rosebud, while he accompanied Colonel Gibbon's column along the Yellowstone and then up the Big Horn.

In the early morning of that fatal day of june 25, 1876, Colonel Custer sighted the Indian village in the valley of the Little Big Horn. Lest his prey escape him, he decided to divide his command and attack from various angles. He took personal command of five troops, gave three each to Major Reno and Captain Benteen, and left one under Captain McDougall to guard the pack train. They had crossed the divide between the Rosebud and the Little Big Horn and were descending a branch of the latter stream. Custer made a swing to the right to get around the village to strike it from the lower, or northern, end. Reno turned to the left to attack the camp from the upper side.

They were all unaware of the magnitude of the force before them, not realizing that the valley contained one

spirited account of the battle. Grinnell, in his *Fighting Cheyennes*, 316-332, gives the Cheyenne account of the engagement. See also, Bourke, *On the border with Crook*, 283-322, and J. F. Finerty, *War-path and bivouac or the conquest of the Sioux*, 121-141.

of the largest gatherings of warriors ever assembled in the West. Crazy Horse, Sitting Bull, Dull Knife, Two Moons, American Horse and many another famous fighter were there. Many of the Indians here had been in the fight with Crook eight days before and their blood had not yet cooled. They were ready for more soldiers.

Major Reno met the Indians first. He had crossed the river and moved some distance down the valley when the Indians charged him. They swarmed about in such overwhelming numbers that he ordered a retreat, and recrossing the river, took refuge on the bluff at the east side of the valley. Already thirty-two of his men had been killed and seven wounded. Benteen and McDougall joined him here.

They now heard firing to the northward and presently the main body of Indians dashed off in that direction. Apparently, Custer was engaged. But Reno remained where he was. Finally, he moved cautiously north along the bluffs, but before he had gone far the noise of firing had ceased and the Indians were turning back toward him. He returned to his first position on the bluff and entrenched. The Indians came back and again attacked him in the late afternoon. With barricades of dead horses and boxes from the packs he held his position, though he suffered a loss of eighteen killed and forty-six wounded.

As darkness came, the Indians withdrew to hold scalp dances in the valley. But before daylight the next morning they renewed the attack, first with long-range fire and then in a terrific charge. But Reno held his position. In the afternoon of the 26th the Indians fired the grass in the valley and began moving off toward the Big Horn mountains. The approach of General

Terry with Gibbon's column was doubtless a factor inducing the Indians' withdrawal.

On the morning of the 25th, Terry had begun moving up the valley of the Big Horn. The next day he reached the Little Big Horn branch and pushed eleven miles up this stream. The following day he continued nine miles farther and reached the deserted battle field.

The whole ghastly story was revealed in the naked and mutilated bodies of Custer's men, strewn along the trail and over the hillside. Not a single man of the 268 had survived to tell exactly what had happened. This uncertainty, the magnitude of the disaster, the charges and counter charges of participants, have combined to make this the most famous and widely discussed tragedy in that long line that has marked the conflict between the red man and the white for possession of western America. These controversies are beyond the scope and the dimensions of this book. Suffice it to say that Custer, having made a longer circuit than Reno, did not engage the Indians until after they had met and defeated Reno. The warriors had then turned their full fury upon Custer, and with their overwhelming numbers had wiped him out.[712]

Terry and Reno, having joined forces on june 27, buried the dead. They carried the wounded to the mouth of the Little Big Horn and placed them on the steamboat Far West, to be taken down to Fort A. Lincoln. Terry's united command then moved back down the valley to the Yellowstone river and encamped there on july 2.

General Terry attempted to open communication

---

[712] In the main we have followed the account as given in the official *Record of engagements,* etc., 61-66, supplementing it with data from other more extensive recitals. The literature on this subject is too extensive for listing here.

with General Crook and finally succeeded. Exchange of intelligence revealed that they had experienced much in common; both had been repulsed by the Indians and now both were awaiting reinforcements. But it took time to gather men from various frontier posts and to get them in motion. In the meantime the Indians had scattered to hunt for food.

The flight of Indians from the agencies to join the hostiles in the spring of 1876 had induced the interior department to accede to the war department's renewed request for placing the Sioux agencies under the military. When this was done in july, a count of Indians at the agencies revealed that from one-third to one-half were absent, presumably having gone with their ammunition and supplies to the hostile camps.[713] In mid july one such band of Indians was intercepted by Colonel Merritt at Hat creek, Wyoming, and was chased back to the Red Cloud agency.

Having received reinforcements, General Crook, on august 5, moved to Tongue river and then toward the Black Hills, seeking hostiles. On september 9 a battalion under Captain Mills attacked and captured American Horse and his village.[714] Crazy Horse, coming to the rescue, arrived too late to save his lieutenant. Minor engagements that followed, between the forces of Crook and Crazy Horse, were indecisive.

Colonel Nelson A. Miles was now summoned from the Southwest. He made preparations for a winter campaign, equipping his men as if he were "organizing an expedition for the arctic regions." [715] After pursuing the Indians for some time the hostiles raised a flag of

---

[713] *Record of engagements*, etc., 67.

[714] Finerty, *op. cit.,* 249-264.

[715] *Personal recollections and observations of General Nelson A. Miles*, 218.

truce. Sitting Bull and Miles met in conference. The
chief wanted the troops withdrawn from his country
and the fighting would then cease. But Miles would
accept nothing but an unconditional surrender. So the
fighting continued. On october 27, over four hundred
lodges, comprising about two thousand Indians, surrendered to Colonel Miles. But Sitting Bull and his
immediate following were not among them.[716]

In the meantime General Crook, after putting down
a threatened uprising at Red Cloud agency, organized
another Powder River Expedition from his Fort Laramie base. It was composed of ten troops of cavalry,
under Colonel R. S. Mackenzie and eleven companies
of infantry and four of artillery under Lieutenant-
colonel R. I. Dodge. From a cantonment established
near old Fort Reno, Colonel Mackenzie moved north
and struck Dull Knife's Cheyenne village on the Crazy
Woman fork of Powder river, november 25. He took
the village, destroyed the supplies, captured and slaughtered a large herd of horses. The weather turned extremely cold. Mackenzie returned to Crook's base on
Powder river and the destitute Cheyennes made their
way north to find succor in Crazy Horse's camp.[717]

From his cantonment at the mouth of Tongue river
Colonel Miles continued to press the Indians under
Sitting Bull and Crazy Horse. On december 29, 1876,
he moved against the latter, reported to be in the
Tongue river valley. The Indians deserted their winter
camp. Sharp skirmishes occurred on january 1 and 3,
followed by a larger engagement on the 8th. After
routing the Indians the troops returned to their base
at the mouth of Tongue river.

---

[716] *Record of engagements*, etc., 72.
[717] Grinnell, *op. cit.*, 355-368, gives the Cheyenne account.

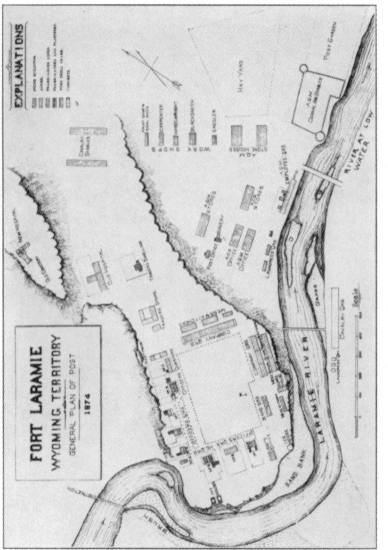

FORT LARAMIE, WYOMING TERRITORY, 1874
General plan of the post

Through some prisoners captured from Crazy Horse's village on january 7, negotiations were opened with the Indian leaders in february, 1877. They were told that if they did not surrender to Miles or at the agencies the white campaign would be resumed. Further resistance appeared hopeless. So Indian hostages were given, and about three hundred Indians surrendered to Miles on april 22. 'The larger part of the bands, numbering more than two thousand, led by Crazy Horse, Little Hawk, and others, moved southward and surrendered at Red Cloud and Spotted Tail agencies in may." [718]

In the meantime Sitting Bull, unwilling to surrender, led his band to the north and took refuge in Canada. There he was to stay two years before returning to surrender.[719]

One part of Crazy Horse's band, led by Lame Deer, refused to follow their principal chief to the agency. Miles, learning of this deflection, went in pursuit. He caught up with Lame Deer's band on may 7. A fight followed, in which Lame Deer was killed. The remnants of his band were so persistently pursued that they finally surrendered at the southern agencies during the summer and early fall of 1877.[720]

While the military had been forcing submission, white lawmakers were writing their desires into congressional statutes. An Act of august 15, 1876, making appropriations for the Indian department, stipulated that no annuities should be paid to Sioux bands engaged in hostilities and that thereafter none should be paid until after the Sioux had ceded that portion of their

[718] *Record of engagements*, etc., 77.

[719] General Miles' recollections, *op. cit.*, 244.

[720] *Ibid.*, 255.

reservation west of the 103d meridian – the coveted gold region of the Black Hills.[721]

A commission, headed by G. W. Manypenny, was appointed on august 24, 1876, to obtain concessions from the Sioux in conformity with the above Act. It proceeded to the agencies in september and succeeded in devising an agreement and getting it signed. By it the Black Hills territory of the Dakotas, lying between the North and South forks of the Cheyenne river, was ceded to the whites. The agreement was submitted to congress and the president and was enacted into law, february 28, 1877.[722]

Most of the Northern Cheyennes were taken south to the Indian territory in 1877. Not liking the climate and conditions there, they broke away in the following year (1878), under Dull Knife and Little Wolf, and struck for their former home to the north. Troops were sent after them. The Indians began raiding for food and soon a trail of blood followed their path across Kansas. After crossing the Platte river the two chiefs separated, each leading his own following. Dull Knife and his band, numbering about 150, were captured by troops in october and were taken to Camp Robinson, northwestern Nebraska. When they were about to be returned to the Indian territory, in january, 1879, they made another break for freedom. About half of them were killed in the attempt; the others were finally confined on reservations. Little Wolf's band fared better. Although finally captured, in march, 1879, they were

---

[721] C. J. Kappler, *Indian affairs, laws and treaties,* I, 166.

[722] *Ibid.,* I, 168-172. The report of the Sioux commission and the agreement they made appear in the *Annual report of the commissioner of Indian Affairs* (*1876*), 330-357. The old fiction of treating the Indian tribes as foreign nations, negotiating treaties and having these ratified by the senate had been done away with. The agreement of 1876 was enacted by both houses of congress.

permitted to remain in the north, in the region of their old home.[723]

At last the power of the Indian was broken. He had made a determined stand in defense of his land and of his ancient manner of life. But the odds were all against him. The irresistible press of the white man with his unquenchable desire for land could not be stayed. The wild Indian was forced to submit and to be corralled on a reservation.

[723] Grinnell, *The fighting Cheyennes,* 385-411.

Last Years

The rush to the Black Hills in 1875 and 1876 had given new importance to Fort Laramie. It was the gateway on one of the principal trails to the new gold region, the one leading from Cheyenne. Wagons, freighted with mining tools, baggage and supplies, creaked along the newly opened road, while hopeful goldseekers trudged beside them on foot.

The bridge over the North Platte near Fort Laramie, completed during the winter of 1875-76, invited travel over the Cheyenne to Deadwood route.[724] And Cheyenne business houses, awake to outfitting profits, advertised the route and assured customers that the road was well guarded. But though troops from the fort were constantly employed in scouting and escort duty, many depredations were committed by Indians in the spring and summer of 1876.[725] Indeed, outside calls for protection sometimes left the fort well nigh undefended. Though there were nominally three companies at the post in july, 1876, it is asserted that one day but thirteen men reported for duty.[726]

Chief Spotted Tail, father of the princess buried at

---

[724] The congressional Act of june 23, 1874, appropriated $15,000 for the building of this bridge. The request that part of the tolls collected be set aside to keep the bridge in repair was referred through the war department to congress and was refused. House of representatives, *Report no. 829,* cong. 44, sess. 1.

[725] Cynthia J. Capron, "The Indian border war of 1876," in *Journal of the Illinois state historical society,* XIII, 477-479. Mrs. Capron, wife of Lieutenant Thaddeus H. Capron, lived at Fort Laramie in 1876.

[726] *Ibid.,* 494.

the post, paid Fort Laramie a visit in june, 1876, while on his way to Denver. Writes an officer's wife at the barracks: "He was dressed in green pantaloons trimmed at the side with Indian ornamentation; a pair of small moccasins elaborately beaded, a large, dark blue blanket tidily disposed, having a white stripe down the middle of the back. His hair is smooth and black." For ten years the Sioux chief's daughter had lain in the white man's cemetery "where her spirit could hear the martial music." But upon Spotted Tail's return from Denver, "he sent the remains of his daughter home to the agency, which some consider a sign of future hostility." [727]

Another person who passed the fort at this time was Buffalo Bill Cody, going north with the Fifth cavalry to act as guide and destined shortly to have his famous duel with Yellow Hand. "I remember his fine figure," writes Mrs. Capron, "as he stood by the sutler store, straight and slender, with his scarlet shirt belted in and his long hair distinguishing him as the well known character, so much more widely known since." [728]

In the spring of 1876, an attempt was made to open the Cheyenne and Black Hills stage line. But the Indians were so hostile, running off horses and destroying stations, that it was july before the first coach reached Custer City. Upon its return trip the stage was captured by Indians, the horses stolen and the driver killed. In august Dick Seymour and Charley Utter established a Pony Express line between Fort Laramie and Deadwood, charging twenty-five cents per letter. But the service was short-lived. As conditions improved in the

[727] Mrs. Capron, *ibid.*, 487. J. G. Bourke, in his *On the border with Crook,* 399, tells the story that a hospital steward got the bones at night and was going to make of them an articulated skeleton. Then the chief came for the remains of his daughter and the bones had to be returned. The story has the mark of fiction.

[728] C. J. Capron, *op. cit.*, 488.

fall and the treaty was signed with the Sioux, regular mail and passenger service by stagecoach was established.[729]

After the Indian troubles were quieted, a new danger threatened – road agents. On march 25, 1877, the first holdup occurred. Sam Bass and other outlaws waylaid the stage and killed the driver, Johnny Slaughter.[730] The robberies became so frequent and the risks so great that the stage company had a specially designed treasure coach built for hauling bullion and other treasure from the Black Hills to Cheyenne. It was "a steel lined affair, considered to be bullet proof, and so arranged that the guards from the inside could shoot out through the port holes and stand off an ordinary crew of highwaymen." [731] But even this wheeled fortress did not escape robbery. Special guards were employed to accompany the treasure coach. Quick Shot Davis and Stuttering Brown made names for themselves in this service, though Brown was killed by the robbers.[732]

One stage holdup that occurred near Fort Laramie, was of a different sort. Some law officers were returning two prisoners – members of a holdup gang – from Cheyenne to Deadwood. The coach stopped at Fort Laramie for supper. After it had started on and gone about a mile, it entered the trees by the Platte river. Suddenly the cry, "halt," rang out. The driver stopped his team and the occupants of the coach were forced out. The prisoners were taken, ropes were put about their necks and they were hanged to a tree. The masked men then disappeared in the woods.[733]

With the settlement of the Black Hills there devel-

---

[729] Jesse Brown and A. M. Willard, *The Black Hills trails*, 422, 460-461.
[730] *Ibid.*, 245-248.
[731] *Ibid.*, 263.
[732] R. B. David, *Malcolm Campbell, sheriff*, 57.
[733] Brown & Willard, *op. cit.*, 301-305.

oped in Cheyenne a strong feeling that the new mining area should be annexed to Wyoming. Business interests in the territorial capital financed the publication in 1877 of *The Hand-book of Wyoming and guide to the Black Hills and Big Horn regions for citizen, emigrant and tourist.* The author, Robert E. Strahorn, was a newspaper correspondent who had been prominent in accompanying the troops and reporting the campaign against the Sioux. He expressed the attitude thus (p. 239): "The interests of Wyoming and the Black Hills region are so thoroughly alike and harmonious that it is simply folly to talk of their being wholly sundered by any such action as the creation of a separate territory. But as interested parties are at work to destroy so much of this natural identity as they can, it may be well to give Wyoming's status in the case more publicity. Cheyenne and Wyoming have, with work, money and influence, done more to bring about the settlement and development of the [Black] Hills than all adjacent states and territories combined. Our public men have secured legislation; our capital and energy have built roads and telegraph lines; have opened mines and constructed mills, and have, from the first, furnished more swift and reliable means of communication and more hearty support to all Black Hills enterprises than all other commonwealths together. And why? Simply because our interests have been one, and our commercial relations are as natural as the law of gravitation."

In the late 'seventies and early 'eighties the Fort Laramie scene was undergoing a change. The Indian wars were over, the settlement period had begun. Ranchers were acquiring holdings, and the great expanses of Wyoming grass, which had once fed buffaloes, now pastured great cattle herds.

The needs of ranches and towns for wood and lumber, threatened the supply upon which Fort Laramie depended. To prevent its depletion, appeal was made to Washington, which resulted in the setting aside of a wood and timber reservation by executive order of february 9, 1881. It embraced sixty-two sections of land in the Laramie mountains, about thirty-five miles west of the fort.[734]

The building of new structures and repair of the old continued at the post during the early 'eighties. A new frame bathhouse, to cost $3,370.74, three double sets of officers' quarters (to be built of concrete), costing $7,443.72, and two single sets of officers' quarters, costing $6,000.00 were authorized in 1880. In addition, repairs to an estimated total of $10,488.77 were provided for.[735]

An inventory of march 31, 1882, giving the number and condition of buildings, lists fifty structures at the fort. Of these, twenty-three were frame, ten were constructed of concrete, ten of adobe, three of adobe and frame, and four of logs. Twenty-one of the buildings were reported in good repair, fifteen in fair condition, and the remainder in various stages of dilapidation.[736] The building of a new commissary storehouse, at an estimated cost of $7,170.31, the expenditure of $15,743.80

[734] The reservation comprised the following: Township 25 north, range 21 west, excepting the school sections 16 and 36; sections 5, 6 and 8 in township 24 north, and sections 5, 6, 7, 8, 17, 18, 19, 20, 29, 30, 31, and 32 in township 25 north, both in range 70; and sections 1, 2, 3, 4, 5, 6, 7, 8, 9, 10, 11, and 12 in township 24 north, range 71 west of the 6th principal meridian, Wyoming. General orders no. 60, Adjutant-general's office, Washington, june 10, 1890. See also the letter of secretary of war Alexander Ramsey to the secretary of the interior, dated february 11, 1881.

[735] Quartermaster-general's office records, no. 4843 (1880). Records housed at Fort Myer, Virginia, in 1936.

[736] The statement, found at Fort Myer, Virginia, is reproduced below as appendix B.

on repairs, and an appropriation of $4,347.15 for completing the water system were proposed in 1882.[737]

The assistant-quartermaster at Fort Laramie wrote on april 12, 1883: "The post has been in such a poor state of repairs that all available labor and material has been in constant demand to render officers and men decently comfortable. The following repairs are much needed during the following year." Itemized needs, filling seven large pages, are then given, at an estimated cost of $11,798.99.[738]

Colonel John Gibbon, commander at the fort, recommended in 1884 the construction of a granary costing $903.00, non-commissioned staff officers quarters at $4,182.54, and an administration building at $7,902.75. Also a steam laundry was asked for "as a means in part of ridding the army of camp women." During that year several buildings were erected from old materials, a new concrete bakehouse was built, and the concrete commissary building, begun in 1883, was completed.[739]

On september 6, 1884, the Acting-adjutant-general writes: "I have the honor to inform you that the secretary of war authorizes the expenditure of $1,800.25 for repairs to the upper bridge and the construction of a new bridge across the Laramie river at Fort Laramie, Wyoming territory, as recommended." During the winter of 1884-85, a telegraph line was strung, connecting Fort Laramie with Fort Robinson, sixty-seven miles to the east. It was constructed under the superintendence of Lieutenant H. W. Wheeler, the poles being cut by soldier labor.[740]

---

[737] Archives and claims department, Fort Laramie, 1882. Records at Fort Myer, Virginia.

[738] Fort Laramie records at Fort Myer, Virginia.

[739] *Ibid.*

[740] H. W. Wheeler, *Buffalo days,* 232.

Improvement requests continued to mount, though the buildings numbered sixty-five in 1885. The expenditures recommended of this year were as follows: bathhouse, $1,145.62; quartermaster storeroom, $5,294.66; granary, $1,179.45; shops, $1,589.38; two double sets of officers' quarters, $9,725.12; barracks for six companies, $19,352.50; fences, woodsheds, etc., $1,335.81; ice house, $1,534.81; quartermaster stable, $5,200.29; and administration building, $5,815.97. In addition, a special request was made for 3,600 feet of three-inch iron pipe and six hydrants for supplying water in case of fire and for irrigation at the post. The cost of this supplemental water supply was estimated at $1,200.[741]

As an indication of the red tape involved in procuring supplies, we cite the case of a request made by the commanding officer of the fort in 1885 for window blinds for the new administration building, school room, chapel and courtmartial room. The request went from one department head to another from december 25, 1885, to february 11, 1886. After fourteen endorsements it was finally disapproved by order of the secretary of war.[742]

The garrison maintained at Fort Laramie during the 'eighties varied somewhat. Colonel Wesley Merritt, with Companies A, G, I, and K of the Fifth cavalry and companies D and K of the Fourth infantry, aggregating 346 men, were stationed at the fort in 1880.[743] The same commander with six companies of soldiers were reported in 1881.[744] In december, 1882, the aggregate force was 318, comprising companies A and K of the

---

[741] Fort Laramie records at Fort Myer.

[742] *Ibid.*

[743] Annual report of the Adjutant-general, in the secretary of war's annual report of 1880, vol. I, p. 12.

[744] *Ibid.*, for 1881, vol. I, p. 82.

Fifth cavalry and companies D, F, J, and K of the Seventh infantry.[745]

The garrisons at the fort for the years 1883 and 1884 were reported as seven companies of the Seventh infantry, commanded by Colonel John Gibbon.[746] Then Colonel Henry C. Merriam assumed command and was in charge of the fort from 1885 until the post was ordered abandoned. The garrison through these last years was composed of from four to six companies of the Seventh infantry.[747]

The beginning of the end for Fort Laramie was apparent in 1886. On february 9 Major-general J. M. Schofield wrote: "The fact that Elkhorn valley railroad will pass Fort Laramie at a distance of forty-five miles, while Fort Robinson is immediately on that road, greatly diminishes the value of the former and increases that of the latter post.

"Even if another railroad should hereafter be extended along the valley of the North Platte to and beyond Fort Laramie, Fort Robinson would still remain much the most important station because of its closer proximity to the Sioux reservation.

"Hence I suggest the construction of additional barracks and quarters at Fort Robinson and a corresponding reduction of garrison at Fort Laramie.

"It would manifestly be unwise to expend money in repair of the old buildings at Laramie."[748]

The same attitude is voiced by Colonel H. C. Merriam, commander of Fort Laramie, in a report of september 4, 1886: "The buildings at this post are nearly all very old structures of various materials, and plans,

[745] Fort Laramie post returns, Adjutant-general's office, Washington, D.C.

[746] Reports of the Adjutant-general, in the secretary of war's annual report of 1883, vol. I, p. 62, and annual report of 1884, vol. I, p. 60.

[747] Annual reports of the Adjutant-general.

[748] Adjutant-general's office, Fort Laramie files, 1886, Washington, D.C.

FORT LARAMIE, 1902

and generally inferior construction. With few exceptions they are in very bad condition, leaky, crumbling, and unsightly, as well as uncomfortable, requiring constant patching.

"Plans and estimates for new buildings, submitted in april '86 have not received favorable response. A small sum ($2,000) two thousand dollars has been furnished for repairs during the current fiscal year. Even that sum could be applied more intelligently, with regard to the best interests of the service, if some light could be given respecting the probable permanency of occupation of the post.

"In view of new railroad construction, and the consequent distribution of troops it appears to me this post has lost its significance, as a military location, and that no considerable expenditure for construction or repair of buildings would be justified." [749]

The government, however, did not act immediately upon these recommendations. During the two succeeding years there continued to be some uncertainty as to the future of the post. Repairs were reduced to a minimum.[750] Then in 1889 came the final decision:

GENERAL ORDERS NO. 69

Headquarters of the army, Adjutant-general's office, Washington, D.C.

Washington, august 31, 1889

The following recommendations of the Major-general commanding, having been approved by the secretary of war, are published for the information of all concerned:

The garrisons of Fort Laramie, Wyoming territory; Fort Hays, Kansas; and Fort Lyon, Colorado, will be withdrawn, and the several posts named will be abandoned, and the troops thus withdrawn will be assigned to other stations by the division commander. . . .

---

[749] *Ibid.*

[750] The report on the condition, capacity, etc., of public buildings at Fort Laramie, march 13, 1888, gives a detailed list of buildings, etc., and an estimate of repair costs for each structure.

The commanding general, division of the Missouri, will give the necessary orders to carry these changes into effect as soon as it can be done with due regard for economy.

By command of MAJOR-GENERAL SCHOFIELD,

Official Ass't-adjutant-general

THOMAS WARD, *Acting-adjutant-general*.[751]

A message from Governor Warren of Wyoming may have had some effect in postponing the abandonment until the spring following. "If consistent with the necessities and conveniences of the army," he writes, on november 9, 1889, "I respectfully suggest that these companies may be allowed to remain until next spring or summer.

"Fort Laramie is situated nearly 100 miles from the county seat of Laramie county [Cheyenne] and there is in that vicinity but one justice of the peace – and no other civil officers." [752]

The last regular garrison at the fort, composed of companies C and E under Captain Levi F. Burnett, marched away from the post toward Fort Logan, Colorado, on march 2, 1890. Lieutenant G. W. McIver with a small detachment was left to ship the movable property.[753] Lieutenant C. W. Taylor with fourteen men came over in march from Fort Robinson to dismantle the buildings and dispose of the possessions.[754] On the 9th of april, he sold the buildings and fixtures at public auction.[755]

On april 20, 1890, Fort Laramie was abandoned as a military post and all unsold property was turned over

---

[751] Records in Adjutant-general's office, Washington, D.C.

[752] Records in the department of the interior, lands division, Washington, D.C.

[753] Post returns, Adjutant-general's office, Washington, D.C.

[754] *Ibid.*

[755] Fort Laramie file, Indian lands, general land office, interior department. This record is reproduced in appendix C, below.

by Lieutenant Taylor to John Fields, custodian appointed by the military department.[756] Seven weeks later, the war department issued its final order regarding the fort.

> Headquarters of the army, Adjutant-general's office
> Washington, june 10, 1890
> The following order from the war department is published for the information and guidance of all concerned:
> War department, Washington, D.C.
> By authority of the president of the U.S., dated may 28, 1890, and under the provisions of the first section of the Act of congress approved july 5, 1884, entitled "An Act to provide for the disposal of abandoned and useless military reservations." The military reservation of Fort Laramie, Wyoming, declared by the president, june 28, 1869, enlarged by executive orders of april 2, 1872, and reduced by Act of congress, approved august 14, 1876; also the wood and timber reservation of said Fort Laramie, Wyo., declared by executive order february 9, 1881, are hereby transferred and turned over to the secretary of the interior for disposition, as provided in subsequent sections of the aforesaid act, the same being no longer required for military purposes.[757]

The military story of Fort Laramie was at an end – but not the story of old Laramie. To preserve the name, following the building of the Burlington railroad along the North Platte in the early 'nineties, a new town opposite the mouth of the river, about two miles from the fort site, was called Fort Laramie. About twenty-five years before (1867), Laramie city had been established by the west-building Union Pacific railroad, some two hundred miles up the river from the old fort. Today it is a progressive city, seat of the university of Wyoming.

After the interior department took over the Fort

---

[756] Post returns, Adjutant-general's office, Washington, D.C.

[757] General orders book, 1890-91, Adjutant-general's office, Washington, D.C. General orders no. 60.

Laramie military reservation, the land was thrown open to entry. John Hunton, who had come to the fort in 1867 and was the last sutler at the post, homesteaded the main part of the ground on which the fort stood. Already, at the final auction, he had purchased a number of the buildings and various items of equipment. Subsequently he obtained additional pieces of land acquired by other persons, and developed a ranch at the fort site. Here he lived the rest of his life, for near forty years a walking embodiment of the lore of old Fort Laramie. After his death in september, 1928, at the age of 88, the land and remaining buildings passed into other hands.[758]

To preserve the fragments of the old post, the Historical Landmark Commission of Wyoming, created in february, 1927, by act of the state legislature, undertook to procure the Fort Laramie site.[759] The private owners of the property asked a price considered unreasonable by the Commission, and recourse was had to the courts. Title was finally acquired by the state of the site, comprising some 214 acres of land with buildings and ruins. The National Park Service has indicated a desire to take over the historic ground and the State of Wyoming, through the Landmark Commission, has offered it to the nation.[760] At present (september, 1937) the indications are that the National Park Service will take over the site and that it will be established as a National Monument.

In 1913 a monument was erected on the old fort grounds, commemorating the Oregon trail and the

---

[758] See a long article about the fort by Mrs. Agnes W. Spring in the *Wyoming State Tribune and Cheyenne State Leader,* august 5, 1929.

[759] *First biennial report of the historical landmark commission of Wyoming, 1927-1928,* 18.

[760] Letter of Dan W. Greenburg, Secretary-Director of the Wyoming State Planning Board, dated september 19, 1937.

most famous outpost on its course. In 1930, the hundredth anniversary of the first employment of wagons on the Oregon trail was observed at Fort Laramie. Plans for celebrating the centennial of the founding of the fort (1934) failed to materialize because efforts toward public acquisition of the site were unsuccessful.

Today, the building of large canals and reservoirs has diverted much of the water from the Laramie and North Platte rivers and has resulted in the development of a rich agricultural area in the valleys of the two streams.

The historic old fort is crumbling to the ground. A few buildings, in varying stages of decay, still survive. One of the two-story barracks is the best preserved of the structures. The long double-decked veranda still stretches along its entire front – save for a few fallen spans. Of other barracks, only the foundations and parts of the dried-mortar-like concrete walls remain. The adobe sutler's store, with a re-modeled roof and altered interior, is now used as a ranch house. The old jail sets like a "dug-out" in the gravel bank by the river. Its heavy door and barred windows have been defaced by relic hunters, but the thick rock walls of the basement cells could imprison still.

Of all the remnants of the fort none so embodies the past of Fort Laramie as does Old Bedlam, first officers' quarters of the ancient post. It is the one survival of the original military establishment. Built in 1849, it was for years the center of the social life of the fort. In his historical novel, *Laramie, or the Queen of Bedlam,* Captain Charles King has recreated the life in the barracks and woven romance about Bedlam. He has helped the name to live, in this picture of another day.

Weathered and sagging now, Old Bedlam squats on the silent plain like a withered and ancient squaw deserted by her tribe. The frame sways and the joints creak before the wind. The roof droops, as a head bowed down; the porches as hands sag to the lap of earth; and the sightless eyes of broken windows see only what they remember.

Nature, better than man, has preserved her landmarks in this land. Chimney Rock still points its clay finger to the sky; Independence Rock rests like a giant turtle in the sun; and Laramie Peak, with beetled brow looks out on the eternal plains.

But the fort that once presided here has relinquished rule. The Indians come no more to the post, their travois laden with buffalo robes. Packs of furs are never launched in bullboats on the Platte. The white-topped caravans circle no more beside the Laramie, nor does the handcart pioneer look longingly after the rider of the Pony Express. The dust of the Great White Medicine Road rests beneath a black velvet boulevard. The adobe-encircled corral is lost in a field of sugar beets and one looks in vain for the commissary walls in the cornfield. The parade ground is gray with weeds and fenced with the ruins of buildings.

Beside the trickle that was once the ferried Laramie, the dwindling remnant of a once proud fort dreams in the sun. Today Fort Laramie is only a shell, but like a sea-born shell, it still resounds with the music and voices that nurtured it. In the high Wyoming winds, it whistles and moans with the throb of Sioux tom-toms and the ghost-like music of forgotten fifes and drums.

Appendix A

Description of Fort Laramie, 1875

Reports of Assistant Surgeons H. S. Schell and R. M. O'Reilly, United States Army

Fort Laramie is situated on the west bank of Laramie river, one and a half miles above its junction with the Platte; latitude, 42° 12′ 38″ north; longitude, 27° 28′ 26″ west; elevation above the sea, 4,519 feet. The reservation, as declared by the president, includes fifty-four square miles.

For history of the post, see circular No. 4, page 346.

The general plan of the post is shown in the plate opposite. Including the band quarters, there are barracks for seven companies. The barrack on the northeast side contains quarters for three companies. The entire length of the building is 287 feet, but a portion of each set of quarters is occupied by a room for the first sergeants and a baggage room, so that the net size of each room assigned to a company is 81 feet long, 30 feet wide, and 11 feet high. These rooms are ceiled with half-inch boards, but not plastered. The building is of framed timbers, filled in with adobes, plastered inside and weatherboarded outside. They are one story high, raised about two feet above the ground, but without cellars. Each room contains twelve windows, six on a side. The rooms were constructed when the companies were filled to the maximum. They contain 26,730 cubic feet of air-space each.

Of the two barracks on the southeast side of the parade, the first contains quarters for three companies, the second for one company. These buildings are constructed in every respect like the foregoing, except that the net size of the rooms in the first is 103 by 29 feet, having an air-space of 46,298 cubic feet, and that of the other building 70 by 28 feet, with an air-space of 21,560 cubic feet. The middle set is not occupied. The barracks are all in good repair, heated by means of stoves, well lighted and ventilated, and are furnished with single iron bunks. In the rear of each set of quarters is a commodious kitchen and mess-room. There are but two in rear of the barracks first de-

scribed. One is divided into two portions. The east end is used as
kitchen and mess-room by the company occupying the quarters on
the west end of the barracks, and the other is divided between the
other two companies. Kitchens for the other sets of quarters are simi-
larly arranged, and all are provided with cooking-stoves, tables, and
benches.

There are two new sets of cavalry barracks, built of concrete, two
stories high. These are constructed on the general plan recently
ordered for barracks, except that the first story is only 10 feet and
the second story 9 feet high. This is a very serious error, as it reduces
the air space in the dormitories, makes them look low, and not sym-
metrically proportioned. The ventilation also is defective, there being
only two very small shaft-ventilators in each dormitory.

An adobe-lined, shingle-roofed, frame building, 297 by 30 feet,
on the south side of the river, was occupied by the two cavalry companies as quarters, until the completion of the new barracks. This
building is now being changed into quarters for laundresses.

The officers' quarters are, for the most part, fine examples of
growth by accretion. They are generally commodious and comfortable. Referring to the plate, No. 1 is a two-story-and-a-half frame,
lathed and plastered, 45 by 75 feet, containing two sets of quarters.
Each set has a hall, two good-sized rooms, a kitchen and dining-room,
and two store-rooms on the first floor. This was originally built for
commanding officer's quarters, and has but one staircase to the attic.
No. 2 is a frame building, adobe-lined, 65 by 16 feet, with veranda
in front. No. 3, the commanding officer's quarters, is a frame building,
lathed and plastered, 45 by 35 feet, with an extension for kitchen,
&c. No. 4 is a one-story frame, adobe-lined, 44 by 20, and contains
three rooms. Nos. 5, 6, and 7 are one-story adobe buildings, with
verandas in front. No. 8 [Bedlam] is a two-story frame, containing
four sets of quarters. No. 9 is a one-story adobe, 92 by 19 feet, containing two sets of quarters. No. 10, on the bank of the river, originally
intended for quartermaster's employes, is a frame building, adobe-
lined, in which seven officers are quartered.

The guard-house is an adobe building, 42 by 18 feet, containing
two rooms, one for the officers, the other for enlisted men. The prison
is constructed of stone, 20 by 36 feet, one story high in front, and
two stories in rear. The upper story contains two rooms, plastered
and ceiled. The basement room is of rough stones, whitewashed, has
one door and a window toward the river, and on the opposite side,

OLD BEDLAM, 1902

at the top, two small windows for ventilation. Two cells are partitioned off, on the south side, for refractory prisoners. The prisoners are kept in the basement room, which contains no furniture. This room is neither warmed nor lighted. The situation of the guard-house is badly selected.

The commissary and quartermaster's store-houses are five in number, all wooden buildings, rough boards and battened, excepting the clothing-room, which is frame, and in good condition. Two commissary buildings are each 120 by 30 feet, and 9 feet to eaves. A similar structure is occupied by the quartermaster as an office and issuing store-house. The grain-house is 50 by 100 by 20 feet, and has a capacity of 100,000 cubic feet. In addition to the above, an old frame building, which was formerly used as barracks, is now converted into a store-room for the use of the quartermaster. The ice-houses for the post, two in number, will hold, together, 386 tons of ice. The carpenter-shop, wheelwright-shop, blacksmith-shop, saddler-shop, paint-shop, coal-house, &c., are located at the extreme northeast portion of the post, are new, admirably constructed for the purposes for which they were intended, and are kept in good order.

A new hospital, for twelve beds, is in process of construction at this post. It is on the regulation plan for twenty-four beds, and is built of concrete. Though still in an unfinished condition, the building was occupied in december, 1874.

The water-supply at this post is ample. The Laramie river, which bounds one side of the garrison, is a constantly running stream of an average width of 30 feet and depth of 2 feet. Its gravelly bed is always plainly visible through the clear water except in the time of the spring freshets. The water used for culinary and household purposes in the garrison is chiefly obtained from the Laramie river above the post, and is hauled around in a large tank on wheels, and dispensed as necessity may require. Good water may be obtained anywhere in the valley of the Laramie by digging 8 or 10 feet, but all the old wells seem to have fallen into disuse, except one in the post garden, which furnishes very cold, clear water in the summer-time. There is also a spring in the bank of the river, in the rear of the telegraph-office, which furnishes good water.

It is probable that water might be brought directly into the post by means of an acequia a mile and a half long, and the question of its practicability, &c., has been frequently agitated, but as yet no steps have been taken for putting it into execution. . . [An analysis of the water follows].

The means of extinguishing fire throughout the garrison consist in an ample supply of water-barrels, which are kept standing constantly filled at all the buildings. About four hundred gallons of water are kept on hand at the hospital, and fire-buckets hung in every room. Many of the buildings are also provided with fire-ladders as well as buckets.

The post is drained naturally. It stands on an elevated bench containing about ten acres, the sides of which slope in all directions, except toward the bluffs back of the hospital, where the soil is gravelly and moisture sinks out of sight immediately. There is no artificial drainage at the post. All refuse, slops, &c., are collected daily and thrown into the river below the post.

The men bathe freely and constantly, in pleasant weather, when off duty, in the stream above the post. There are many places in the river where the water is 10 to 12 feet deep, affording opportunities for swimming. No bath-houses have as yet been erected.

The post cemetery is located about half a mile from the post. There is a post garden, containing about three acres, which is cultivated by enlisted men under the direction of the post chaplain.[1]

The corral incloses about 2 acres of ground with an adobe wall 10 feet high and 2 feet thick; it has also strong bastions at two diagonal corners, and would serve as a stronghold in case of an attack by Indians.

There is a post library in the Adjutant's office containing about 300 old, nearly worn-out books; a number of papers and periodicals are subscribed for from the Post fund and kept in the library room, to which the enlisted men have access. The hospital library also comprises about 300 volumes, a majority of which are religious works.[2]

---

[1] A report on the hygiene of the u.s. army with descriptions of military posts (circular no. 8, war department, Surgeon-general's office, 1875), 355-357.

[2] The last two paragraphs are from Dr. Schell's report of 1870, in circular no. 4, and cover points not mentioned in the report of 1875.

Appendix B

LIST OF THE BUILDINGS AT FORT LARAMIE IN 1882

	Material	How used	Condition	Capacity
No. 1.	Concrete	Officers' quarters	Good	5 Rooms
No. 2	"	" "	"	5 "
No. 3	Adobe	" "	Very poor	6 "
No. 4	"	" "	Fair	3 "
No. 5	"	" "	Medium	2 "
No. 6	Frame	" "	Good	6 "
No. 7	"	" "	"	6 "
No. 8	Concrete	" "	"	5 "
No. 9	"	" "	"	5 "
No. 10	"	" "	"	5 "
No. 11	"	" "	"	5 "
No. 12	"	" "	"	9 "
No. 13	Frame	" "	"	6 "
No. 14	"	" "	"	4 "
No. 15	"	" "	"	4 "
No. 16	"	" "	"	4 "
No. 17	"	" "	"	4 "
No. 18	"	" "	"	4 "
No. 19	"	Fire engine room, chapel	Fair	12x21 ft.
No. 20	"	Court-martial room, Library, Clerk room	"	17x20 ft.
No. 21	Adobe	Schoolroom, Children	"	40x17 ft.
No. 22	"	Band quarters Schoolroom, men Quarters co. D 4th infy.	"	15x17 ft.
No. 23	"	Kitchen, store, mess room, &c.	"	76x25 ft.
		Kitchen, store, mess room, &c.	Good	114x25 ft.
No. 24	Concrete	Guard house	"	
No. 25	Frame	Quarters Troop G, 5th cav.	Poor	96x30 ft.
		Quarters Troop A		96x30 ft.
		Quarters Company K, 4th inf.	Poor	96x30 ft.
No. 26	Adobe	Kitchen and mess, Troop G, 5th cavalry	Fair	50x22 ft.

	Material	How used	Condition	Capacity
No. 27	Frame	Bath, saddler's reading, &c. Rooms, Troop G, 5th cav.	Good	36x15 ft.
No. 28	Adobe	Kitchen and mess room Troop A, 5th cavalry	Fair	76x22 ft.
No. 29	Frame & Adobe	Reading, saddler's, bath, &c. Rooms Troop A, 5th cav.	Good	55x16 ft.
No. 30	Adobe	Kitchen and mess room Company K, 4th infantry	Fair	56x22 ft.
No. 31	Frame	Reading, bath, &c. rooms Company K, 4th infantry	Good	30x15 ft.
No. 32	Concrete	Quarters, Troop I, 5th cavalry	Fair	135x29 ft.
		Kitchen, mess rooms, &c.		135x29 ft.
		Quarters, Troop K, 5th cavalry		135x29 ft.
		Kitchen, mess rooms, &c.		135x29 ft.
No. 33	Frame	Q.M., tool-warehouse	Poor	120x30 ft.
No. 34	"	" " granary	Very bad	100x50 ft.
No. 35	"	" " lumber wareh'se	Fair	120x30 ft.
No. 36	"	" " clothing wareh'se	Very bad	100x50 ft.
No. 37	"	Sut. storehouse	Very bad indeed	120x30 ft.
No. 38	"	" "	Very bad indeed	120x30 ft.
No. 39	"	Q.M. shops	Fair	25x50 ft.
No. 40	"	Blacksmith shop	Poor	25x60 ft.
No. 41	"	Carpenter shop	Fair	25x60 ft.
No. 42	"	Ord. storehouse	Fair	20x60 ft.
		Hospital, bathroom		13x14 ft.
		" ward	Good	27x52 ft.
No. 43	Concrete	Officers' dispensary &c.	Good	39x45 ft.
		Dining room		21x17 ft.
		Kitchen		24x17 ft.
No. 44	Adobe & frame	Q.M. non-commissioned staff, laundresses	Poor	150x23 ft.
No. 45	Adobe & frame	Laundresses—Q.M.	Fair	150x20 ft.
No. 46	Logs	Stables, Troop K, 5th cav.	Poor	264x28 ft.
No. 47	"	" " I, " "	"	300x28 ft.
No. 48	"	" " A, " "	"	310x28 ft.
No. 49	"	" " G, " "	"	220x28 ft.
No. 50	Adobe	Q.M. stables (enclosure)	Very bad indeed	150x100 yds.

[This statement is from the records at Fort Myer, Virginia]

Appendix C

LIST OF PROPERTY SOLD BY LIEUTENANT TAYLOR:

To T. P. McCalley	One steam pump	$14.00
	" " engine	7.50
	" building	3.75
	" water tank	2.25
	" building	2.50
	" writing desk	2.50
	" set chairs	1.00
	" dresser	1.25
To John Hunton	One building	20.00
	" "	33.00
	" "	22.00
	" "	95.00
	" "	36.00
	" "	5.50
	" "	30.00
	" "	10.00
	" "	25.00
	" "	42.00
	Four ice boxes	4.00
	One set flourbins	.75
	" wardrobe	.40
	Two washtrays	1.00
	One building	50.00
	" wardrobe	3.25
	" building	
To B. A. Hart	One building	6.00
	" "	45.00
	" "	100.00

Various Buyers	One building	30.00
	" "	51.00
	" "	35.00
	" "	35.00
	" "	37.50
	" "	31.00
	" "	47.00
	One lot of barb wire	11.75
	" building	13.75
	" "	50.00
	" "	16.50
	" "	26.50
	" "	75.00
	" "	15.00
	" "	16.00
	" "	5.00
To Doty	One building	20.00
	One lot brick, lumber and hardware	46.00
To Dance	One lot brick, lumber and hardware	39.00
To Wilde	One building	24.00
	One lot lumber	21.00
	" building	2.50
	" lot windows	10.75
	" " waterpipe	6.00
	" " hydrants	7.75
	" " pipe fixtures	2.50
	" " panel doors	5.00
	" " lumber	13.75
	" " hay	13.00
	" " hardware	1.75
	" " lumber	3.00
	" building	38.00
	Three bureaus	3.00
	Six bathtubs	13.00
	Two iceboxes	1.35
	Four tables	3.50
	Six "	3.50
	One desk	2.50

To Wilde	Two desks	1.60
	Two "	1.00
	Four saws	1.00
	One washstand	.90
	Two "	.80
	Ten chairs	4.00
	Four "	.50
	One dresser	2.00
	" "	3.25
	" wardrobe	4.00
	" "	1.10
	" flourbin	2.25
	" lot oil	3.25
	" wardrobe	5.00
	" "	5.50
	" sideboard	4.25
	" "	2.45
	" "	1.15
	" lot lumber	10.50

CHARLES M. TAYLOR, 1st Lieut., 9th cav., A. A. QM., U.S.A.
Pursuant to authority of sec. of war

Index